Sex and the Church

MARRIAGE AND FAMILY RESEARCH SERIES

Volume V

Sex
and the
Church

A SOCIOLOGICAL, HISTORICAL, AND THEOLOGICAL
INVESTIGATION OF SEX ATTITUDES

OSCAR E. FEUCHT, *Editor*

HARRY G. COINER, *Associate Editor*

ALFRED von ROHR SAUER, *Associate Editor*

PAUL G. HANSEN, *Research Director*

Issued by the Family Life Committee
of The Lutheran Church — Missouri Synod

CONCORDIA PUBLISHING HOUSE · ST. LOUIS, MISSOURI

The Authors

Oscar E. Feucht, D. D., St. Louis, Mo., secretary of adult education, director of the Family Life Education program of The Lutheran Church — Missouri Synod.

Harry G. Coiner, M. Ed., professor of pastoral theology and education at Concordia Seminary, St. Louis, Mo., chairman of the Family Life Committee.

Alfred von Rohr Sauer, Ph. D., professor of Old Testament interpretation at Concordia Seminary, St. Louis, Mo.

Paul G. Hansen, M. A., pastor of St. John's Lutheran Church, Denver, Colo., part-time instructor in sociology at the University of Denver.

Copyright 1961 by
Concordia Publishing House
St. Louis, Missouri

Library of Congress Card No. 60-53151

MANUFACTURED IN THE UNITED STATES OF AMERICA

Contents

Preface

THERE ARE TWO MAJOR REASONS why this work was undertaken. First, because the church does not and cannot exist in a vacuum, and second, because the problems concerning sex have troubled Christian people for a long time.

The church is always in danger of maintaining a sealed-off existence in its own house of faith. This house, however, stands in the world, and people come into it from the world and go out from it back into the world. In the world of everyday affairs they make their living and have their social existence. Here they are influenced by the moral and ethical patterns of society in any given age. To communicate the Gospel effectively to the people of this generation demands an understanding of the mores of our times.

Today the moral values, not only of America but of much of the world, are affected as perhaps never before by a preoccupation with sex and a confusion about sex. This fact the church cannot ignore. This is witnessed by an increase in sex crimes, juvenile delinquency, divorce, the flood of films and books that pander to low sexual morals, the alarming increase in illegitimate births, and the increase of premarital sex relations, especially among America's youth.

The problem has several causes, among them confusion as to what really is the moral standard with regard to things sexual and the unclear or faulty concepts concerning sex that have been taught at various times in Christendom.

To regain a proper perspective it was felt necessary to review and re-examine all that has been taught in the past — to which we have fallen heir — in the light of the present predicament, to compare this with the situation in which we find ourselves today, and to do this in the light of Biblical principles which grow out of an evangelical interpretation of Scripture. In this way we can learn why we feel about sex as we do, explore our attitudes in the light of sound Christian criteria, and gain new clarity regarding the principles which should undergird our teaching and practice. To go back to a pre-Kinsey world is as impossible as it is undesirable. Like it or not, the church must face the question: What are Christian sex attitudes?

This book is one of a series of six which have been planned, dealing with moral and spiritual issues in the field of Christian family life education. *Engagement and Marriage* appeared in 1959. Other areas being examined are: Mate Selection, Family Authority, Divorce and Remarriage, and Planned Parenthood.

Each subject is being looked at from sociological, historical, and theological points of view because all three points of view have contributed and are contributing to our thinking.

A sociological study of 3,400 couples, 750 unmarried young people, and 1,000 pastors in three Lutheran synods living in various parts of North America, was a part of the study to make it relevant to the current scene. History plays a role in terms of tradition and experience, showing what the church in every era said and did with regard to human sexuality. What we do about sociological and historical facts as Christian persons should depend on theology, that is, on discovering God's will with regard to the use of sex, His creation gift, in a fallen world.

This study cannot claim for itself any degree of infallibility. It does, however, represent years of careful research, the checking and rechecking of data in order to get at well established facts that can give guidance to pastors, teachers, youth leaders, counselors in the church, as well as leaders in the social science fields, so that they can evaluate past and present attitudes and establish teaching and practice on a soundly Christian and Biblical foundation. Correct teaching, however, is not the ultimate end; that end is the healing of minds, the correction of malpractices, the establishment of Christian sex behavior that grows not so much out of the Law as out of the Gospel of Jesus Christ.

The entire project was begun in 1950 as outlined by the Family Life Committee of The Lutheran Church — Missouri Synod. The spadework was done by a research director working with

18 research assistants who gathered significant data in all six areas. The research director then assembled this material in a first draft of approximately 100 pages for each of the six areas. He also conducted the sociological study.

The first draft for this book was then submitted to three pastoral conferences for criticism and to a number of theologians. It then went through a complete revision in the light of the critique. The final draft is the work of the editor and associate editors, who in turn submitted the manuscript to a reviewing committee of ten.

The research director and editors are indebted to many persons who helped them in the production of this volume and who contributed significant counsel at various points in the many-phased process. To all of these persons the Family Life Committee wishes to express its deepest gratitude, especially also to the host of scholars whose work supplied the necessary historical information and insights, to those who helped us with translations from works in other languages, and those who read the final manuscript.

We especially acknowledge the painstaking editing and proof-reading by the Editorial Department of Concordia Publishing House.

The entire project was made possible through a grant by the Synod's Committee on Research, which is herewith gratefully acknowledged.

This book, like its predecessor, goes forth in the hope that it will clarify concepts and assist pastors, teachers, youth workers, marriage counselors, and social scientists as they help individuals, families, congregations, and communities toward Christian sex attitudes on the basis of theologically sound sex ethics.

Oscar E. Feucht, editor

on behalf of

The Family Life Committee
of The Board of Parish Education
of The Lutheran Church — Missouri Synod

The Research Team

and the Fields of Investigation

PAUL G. HANSEN, M.A., RESEARCH DIRECTOR
The Sociological Survey

WILLIAM F. ARNDT, PH. D. († 1957), professor, Concordia Seminary,
St. Louis, Mo.
New Testament passages on divorce, remarriage

EMIL M. BIEGNER, S. T. D., pastor emeritus, St. Louis, Mo.
Writings of the Missouri Synod on marriage and family

GUSTAV M. BRUCE, PH. D., professor emeritus, Luther Seminary,
St. Paul, Minn.
Writings of the Evangelical Lutheran Church

NORMAN F. GIENAPP, PH. D., professor, St. Paul's College, Concordia, Mo.
New Testament on divorce and remarriage

GUNTHER M. JACOBS, professor, Concordia College, Milwaukee, Wis.
Canon and civil marriage laws in Germany
Contemporary German Christian thought on marriage

LUTHER P. KOEPKE, S. T. D., professor, Valparaiso University,
Valparaiso, Ind.
Relation of Old Testament marriage laws to Christian marriage

FRED KRAMER, S. T. M., D. D., professor, Concordia Seminary, Springfield, Ill.
Jewish marriage customs
Sexual ethics in Roman Catholicism and Reformed communions

ERWIN L. LUEKER, PH. D., professor, Concordia Seminary, St. Louis, Mo.
Marriage in the New Testament

HAROLD J. MALESKE, professor, Concordia Senior College, Fort Wayne, Ind.
Writings of the United Lutheran Church in America

ALVIN D. MATTSON, PH. D., professor, Augustana Seminary, Rock Island, Ill.
Writings of the Augustana Lutheran Church

HERBERT T. MAYER, S. T. M., assistant professor, Concordia Seminary,
St. Louis, Mo.
Lutheran confessional writings

CARL S. MUNDINGER, PH. D., professor, St. John's College, Winfield, Kans.
  Writings of Martin Luther

ARTHUR CARL PIEPKORN, PH. D., professor, Concordia Seminary, St. Louis, Mo.
  Lutheran dogmaticians of the 16th to 18th centuries

CARL F. REUSS, PH. D., Social Welfare Department, American Lutheran
    Church, Columbus, Ohio
  Statements of the American Lutheran Church

WALTER R. ROEHRS, PH. D., professor, Concordia Seminary, St. Louis, Mo.
  Old Testament on engagement, marriage, parenthood

ALFRED VON ROHR SAUER, PH. D., professor, Concordia Seminary, St. Louis, Mo.
  Old Testament on family authority, divorce, remarriage

THEODORE SCHABACKER, pastor, Grace Lutheran Church, Boulder, Colo.
  Writings on the family by social scientists

GEORGE V. SCHICK, PH. D., professor, Concordia Seminary, St. Louis, Mo.
  Old Testament passages relating to mate selection and sex attitudes

OTTO E. SOHN, professor, Concordia Seminary, St. Louis, Mo.
  Writings of the Missouri Synod on pastoral theology

LEWIS W. SPITZ, SR., PH. D., professor, Concordia Seminary, St. Louis, Mo.
  Patristics — writings of the church fathers

AUGUST R. SUELFLOW, S. T. M., director, Concordia Historical Institute,
    St. Louis, Mo.
  Old Missouri Synod congregational records

Acknowledgments

The editorial committee is grateful to the publishers and editors who have given permission to quote from the following publications:

Althaus, Paul, Erlangen, Bavaria: *"Die Begegnung der Geschlechter,"* n.d.

American Social Health Association, New York: Theodore M. Hesburgh, "Sex Education and Moral Values" in *Social Hygiene Papers,* 1957.

Association Press, New York: Roland H. Bainton, *What Christianity Says About Sex, Love, and Marriage,* 1957.

Association Press, New York: Sylvanus M. Duvall, *Men, Women, and Morals,* 1952.

Augsburg Publishing House, Minneapolis: G. M. Bruce, *Marriage and Divorce,* 1930.

Augustana Book Concern, Rock Island, Ill.: A. D. Mattson, *Christian Ethics,* 1938.

Baker Book House, Grand Rapids, Mich.: Alexander C. DeJong, *The Christian Family and Home,* 1959.

De Graff, John, Inc., New York: E. O. James, *Marriage and Society,* 1952.

Harper & Brothers, New York: Mary Alice and Harold Walker, *Ventures of Faith,* 1959.

Harper & Brothers, New York: Derrick Sherwin Bailey, *The Mystery of Love and Marriage,* 1952.

Harper & Brothers, New York: Derrick Sherwin Bailey, *Sexual Relation in Christian Thought,* 1959.

Longmans, Green & Co., Inc., New York: Thomas Gilbey (T. G. Wayne), *Morals and Marriage: The Catholic Background to Sex,* 2nd ed., 1952.

The Macmillan Co., Chicago: C. S. Lewis, *Mere Christianity,* 1958.

McGraw-Hill Book Company, Inc., New York: Lewis M. Terman et al., *Psychological Factors in Marital Happiness,* 1938.

Muhlenberg Press, Philadelphia: Marjory Louise Bracher, *Love Is No Luxury,* 1951.

Muhlenberg Press, Philadelphia: Harold C. Letts, ed., *Christian Social Responsibility,* 1957.

Oxford University Press, New York: William Graham Cole, *Sex in Christianity and Psychoanalysis,* 1955.

Philosophical Library, New York: David R. Mace, *Hebrew Marriage,* 1953.

Prentice-Hall, Inc., New York: William E. Hulme, *God, Sex and Youth,* 1959.

Fleming H. Revell Company, Westwood, N. J.: Dwight Hervey Small, *Design for Christian Marriage,* 1959.

Seabury Press, Greenwich, Conn.: Reuel L. Howe, *The Creative Years,* 1959.

Vadian-Verlag, St. Gallen: R. Hirzel, *Wir Männer und die Frauen,* 1949.

CHAPTER 1

The Nature and Purpose
of This Study

SELDOM HAS A WORD in our language describing something good and beautiful in itself become associated with so much disillusionment, evil, and impurity as the word *sex*.

The word sex is used with broad and varied meanings. It can identify either of the two divisions of organisms formed on the distinction of male and female; a portion of the human race, males or females collectively; the character of being a male or female; all the things which distinguish a male from a female. Furthermore, the word sex can refer to anything connected with sexual gratification or reproduction or the urge for these, especially the attraction of individuals of one sex for those of the other. The legitimate expression of the qualities of femininity or masculinity in common parlance today is often referred to when the word sex is employed. Sex can mean the proper sexual love in marriage or lusting sexuality, namely, undue preoccupation with what is sexual.

Sex is a good word. However, the word has been used and abused in such fashion that the Christian context of the word has been largely lost, even among Christian people. William E. Hulme says, "This is the Christian definition of sex: that God created people as men and women for the purpose of the marriage companionship and the creation and development of new life." [1]

---

[1] William E. Hulme, *God, Sex and Youth* (New York: Prentice-Hall, 1959), p. 19.

The word comes from the Latin *sexus* meaning "gender" (maleness or femaleness), probably from the root form *secare*, to cut, meaning thereby a division or segment of mankind.[2]

Sex in God's Design

The Bible establishes the unitive and procreative function of sex and makes it an integral part of the created nature of man. "So God created man in His own image, in the image of God created He him; male and female created He them. And God blessed them, and God said unto them, Be fruitful, and multiply, and replenish the earth, and subdue it" (Gen. 1: 27, 28). "And God saw everything that He had made, and, behold, it was very good" (Gen. 1: 31). "And the rib, which the Lord God had taken from man, made He a woman and brought her unto the man. And Adam said, This is now bone of my bones, and flesh of my flesh. . . . Therefore shall a man leave his father and his mother and shall cleave unto his wife; and they shall be one flesh. And they were both naked, the man and his wife, and were not ashamed." (Gen. 2: 22-25)

David R. Mace's comment on this Scriptural account of man's creation is concise: "The Bible has no hesitation in declaring that the sexual nature of man was deliberately created as part of the divine purpose. The hand of the Creator did not falter or slip at this point. The Hebrews accepted this view of sex whole-heartedly. For them the sexual union of husband and wife was a blessing bestowed by God for man's enjoyment and use."[3]

When, at a certain stage of the creative process, God said, "It is not good that the man should be alone; I will make him a helper fit for him" (Gen. 2: 18 RSV), this was more than a passing comment. Adam was alone, and with him in such a state there would have been no possibility of the subsequent covenant relationship between God and His people.

God created man as male and female. To fulfill the divinely given nature, it is "not good" for either man or woman to be

---

2 *Webster's New International Dictionary of the English Language,* 2d edition, unabridged (Springfield, Mass.: G. & C. Merriam Co., 1949); *Harper's Latin Dictionary,* ed. E. A. Andrews, revised, enlarged, and in great part rewritten by Charlton T. Lewis and Charles Short (New York: American Book Co., 1907).

3 David R. Mace, *Whom God Hath Joined* (Philadelphia: Westminster Press, 1953), p. 38.

alone, but to cleave to each other and be one flesh. "The Bible begins by telling us that God chose to make the human race in the form of individuals of two different kinds, so that they might meet and love and marry and complete each other. And on all this God looked with satisfaction and blessed it." [4]

Thus by faith we accept our sexual life as a divinely given part of our natural creation. There is no reason why as human beings we should be ashamed of this "power of fruitfulness" or should treat sexual attraction as something that should be hardly more than tolerated.

Martin H. Scharlemann observes:

> The very fact that the divine image and the creation of man and woman are mentioned in the same breath, so to speak, suggests that man was endowed with sex to permit him to share in God's creative activity. Sex is an integral part of God's plan of creating and preserving life among those beings which He intended to be the very crown of visible creation. . . . From this we must conclude that sex is a divine blessing of immeasurable worth and consequence, which, like other gifts from God, and possibly to a higher degree, should be "received with thanksgiving by those who believe and know the truth" (1 Timothy 4:3). [5]

David R. Mace further comments:

> Only in recent years have we been able to see a gradual but welcome change in the generally accepted Christian attitude toward sex. . . . Many of us were brought up under the still lingering influence of the old tradition. Somewhere in our deepest thoughts and feelings there may still lurk doubts about the wholesomeness of the sexual side of marriage. There may still seem to us to be something just a little unclean or shameful or discreditable about the fact that we have sexual intercourse from time to time with our wives or husbands. It cannot be strongly enough asserted that there is no authoritative Christian truth that gives any support to such feelings or attitudes. [6]

The attitude of the Christian church when facing the fact of sex has been a strange mingling of "lights and shadows." Sometimes a distorted fear of sex, sometimes unclear and false concepts, and sometimes unhealthy influences contributed toward

---

[4] Ibid., p. 18.

[5] Martin H. Scharlemann, "The Biblical View of Sex," in *The Lutheran Scholar,* XIV (Oct. 1957), 579.

[6] Mace, pp. 38, 39.

confusion more than to clarity concerning the marital relationship. Throughout its history Christianity has wavered between
the wholesome naturalism of the Hebrew family and the disturbing dualism of the Hellenistic age, which relegated the whole
matter of sex to a secondary position because it belonged to
the body, as being of an inferior order for a reasonable creature
like man.

Modern Focus on Sex

Particularly our Western culture today raises many searching
questions as to the meaning and purpose of sex. Thoughts on the
subject during the last half century have shifted back and forth
between attitudes of repression and permissiveness. As one
studies the resulting confusion of ideas, attitudes, and practices
with regard to sex, it becomes clear that to some degree all men
sense the mystery and sanctity of sex, yet continue to exploit
the pleasures, evade the responsibilities, and miss the fulfillment
that are part of the sex relationship.[7] "In the long history of
mankind, some have sought for the meaning of sex in sexual
expression; some have confined the meaning of sex to its propagative function; others have put their faith in romance as the
guide for sexual fulfillment; still others accept it as a biological
necessity only; and countless others have become victims of its
dynamic power for demonic ends." [8]

There are those who contend that sex has become a mess
because it was hushed up. Sex has not been hushed up but
chattered about for centuries, and it is still in a mess. The facts
warrant the general conclusion that a rather large-scale deterioration has taken place in the attitude of contemporary society
toward sex. Pitirim Sorokin's analysis of the sex mores of
America gives abundant evidence for the growing practice of
premarital intercourse and the increasing number of extramarital
relations, which often result in divorce, desertion, abortion, and
illegitimate children. It is Sorokin's firm belief that sexual promiscuity leads to a general breakdown of sex ethics and is fos-

---

[7] Dwight Hervey Small, *Design for Christian Marriage* (New York:
Fleming H. Revell Co., 1959), p. 80.

[8] Reuel L. Howe, "A Pastoral Theology of Sex and Marriage," in *Sex
and Religion Today*, ed. Simon Doninger (New York: Association Press,
1953), pp. 97, 98.

tered by our pulp magazines, bathing beauty contests, realistic and/or sophisticated novels, lewd entertainment on the stage, and by suggestive movies as well as television programs. He asserts that all this is taking its toll in terms of physical and mental debility and errant behavior. The debasement of sex and failure to put it to its proper use produces mental tensions and results in the reduction of the creative activity of the individual as well as the destruction of his integrity and personal habits.[9]

Martin J. Heinecken states that —

There is a deep-seated malady, something gone wrong with the basic orientation toward sex, so that it is high time that the church cease lamenting and denouncing and give a theological diagnosis and suggest a theological cure, in positive, constructive terms. We are confronted with a desperate flight into sensuality and the frantic multiplication of piecemeal satisfactions because the quality of life has lost its eternity. We are confronted with an unprecedented phenomenon which makes us realize the tremendous, disintegrating power of sex gone astray, because it strikes at the very roots of man's being.[10]

Alexander C. DeJong points up the strange paradox with regard to sex in the modern world:

Today we are faced with a strange and tragic situation. Our generation is both sex-sodden and sex-starved. On the one hand our age is soaked with sex literature. Books and magazines dealing with the techniques of sexual satisfaction within marriage pour off the presses. Detailed information can be bought for the price of a quarter. Nothing is left to one's imagination. If knowledge alone were sufficient to achieve sexual adjustment in marriage, every couple could be happy. The appalling divorce rates of our day, however, underscore failure at this point.

On the other hand our generation is sex-starved. With vengeance modern man has cast aside the cloak of Victorian silence. He hotly pursues sexual knowledge and in his pursuit loses the real meaning of sex. He has divorced sex from its religious and moral contexts. Sex has been abstracted from the marriage situation as a divine institution. Secularizing

---

[9] Pitirim A. Sorokin, *The American Sex Revolution* (Boston: Porter Sargent, 1956), pp. 7, 62, 63, 65.

[10] Martin J. Heinecken, "A Theology of Marriage" (unpublished paper, delivered at the Seminar on Christian Education and the Family, St. Olaf College, Northfield, Minn., 1957).

sex is as disappointing and meaningless as every other process of secularization.[11]

Although causes which influence the level of sex morality are not easily identifiable, the widespread influence of Sigmund Freud warrants serious consideration. William G. Cole discusses Freud's teachings and summarizes: "Freud saw man as a totality, with sex as one part, perhaps the most important part of his nature. He proclaimed that sex was natural, that procreation was secondary to pleasure, and he cautioned society against too severe restrictions on sexual instincts." [12]

The causes for the low level of sex attitudes and morality today are hidden from us, no doubt, within the complex ferment of the culture of our time. We are living in an age of tremendous social, political, and intellectual change. The foundations of religion, morality, political institutions, social theory, the very notion of the nature of man — all have been shaken with a great violence. The most general cause for a low level of sex attitudes and morality is the weakening of the moral and spiritual sanctions which support high ideals of love and sexual expression. Religious sanctions of obedience and loyalty to God mean very little, if anything, in a secular society. Social pressure bears little restraint when a new technology of sex, prophylaxis, and contraception removes the triple terror of conception, infection, and detection. Added to this, there is additional freedom and protection in the anonymous stranger-patterns created by the automobile, the motel, and the apartment house. Public opinion is less hostile to illicit unions and even to perversion than it has been for a long time. The Christian churches are not free from blame in all of this, largely because of their failure to do much in a positive way to remove the confusion, ignorance, and unhealthy guilt associations which surround sex like a fog not only in our Western culture but also in many other areas of the world.

While America was curiously obsessed with the matter of sex, on the one hand treating it as if it didn't exist, yet on the

---

[11] Alexander C. DeJong, *The Christian Family and Home* (Grand Rapids, Mich.: Baker Book House, 1959), p. 37.

[12] William G. Cole, *Sex in Christianity and Psychoanalysis* (New York: Oxford Univerity Press, 1955), p. 235. Note: Space limitations do not permit an evaluation of Freud's work in this volume.

other hand exploiting it in numerous ways, Alfred C. Kinsey and his associates were discovering some facts about sexual behavior. Though many doubts have been expressed, both in the press and elsewhere, as to the validity of the Kinsey findings, it is probably fair to say that, insofar as statistical studies can give us accurate information, the Kinsey books are reliable for the type of study made. In any event, for good or ill, the lid is off. According to Kinsey's data, Americans are not sexually chaste, and their sexual behavior is not nice.

Though Kinsey's findings do not in any basic way invalidate the nature of the Christian view of sex, it is not possible for Christians to return to a pre-Kinsey era and ostrichlike insist that there is no problem about which they should be concerned.[13]

Seward Hiltner in an appraisal of the strengths and weaknesses of the Kinsey reports asks: "Is there anything in Kinsey's findings that suggests we put the Christian view of sex on the shelf as irrelevant to modern life?" Hiltner answers with an unqualified *no*. "Is there anything in these findings that brings judgment on what Christians are thinking as well as doing, not thinking or not doing, about sex today?" he asks again. His answer is an unqualified *yes*.[14]

Speaking to the same point, W. Norman Pittenger says, "For the Christian, the Kinsey reports have a particular significance. Not only do they show the plain truth that the moral standards of our fellow Americans and even of our fellow Christians, as of ourselves, are less than the most humanistically minded Christian ethic will allow . . . they also make it clear that a genuine Christian understanding of the meaning of human sexuality is almost entirely absent from most nominal Christians." [15]

The exploitation and perversion of sex is of concern to Christians because of the spiritual and moral implications. The beauty and rightness of a God-given aspect of life may be perverted and is being perverted. There is a fine line between that which

---

13 For an evaluation both of the Kinsey reports and of sex practices in America by other authorities in the field, see Jerome Himelhoch and Sylvia F. Fava, eds., *Sexual Behavior in American Society: An Appraisal of the First Two Kinsey Reports* (New York: Norton, 1955).

14 Seward Hiltner, *Sex Ethics and the Kinsey Reports* (New York: Association Press, 1952), p. 206.

15 W. Norman Pittenger, *The Christian View of Sexual Behavior* (Greenwich, Conn.: Seabury Press, 1954), p. 17.

is holy and sublime and that which is sinful and ugly. With the easy explanation that sex is nothing to be ashamed of, some people justify lust and license as the right way of living. They assume that every gratification of sex is good merely because man is physically endowed to satisfy this hunger, and thus they condone adultery and fornication as normal and desirable. It may therefore be as misleading to say that sex in itself is good as to say that sex is always bad. What we are concerned about is the right expression or use of sex. While the Christian will identify himself with God's saving plan and thus see his own sexual life in this light, the person who lacks faith will be tempted to appreciate sex on account of the pleasure which it carries with it, or the biological importance it has for the propagation of the human race. Both of these latter views are fragmentary. The Bible is explicitly clear on the privileges and blessings of sex, confirming the desire which one person has to have union with a person of the opposite sex, and states that this divinely assigned function is to bring about the "oneness of the flesh" of the two persons. At the same time the Bible is just as explicitly clear on the judgment which inevitably attends willful and sinful exploitation of sex. Chastity [16] of life is to be the badge of the Christian and serve to set him apart from the world so that his witness to the saving and keeping power of Christ will be effective. His life is to demonstrate the "bringing into captivity every thought to the obedience of Christ." (2 Cor. 10: 5)

The Christian and Sex

The consideration of a Christian view of sex begins for Lutherans on a solid confessional base. The Apology of the Augsburg Confession (XXIII, 7, 12) states: "Gen. 1: 28 teaches that men were created to be fruitful and that one sex in a proper way should desire the other [*et sexus recta ratione sexum appetat*]. For we are speaking not of concupiscence, which is sin, but of that appetite which was to have been in nature in its integrity, which they call physical love [*storgeen physikeen*]. And this love of one sex for the other is truly a divine ordinance. . . . The natural desire of sex for sex is an ordinance of God in nature and for this reason is a right [*et propterea ius est*]; other-

---

[16] Chaste: "Innocent of unlawful sexual intercourse." (*Webster's New Collegiate Dictionary*, 1959)

wise, why would both sexes have been created?" This affirms that there is nothing to be ashamed of in the fact that the human race reproduces itself in a certain way, nor in the fact that sexual activity gives pleasure. According to the Bible the body is to be used, not abused, to be enjoyed, not punished. Christianity teaches redemption of the whole person, which in every activity is to glorify God. (Rom. 12: 1, 2; 1 Cor. 10: 31; 6: 19, 29)

The Biblical view of sex is based on the premise that man is a sinner and that in his sex life as in other areas of life he stands in need of God's forgiving love and transforming grace.

Roland H. Bainton is careful to affirm that Christianity like Judaism has never condemned sex. Because the creation is good, life is good, the continuance of life is wholesome, and the means which God has instituted for its ongoing cannot be evil. Sex in Christian treatment has never been considered by itself or apart from the context of marriage, procreation, family, and the ordinary life of men and women. Broadly speaking, the church [17] like the synagog has taken a middle course between the extremes of asceticism and license. Though sex is not to be repudiated as defiling, yet it dare not be indulged in promiscuously or for private gratification apart from social responsibility, and above all not as a device for exciting emotional upheaval in the interests of religion. Sex is good but capable of abuse, and like every good is to be disciplined and subordinated to an entire way of life.[18]

Premises of This Study

This study is built upon the following premises:

First, that sex is an important aspect, area, dimension, or relationship of life which — no less than other important things — requires careful and critical consideration in the light of Christian truth.

Second, that there is emerging a kind of thought and concern about sex in relation to the total person under God, a structure of thinking and teaching which unites what modern knowledge and insight have given us with the traditional concern and intent

---

[17] Here and elsewhere in this study the word *church,* standing alone, is used for the Christian church throughout the ages, or the church dominant at the time, e. g., in the Middle Ages.

[18] Roland H. Bainton, *What Christianity Says About Sex, Love and Marriage* (New York: Association Press, 1957), pp. 9, 10.

of Christian doctrine, which needs to be described forcefully
and adequately enough so that the thinking of the church might
be deepened and expanded.

Third, that several factors in our modern society are causing
a deterioration of personal relationships, including the physiological and psychological aspects of such relationships; and that
these factors ought to be clearly seen (in their sexual aspect as
in any other) and made an item of concern and action.

Fourth, that Christian pastors and teachers will appreciate
a sound Biblical basis for effective Christian sex education, marital counseling, and pastoral care. The Christian pastor and
teacher should not be speechless or helpless before the power
and mystery of sex, but rather articulate and able to hold before
his people a Christian view of sex and marriage.

In general, that there are some old facts and new facts about
which there should be an expanded openness of discussion, some
deepening understanding of Christian points of view, and therefore something new to be said.

It is certainly our concern that the sexual life of man be interpreted from the Christian perspective. To discuss sex fully
and frankly on a secular level only, outside the Christian context, would mean losing Christian contact with a vital area of
man's experience and by so much would pervert Christianity
itself.

To help create a Christian dimension in thinking about sex
in the modern world the church must sound a clear and certain
note on the sexual nature and life of man.

THE ISSUES CONFRONTING THE CHURCH

We are living in what has been called a "sensate culture." [19]
"In all spheres of this life sex sticks out, especially in its 'free,'
abnormal, and raw forms, as the central feature of our cultural
landscape, as the obsessive preoccupation in our personal and
social life." [20]

This relaxing of sex morals is attributed by students of history to a variety of factors, such as the influence of Freudian

---

[19] Pitirim A. Sorokin, *The Crisis of Our Age: The Social and Cultural
Outlook* (New York: E. P. Dutton, Inc., 1942), Ch. i.

[20] Pitirim A. Sorokin, "The Depth of the Crisis: American Sex Morality
Today," in *Christianity Today,* IV (July 4, 1960), 3.

psychology, the scientific advances of our age, the freer association between men and women, the demoralizing effect of two world wars, the reaction to Puritan taboos, the inflexibility of the church's teaching, the effect of the Kinsey studies, the frustrations of living in modern urbanized society, and the relaxing of strict moral teachings. This study was undertaken to obtain light from the Holy Scriptures, from Christian history, and from pertinent modern studies that will help Christian leaders on the basis of all the relevant facts to find the bases for a Christian interpretation of sex.

It is time for the church to provide reliable guidance on the basis of Holy Scripture on a number of specific issues. To list these issues is to run the risk of oversimplification on the one hand and overcomplication on the other. Because of the subjectivity involved it is difficult to categorize and define clearly in the area of sex attitudes. However, the following are subjects concerning which a great many Christian people, and particularly professional church workers, have expressed doubt and uncertainty and a desire for clarification.

1. *What is the place of sex in God's design?* Why did God create mankind male and female? Why did God endow human beings with the sexual drive? Can the mature male or female normally become a "completed" person unless he or she leads a life in a married relationship to a member of the opposite sex? Is sex a mere biological urge, or does it have significant psychological and spiritual functions as well?

2. *What is the "proper" place of sex in marriage?* Must the propagative purpose be the dominant one? Are there other legitimate purposes for the marriage union? Are children a part of the *esse* (essence) of marriage — or its *bene esse* (blessings)? Is the "creative" power of marriage limited to the capacity for procreation? Should any distinction be made between the function of sex before the fall into sin and sex after the fall? In what way has the gift of sex been blighted by sin? What are the purposes and benefits of sex in Christian marriage?

3. *What is the "proper" place of sex outside marriage?* Is sex expression never moral or right outside marriage? Does marriage alone make the sexual function acceptable to God? Is the extramarital sex relation ever justified? Is this an unforgivable sin?

What is the Christian attitude toward sexual sins? Can there be a "life together in love" in which sex does not play a role? How does sexuality [21] play a role in all of life? How should a person outside marriage act toward persons of the opposite sex?

4. *When is sexual desire sinful (lust)?* What is moral or immoral in the realm of sex? At what point does sexual appetite become a transgression against the will of God? Are bodily desires to be considered natural and proper, or are they improper and sinful? When is looking at a person of the other sex "lustful desire"? When is sexual desire sin and to be denied? When is it proper and therefore to be expressed and fulfilled? What is the essence of the Moral Law in relation to the commandment "Thou shalt not commit adultery"?

5. *What is the relation of love to sex?* In what ways does the instinctive sex relation of animals differ from the sex relations of human beings? What is the nature of the chain reaction from love to sex or from sex to love? How do *eros, philia,* and *agape* relate to one another in marriage? Why must we distinguish between mere romantic love and more mature love? What is the relation between conjugal love and the love of parents, of brothers and sisters, of friends?

6. *What should the church teach regarding aberrations in sex practices?* What is the Christian evaluation of such practices as extramarital sex experiences? prostitution? homosexuality? masturbation? other perversions and deviations? Is it wrong under all conditions except in marriage to satisfy the sexual desire?

7. *What is the place of chastity, modesty, and shame in matters of sex?* The New Testament warnings against immorality have been emphasized in the church for centuries in various expressions of restraint, especially in postapostolic asceticism and in the Puritan movement. Are these concepts outmoded by modern freedoms? How can the church help its people practice Christian modesty and chastity?

8. *What should be the Christian attitude toward the modern emphasis on sex?* Many social and moral forces, scientific discoveries, and humanistic philosophies in modern society account

---

[21] Sexuality is used here as the constitution and life of the individual as a sexual being.

in part for the present emphasis on sex and contribute toward the lowering of Christian standards. How shall the Christian evaluate these forces and deal with them? How can the church counteract the exploitation of sex and help preserve Christian standards of sex morality in our society?

9. *What should be the church's responsibility and role in sex education?* Should sex education be discouraged? Does it lead to irresponsible freedom? Pastors and congregations have been divided in their answers. Can sex education be entrusted entirely to parents and the home? What role should be given to secular agencies? to public schools? to church schools? To what extent is this a responsibility of the local congregation? If the bare communication of biological facts is inadequate educationally, and spiritual values and attitudes are the most important considerations, must not the church play an important part in education for marriage and family living, including sex education?

10. *What is a Christian interpretation of sex?* How does the Christian view differ from the purely social, the biological, the secular points of view? Is it to be naturalistic? What view of sex is most in harmony with God's original design? How can the Christian keep from prudery on the one hand and from moral laxity on the other? Just when is the use of sex sanctified to the Christian?

CHAPTER 2

The Treatment of Sex in the Old Testament

ATTITUDES TOWARD SEX in the Old Testament are to a large extent inferential in character; that is, they must be derived from the observation and analysis of people's behavior. It is particularly hard to determine sex attitudes in the Old Covenant, because incidents involving sex behavior are so often recorded without comment. Still there is sufficient evidence to warrant a number of significant conclusions. In this chapter the conclusions will be grouped under two headings: The Use of Sex Which God Approves, and: The Abuse of Sex Which God Condemns. Under the use of sex it will be noted that (1) sex is very good in God's sight; (2) sex for pleasure is approved; (3) sex play is legitimate; (4) sex is openly discussed. In connection with the abuse of sex four areas will be treated: (1) fornication, (2) adultery, (3) harlotry, (4) other irregularities.

THE USE OF SEX WHICH GOD APPROVES

Sex Is Very Good in God's Sight

That the gift of sex is part of God's creation is clearly stated in the words "male and female created He them" (Gen. 1:27). It is also clear that sex is included among those things of which the Scripture says: "God saw everything that He had made, and behold, it was very good" (Gen. 1:31). Furthermore, when the Lord said, "It is not good that the man should be alone" (Gen. 2:18), He meant that it would be good for man to have a mate, such as the other creatures had; that man might have

14

a partner "after his kind" who would be his sexual counterpart. It is interesting to note that the Old Testament has no word for bachelor and that the Arabic word for bachelor means solitary one.[1]

Nor is the fact that God approved of sex brought into question by the account of the Fall. It has been suggested that Adam and Eve fell into sin by engaging in the sexual act. This argument, however, is based to a large extent on a faulty interpretation of Psalm 51:5. In this passage the Psalmist does not say that his mother became guilty of a sinful act when she conceived him, but rather that like all other human beings she was in a sinful state or condition at the time of his conception.

Sex is also good in the sight of God because it is closely linked to another divine blessing, the gift of children. It pleased God to arrange for the procreation of children through the sexual act. He did not intend to make this the sole purpose of the sexual act; He combined the blessing of children with the blessing of sexual enjoyment. The promise of children came to be one of the highly cherished blessings of the Old Testament (Gen. 13:16; 15:5); the possession of children became the mark of a happy man. (Psalms 127, 128)

By the same token the withholding of children was considered a grievous misfortune. To explain the childless marriage the Hebrew spoke of the barrenness of the wife but did not refer to the possible sterility of the husband.[2] It was said of Hannah that her womb was shut up (1 Sam. 1:5). When barren Rachel told Jacob to give her children or she would die, Jacob reminded her that such a gift of children was God's prerogative, not his (Gen. 30:1, 2). Whatever may have happened to Jephthah's daughter, whether she was put to death or devoted to the Lord in some other way, her greatest sorrow was this, that she was to remain a virgin and never know the joys of a wife and mother (Judges 11:37). By inference and implication these incidents tell us that sex and marriage came from the hand of God; that they are no less holy or worthy than any other divine gift; that Christian men and women may use them as they use all of God's gifts, namely, to His glory.

---

1 Ludwig Köhler, *Hebrew Man* (New York: Abingdon, 1953), p. 76.

2 Köhler, pp. 42, 43.

Sex for Pleasure Is Approved

The first two chapters of Genesis have been contrasted in various ways. Among other things these chapters speak of the two purposes of sex. Genesis 1 associates sex with the procreation of children (vv. 27, 28) but has nothing to say of marriage as such. Genesis 2 adds the significant feature that sexual union is a blessing in itself (vv. 18, 24), that cohabitation is approved by God. The assistant that God had in view for man was not merely a friendly man-to-man associate but rather a female counterpart who would complement him and be a helpmeet for him. That is why God also said that a man should cleave unto his wife, that is, cling to her in love, be bound to her by a mutual attraction. God crowned the whole institution of sex with the glorious capstone: "They shall be one flesh." This blessed injunction of Genesis 2 is just as important as that in Genesis 1 which bids people to be fruitful and multiply. In this one-flesh union man and his helpmeet were to experience the ecstasy of sexual completion, they were to share in the fusion of their entire personalities. Thus they were to enjoy the truly God-given purpose of sex.[3]

But the pleasure of sex itself is closely associated in the Old Testament with the joy of having children. To Eve it is said that her desire (Moffatt translates "craving") for her husband will be so strong that she will be willing to obey him and to suffer the pains of childbirth for the sake of this yearning and attraction (Gen. 3:16).[4] Sarah reacted to the promise of a son in her old age by saying: "After I am waxed old shall I have pleasure?" (Gen. 18:12),[5] which can refer to the gratification of sexual desire. Isaac and Rebekah also shared the pleasure of sex; it was Isaac's sporting with her, fondling her, making love

---

[3] David R. Mace, *Hebrew Marriage* (New York: Philosophical Library, 1953), pp. 143, 144. Mace tells us that until the cult of the Essenes was founded, about the time of Christ, there was no sign that celibacy was approved or even tolerated among the Jewish people. There was no place in Hebrew society for the "single" person. Hebrew society so ordered community life that no one was likely to be left in the condition of prolonged sexual frustration.

[4] Note the word "yet" in the RSV translation of the Hebrew. So also the German translation by Hermann Menge.

[5] The word for pleasure in Hebrew is *ednah;* in Greek, *hedone.*

to her,[6] which indicated to Abimelech that Isaac and Rebekah were husband and wife (Gen. 26:8). In early Israel, when a man's having more than one wife was apparently tolerated,[7] it was clearly stipulated that, as every wife was entitled to her fair share of food and clothing, so she was to be given her due portion of sexual enjoyment by the husband (Ex. 21:10; RSV translates: "her marital rights").

Approval of sexual pleasure is also implied in the regulation that a newly married man was exempt from military service for one year (Deut. 24:5), in the wise man's advice to be happy with a youthful wife (Prov. 5:18), and in the fact that the sheer delight of sex is the obviously dominant theme of the Song of Solomon (1:2; 2:6, 7; 4:5; 7:1-3; etc.).

There are, however, a number of circumstances or situations described in the Old Testament in which the enjoyment of sex was to be held in abeyance. When God prepared the people for the reception of the Law at Mount Sinai, He specifically told them to wash and to have no sexual relations (Ex. 19:15). Ahimelech refused to let David's men eat the hallowed bread at Nob until he had the assurance that they had had no relations with women (1 Sam. 21:4). The Levitical law forbade husbands to have relations with their wives not only during their menstrual periods but also for a period of forty or eighty days after childbirth, depending on whether the child was a boy or a girl (Lev. 18:19; 12:2, 5).[8] It would be unwarranted, however, to conclude that these instances show that sexual relations are in any way wrong. In the first two cases sexual abstinence was, like fasting, part of the preparation for worship; in the latter two abstinence was required mainly because the woman was considered to be ceremonially unclean.[9] Cultic and hygienic regulations thus set up temporary restrictions on sexual enjoyment but in no way constituted disapproval of it. Most interpreters regard these regulations regarding sex as belonging to

---

[6] We might even say "Isaacing her," inasmuch as the Hebrew verb form *mezacheq* is derived from the same root as that used in the name Isaac (*Yizchaq*).

[7] Köhler, pp. 78, 79.

[8] Friedrich Nötscher, *Biblische Altertumskunde* (Bonn: Peter Hanstein, 1940), p. 336.

[9] Note the emphasis on uncleanness and purification in Leviticus.

Israel's civil and ceremonial ordinances and not to moral law.[10] Regulations regarding health, sanitation, and ceremonies for worship are so intermingled in the Old Testament that it is difficult to distinguish one from the other. It seems that the Lord merely stressed the need for cleanliness (in a world where sanitation was scarcely known otherwise) by attaching it very closely to personal holiness and the right to worship God.

That sexual pleasure is good is also emphasized by the fact that God uses the relationship between husband and wife to describe the relationship between Himself and His people. There will be a mutually affectionate response between God and His people comparable to that beautiful attraction that binds husband and wife together (Hos. 2:14-20). God will call His people such pet names as Hephzibah ("My pleasure is in her") and Derushah ("The desired one") to show how dear they are to Him and what pleasure He finds in them. (Is. 62:4, 12)

Sex Play Is Recognized as Normal

Except for the limitations mentioned above (during periods of impurity), husbands and wives were free to enjoy sexual satisfaction as they saw fit. This includes not only the frequency with which they came together but also the manner in which they demonstrated their affection. The sporting, or playing, with Rebekah that Isaac indulged in was a type of sexual expression that was approved (Gen. 26:8). Selomeh's faithful shepherd lover spoke of looking with rapture at her breasts and navel (Song of Solomon 7:1-3).[11] The very phrase that is used in Hebrew of sexual relations, to uncover the nakedness, implies an exciting preparatory activity that is permitted between husbands and wives (Lev. 18:6 ff.). The young man in Prov. 5:18, 19 is encouraged to enjoy the wife of his youth and to be enraptured by her breasts at all times.

The many allusions to the sexual love of man for woman scattered throughout the Old Testament, the contrasts of harlotry with legitimate love-making, and the inclusion in the

---

[10] This is the case also in other cultures of the East. See David Mace and Vera Mace, *Marriage: East and West* (Garden City, L. I., N. Y.: Doubleday, 1960), p. 91.

[11] In the King James Version she is called the Shulamite.

Hebrew Scriptures of the Song of Solomon celebrating sexual love as an allegory of the love of God for Israel only reinforce the assertion that sex play in marriage is considered normal. From these incidents it is rightly inferred that husbands and wives prepared each other for the enjoyment of sex. Such preliminary sexual activity is in accordance with the precedent of the Old Testament. Looking at one another's naked body, or a mutual fondling of the bodies for the purpose of stimulating desire, is a type of sex play that lies within the scope of marital propriety.

Sex Is Openly Discussed

We do not know to what extent sex was discussed among the growing children of the Hebrew people. From the age of five onward the boy lived to a great extent with his father, while the young Hebrew girl received her training with the mother in the female quarters.[12] In either case they were given thorough instruction in the Law of the Lord (Deut. 6:7). It is evident that the Book of the Law speaks very bluntly, frankly, and directly on matters that pertain to sex. Young Joseph is described as being tempted by a seductive woman to have relations with her (Gen. 39:7ff.). Onan is pictured as deliberately pouring his seed on the ground by an act of withdrawal (Gen. 38:9).[13] If the Old Testament writers and those who used the Law for instruction had been prudish or puritanical in regard to sex, they would hardly have included these and similar accounts in the sacred text. The simple candor and forthrightness of the Old Testament narrative suggests that the coming generation was evidently prepared for marriage by a timely discussion of the simple facts of life.[14]

---

[12] Mace, *Hebrew Marriage,* pp. 214, 215; cf. also Köhler, pp. 72, 73.

[13] There are a great many such passages in the Old Testament; for instance: Ezek. 23:20; Jer. 5:7, 8; 13:27; Is. 57:3; Nahum 3:4. The writers do not wish to entertain their readers with sensuous references, for they had serious messages to deliver in all earnestness. But these references presuppose a wide knowledge of sex and an absence of prudery. Where the mind is free from prudery, all of these passages can be read with profit.

[14] "Jewish marriage was founded upon a very clear and natural acceptance of the sex impulse as a constructive force in life. Prudishness never had any place in Jewish teaching." (Stanley Brav, *Marriage and Jewish Tradition* [New York: Philosophical Library, 1951], pp. 4, 5)

THE ABUSE OF SEX WHICH GOD CONDEMNS

While the Old Testament thus recognizes a legitimate use of sex within the estate of marriage which God approves, it also has much to say about those extramarital abuses of sex which God condemns. If a man and a woman are joined as one flesh outside marriage, such a union is clearly wrong in the sight of God. Such illicit unions fall into a number of categories.

Fornication

The word fornication covers those instances in which an unmarried man has sexual relations with an unmarried woman.[15] When this took place and was discovered, the man was usually obliged to marry the woman and to pay her father fifty shekels of silver (Ex. 22:16, 17; Deut. 22:28, 29). If the father was convinced that his daughter was innocent, he was free to withhold her from the marriage and yet to demand the fifty shekels' indemnity from her seducer.[16]

Much more serious was the matter of the girl who lost her virginity in illicit relations with a man but whose loss of virginity was not discovered until she was given in marriage to another man. The husband then had the right to prefer a public charge against her, and if he was proved right, the woman was to be stoned by the men of her city at the door of her father's house. If, on the other hand, the charge was proved false, the husband was whipped, fined a hundred shekels of silver, and obliged to enter into an indissoluble marriage with the woman (Deut. 22:13-21). This severe regulation shows what importance was attached to virginity in the consummation of Hebrew marriage.

Adultery

In contrast to fornication, adultery is an act of infidelity on the part of a married person, either husband or wife. It has been maintained, however, that in the Old Testament a husband's sexual relations with another woman, provided she were unmarried, were not considered adulterous, that the wife alone could be charged with adultery.[17] But such a double standard

---

[15] Mace, p. 226.

[16] Ibid., pp. 228, 229.

[17] Mace, p. 27; cf. also Paul Heinisch and William Heidt, *Theology of the Old Testament* (Collegeville, Minn.: The Liturgical Press, St. John's Abbey, 1950), p. 189.

in sex morality is not a divine directive or teaching in the Old
Testament. It is rather a recorded social phenomenon that has
persisted throughout the Middle East until the present day and
that has had a pronounced effect on our Western sex standards.[18]
The fact that legal custom accorded the man greater sexual liberty in the Near East than the woman is shown by the common
practice of polygyny there throughout the ages. Even the old
Testament speaks of polygyny without reproof (Gen. 4:19; 21:10;
22:24; 30:3 f.; Deut. 21:15; 22:19; 1 Sam. 1:2, 6; 25:43). And
having a female slave or a captive of war as a concubine is not
considered unusual. (Ex. 21:8ff.; Deut. 21:10ff.)[19]

The Old Testament references, however, that accord the man
greater latitude in sexual matters than the woman are to be
regarded not as conveying the will of God but rather as reflecting the mores of that time which the people of God confronted
and which the Word of God eventually brought under control
and then eliminated.[20] There is evidence, for example, that at
Hosea's time the Lord held man and woman equally responsible.
In Hosea 4:14 the Lord says that He will not punish the women
for their immorality, because the men themselves gave their
wives and daughters a bad example by their unchastity. On the
other hand, the double standard in popular tradition and practice seems to have persisted even in New Testament times. Only
the woman, not the man, was brought to Jesus in the story of the
woman taken in adultery (considered by most authorities as
noncanonical, but nevertheless an Agraphon), John 8:3.[21] But
that the real moral offense in adultery, whether committed by
man or woman, is against God is shown by such references as
Gen. 39:7-9; Ex. 20:14; Deut. 5:18; 2 Sam. 12:13; Ps. 51:4;

---

18 Raphael Patai, *Sex and Family in the Bible and the Middle East*
(New York: Doubleday, 1959), p. 159.

19 Cf. Walter Eichrodt, *Theologie des Alten Testaments,* 3d ed. (Berlin:
Evangelische Verlagsanstalt, 1950). Part 3, p. 48; also Hartwig Dierks, *Social
Teachings of the Old Testament* (St. Louis: Concordia Publishing House,
1940), pp. 49—51.

20 Harold H. Rowley, *The Faith of Israel* (London: SCM Press, 1956),
pp. 17—19.

21 Mace, p. 250. As the German jurist Christian Thomasius observed:
"Among all civilized peoples, and in all times, until the date of the Lutheran
Reformation, concubinage was permitted, and even to a certain extent
legally recognized, and was an institution involving no dishonor." (Robert
Briffault, "Free Love," *Encyclopedia of the Social Sciences,* ed. Edwin R. A.
Seligman [New York: Macmillan, 1937], V, 434)

Prov. 6: 23-29. This, of course, is also the evident conclusion from
the many references to God's rejection of idolatry under the
symbol of adultery.

Although death by stoning was for both parties the Old Testament penalty for adultery (Lev. 20: 10-14; Deut. 22: 22-25; Ezek.
23: 45, 47), there is not a single instance recorded in the Old
Testament where this was carried out. This may have been
because *it is so difficult to prove* that adultery has taken place.
In Assyria and Babylonia the possibility was allowed that the
deceived husband could pardon both guilty parties in the adulterous act, but not so in Israelite law.[22] On the other hand, God
Himself gave His approval to this better way by pardoning David
after his sin with Bathsheba (2 Sam. 12: 13, 14) and by enjoining
Hosea to pardon and take his adulterous wife Gomer back.
(Hosea 3: 1)

Harlotry

One of the natural by-products of the double moral standard
in the Near East was harlotry. Prostitution appears to have
been just as much a part of local tradition and practice as
was polygyny. Tamar assumed the role of an ordinary trav-
eling prostitute who solicited business along the way, Gen. 38.[23]
When the Old Testament refers to harlots plying their trade,
it often does so without any rebuke or reprimand. This is
especially evident in the case of Rahab, who is repeatedly
called Rahab the harlot, without any kind of censure. (Joshua
2: 1; 6: 25; Heb. 11: 31)[24]

On the other hand, the fact that Dinah had been used like
a harlot by Shechem so incensed her brothers Simeon and Levi
that they slew all the males in Shechem's family (Gen. 34: 31).
Fathers in Israel were expressly forbidden to let their daughters
practice harlotry (Lev. 19: 29). A girl who had lost her virginity
before marriage was held to have wrought folly in Israel by
playing the harlot in her father's house (Deut. 22: 21). That the
daughter of a priest was specifically forbidden to practice harlotry (Lev. 21: 9) need not be interpreted to mean that any
layman's daughter was free to do this (cf. Lev. 19: 29). It should

---

22 Nötscher, p. 84.
23 Patai, p. 145.
24 Mace, p. 234; cf. Eichrodt, p. 48.

also be noted that the money paid to a harlot was an abomination in the Lord's eyes and was not to be used for a votive offering (Deut. 23:18). The people of Judah were told that they actually polluted the land with their practice of harlotry (Jer. 3:2), and the punishment of Amaziah included this, that his wife would be a harlot in the city (Amos 7:17). Finally the Book of Proverbs condemns the prostitute as one who will rob a man of his money and despoil his whole life. (Prov. 29:3; 2:18, 19)[25]

In addition to what it says about the ordinary harlot the Old Testament has much to say about the "sacred" harlot. When the Israelites entered Canaan, they came into contact with fertility cults, the followers of which indulged in illicit sexual relations as part of their cultic worship. At the entrance to the heathen sanctuaries there were not merely women called Qedeshoth, who offered themselves to the men as part of the religious rites, but also male prostitutes called Qedashim, who made themselves available to the women. It will be readily understood why the Lord vehemently condemned this practice of "sacred" harlotry.

Circumcision was the sacred symbol of Israel's covenant with her Lord. It was therefore almost blasphemous for an Israelite to be joined sexually to a "sacred" harlot, who was in the service of Baal.[26] It must also be remembered that such "sacred" prostitution posed a grave threat to Israel's religion. By these very immoral rites the Israelites were attracted to the Baals and thus lost to Yahweh. Evidence of fierce opposition to "sacred" harlotry may be noted, beginning with the falling away to Baal-peor at Shittim (Num. 25:1-5) and extending through the writings of the prophets. (Is. 1:21; Jer. 2:20; 3:1, 2; Hosea 4:14)

Other Irregularities

Thus far we have spoken of abuses that involve a normal sexual act. In addition to these we must note such abnormal or perverse practices as homosexuality and bestiality. The former is referred to for the first time when the two angels visited Lot at Sodom. At that time the men of the city demanded that the two angels be turned over to them that they might know

---

25 Mace, p. 238.
26 Mace, pp. 222, 223.

them sexually; but Lot tried to dissuade them, charging them
with acting wickedly (Gen. 19:5-7). It was this incident that
gave the name "sodomy" to such perverse sexual relations among
males. Furthermore, the Law specifically forbade a man to lie
with another man as with a woman and called such an act an
abomination (Lev. 18:22; 20:13). The references to cult prostitutes (KJV: Sodomites), on the other hand, really have
nothing to do with homosexuality. There is no evidence that
the Qedeshoth and Qedashim solicited or had relations with
people of the same sex (Deut. 23:17; 1 Kings 14:24; 15:12;
2 Kings 23:7). On the basis of the account of the creation of
Eve it may also be assumed that it is not the will of God that
people of the same sex mingle carnally. That man needed and
received a mate of the opposite sex, such as all of the other
creatures had, shows that this is the normal God-pleasing sexual
relationship (Gen. 2:18). For this reason also God forbade man
to have sexual relationships with any kind of animal. (Ex. 22:19;
Lev. 18:23; 20:15, 16)

The Old Testament speaks very directly and disapprovingly
of incest (Lev. 18:6ff.) and of rape (Deut. 22:25-27). It has
nothing to say about masturbation. The involuntary seminal
emissions that may be referred to in Lev. 15:16-18 and Deut. 23:
10, 11 produce only temporary and only ceremonial uncleanness.
From the fact that men with crushed testicles or a severed penis
were excluded from the congregation of God according to Hebrew law (Deut. 23:1) we may conclude that the Old Testament
ceremonial ordinances did not approve of castration.[27] In the
ideal future even such emasculated persons were to be accorded
a place in the community. (Is. 56:3-5)

Significant is the personal observation of sociologist David R.
Mace, author of one of the most extensive works on marriage in
the Old Testament:

> The entire positive attitude to sex which the Hebrews adopted
> was to me an unexpected discovery. It is true that I had
> always been struck by the unembarrassed plainness of speech
> with which they discussed sexual matters. But I had not fully
> realized that it had its roots in an essentially "clean" concep-
> tion of the essential goodness of the sexual function. This is
> something very difficult for us to grasp, reared as we have

---

[27] Köhler, p. 34.

been in a tradition which has produced in many minds the rooted idea that sex is essentially sinful. That sex can be a gift of God, to be received with gratitude and enjoyed freely, is a truth too long forgotten, and sorely in need of revival.[28]

SUMMARY

1. Sex in the Old Testament is clearly regarded as a valuable gift from God, not only for the purpose of bringing children into the world but also for the satisfaction of one of mankind's deepest needs and for sheer enjoyment.

2. Within the marriage relationship there is no criticism of any type of normal sexual activity. The one basic restriction placed on the satisfaction of sexual desire is that it should occur only within the framework of God's holy institution of marriage. References to uncleanness in connection with sexual functions are largely to be attributed to a desire for sanitation and the close relation between cleanliness and personal holiness in the cultus of Israel.

3. The Old Testament seems to take a discussion and understanding of sex for granted. Many of the narratives and some of the specific precepts could not be understood without a basic knowledge of the physiology of sex.

4. Polygyny was tolerated, and there are evidences in the Old Testament of a double standard in regard to sex practices, but these lack specific divine approval. God speaks out plainly against all adultery, fornication, prostitution, and such perversions as homosexuality.

5. Finally, marriage is viewed as a divinely ordained way by which men and women satisfy physical and emotional needs and provide for the continuation of society. Sex need not be explained or justified or covered with a halo of spirituality. Sex is good in itself.

---

[28] Mace, p. 262.

CHAPTER 3

What the New Testament Says About Sex

THE NEW TESTAMENT follows the example of the Old Testament in expressing positive attitudes toward sex. Some spokesmen of the church have used a number of New Testament references in support of their disparaging statements concerning marriage and sex. But a review of the pertinent material will show that the New Testament regards sex and marriage as among the "good and perfect" gifts of God.

THE NEW TESTAMENT APPROVES OF SEX AND MARRIAGE

The Approval of Jesus in the Gospels

On the positive side one may point to the presence of Jesus Himself at the wedding in Cana and the performance of His first miracle there in order to make that wedding a more joyful occasion. Thereby He certainly placed His stamp of approval on the institution of marriage and on the joy that goes with it (John 2:1-11). Jesus compared His being here on earth to the presence of the bridegroom at a marriage feast and criticized those people who believed that gloom or sadness could be possible on such an occasion (Mark 2:19). John the Baptist also used this same picture in referring to Jesus (John 3:29). Finally we cannot overlook the words of Jesus Himself, which beautifully describe the divine order of creation as an order in which men and women would regularly marry and establish homes and families (Matt. 19:4-6; Mark 10:6-9). The Biblical evidence does not support the view that Mary remained a virgin after Jesus' birth and that therefore the state of virginity is better than that of the married woman. Certainly these references do not cast any reflections on marriage but rather exalt it even more highly than it was exalted in Old Testament times.

The Apostles Echoed the Lord's Approval

St. Paul says that one of the characteristics of the latter times will be the fact that false prophets will arise, and among other things they will "forbid marriage" (1 Tim. 4:3). According to this verse in its context (v. 1) any attempt to forbid marriage in principle is a departure from the faith, in fact, a doctrine of devils. The same apostle, writing both to Timothy and Titus, makes the statement that a bishop should be the husband of one wife (1 Tim. 3:2, 12; Titus 1:6), which implies approval of marriage.[1] Although he himself was not married, Paul declared his right to have a wife if he so desired (1 Cor. 9:5), and he stated that even in situations where it might seem wiser not to marry, because the times were perilous, those who so desired had a right to marry (1 Cor. 7:9, 27-29, 36-40). He also advised the younger women to marry and have children (1 Tim. 5:14). The writer to the Hebrews advises: "Let marriage be held in honor among all, and let the marriage bed be undefiled" (Heb. 13:4).[2] In the Book of Revelation heaven is referred to as an everlasting marriage celebration, and the second coming of Christ is described as the coming of a bridegroom to claim his bride. (Rev. 19:7-9; 21:2, 9)

Alleged Disapproval Is Only Apparent

It is true that there are some New Testament passages which have been used in an effort to show that, although marriage is permitted, it is an institution less holy than the single state. In Matthew 19:12 Jesus refers to some who have "made themselves eunuchs for the kingdom of heaven's sake."[3] This refers to voluntary, self-imposed continence. It is hardly a suggestion

---

[1] Some use these passages to reject polygamy, others to forbid remarriage. Their full implications remain uncertain.

[2] "Marriage is honorable in all" (KJV).

[3] This would undoubtedly not refer to actual sterilization or castration, contrary to Deut. 23:1, but rather speaking figuratively, simply to the act of refraining from marrying.

to others, nor is it even a statement of approval. Since Jesus has
been talking about the difficulties of being faithful in marriage,[4]
it seems evident that He is telling those who find it practically
impossible to live up to His regulations regarding marriage and
divorce to be "eunuchs for the kingdom of heaven's sake," that
is, unmarried rather than to flout the will of God by marrying
and then getting a divorce.

The same thought may be carried over to what Paul says in
1 Cor. 7 (RSV). Being himself unmarried, he writes:

> To the unmarried and the widows I say that it is well for
> them to remain single as I do. But if they cannot exercise
> self-control, they should marry. For it is better to marry
> than to be aflame with passion. (Vv. 8, 9)

> But if you marry, you do not sin; and if a girl marries, she
> does not sin. Yet those who marry will have worldly troubles,
> and I would spare you that. (V. 28)

> So that he who marries his betrothed does well; and he
> who refrains from marriage will do better. (V. 38)

These passages sound very definitely as if the apostle Paul dis-
approves of marriage and grudgingly assents to it only if people
cannot refrain.

But he provides further words of explanation in the same
chapter:

> I think that in view of the impending distress it is well
> for a person to remain as he is. (V. 26)

> I want you to be free from anxieties. The unmarried man
> is anxious about the affairs of the Lord, how to please the
> Lord; but the married man is anxious about worldly affairs,
> how to please his wife. (Vv. 32, 33)

A wife and family might be a temptation for many men to
give up the faith rather than give up life. In this case it would
also be better to remain unmarried than on account of marriage
to lose one's soul.[5] However wonderful a gift of God marriage
might be, no one can deny that it might become an evil if because
of it a man were ready to sacrifice his faith. Even a right hand
or eye could under those circumstances become an evil, according to Jesus. (Matt. 5: 29, 30)

---

[4] See His statement on divorce in Matt. 19: 9, 10.

[5] This would also apply to Rev. 14:4 ("not defiled with women") if
this passage is understood as referring to marriage and not to extramarital defilement.

One scholar suggests that Paul's counsel against marriage in 1 Cor. 7 is based on the view that the end of the world is at hand.[6] He who is single will thus be in a better position to concentrate on the Lord's coming than he who is married. It is interesting to note that among the Essenes who lived in the Dead Sea community of Qumran similar advice on celibacy was given and apparently for similar eschatological reasons.[7]

In speaking of the terrible times that will come before the destruction of Jerusalem and before the end of the world, Jesus also touches on family relationships. He says it will be tragic for those that are with child and for those who give suck in those days (Matt. 24:19). He says that in those days people will exclaim, "Blessed are the barren and the wombs that never bare and the paps which never gave suck" (Luke 23:29). It is quite clear, however, that these passages do not say anything about the undesirability of marriage and the family, but refer only to the special hardships of family life in those last times of great distress.

What attitude toward sex is suggested in the statement of Jesus that in the resurrection, "they neither marry nor are given in marriage but are as the angels of God in heaven" (Matt. 22:30; Mark 12:25; Luke 20:34-36)? It is true that there is no such thing as marriage in heaven, but Jesus does not say men and women will be sexless. He merely says that the institution of marriage, with all of its divine and social restrictions here on earth, will not be necessary in heaven. Further to speculate on the condition of eternal bliss described in the New Testament would be pointless.[8]

---

[6] Frank Moore Cross, Jr., *The Ancient Library of Qumran and Modern Biblical Studies* (New York: Doubleday, 1958), pp. 74, 180.

[7] Ibid., pp. 71 ff.

[8] (1) Noesgen observes that there is no warrant for drawing conclusions from Matt. 22:30 concerning the nature of the human body in heaven (Karl F. Noesgen, *Die Evangelien nach Matthaeus, Markus und Lukas* [München: C. H. Beck, 1897], p. 151); (2) "The entire arrangement of sex, marriage, reproduction and childbirth, and all laws pertaining to these is intended for the earthly life only and not for the life to come" (R. C. H. Lenski, *The Interpretation of St. Matthew's Gospel* [Columbus, Ohio: Wartburg Press, 1943], p. 872); (3) "Marriage is necessary for men in this world, because they die, and the race must be preserved; but in the other world they do not die, and therefore marriage becomes as unnecessary for them as it is for the Angels." (Alfred Plummer, *An Exegetical Commentary on the Gospel according to St Matthew* [London: Elliott Stock, 1909], p. 306)

Sexual Expression in Marriage Assumed and Taught

The New Testament sex ethic is a continuation of Jewish teaching on sex in marriage. "The Jewish attitude tended to induce a healthy, affirmative view of coitus, which to some extent corrected an ingrained disposition to associate venereal acts and impulses with sin and evil," says D. S. Bailey of this period.[9] The virgin state which was emphasized in postapostolic times would have been considered by the orthodox Jew "an impious frustration of the purposes of God."[10] That Jesus made no change in this position is implied by His words: "Have ye not read that He who made them from the beginning made them male and female? . . . For this reason a man shall leave his father and mother and be joined to his wife, and the two shall become one" (Matt. 19:4-6). Jesus nowhere frowned on conjugal happiness. On the contrary His parables using the wedding celebration (taking home of the bride) as a symbol of the joy in the kingdom of God would be pointless unless Jesus accepted and approved also the sexual companionship in marriage. Sexual expression in marriage is plainly taught also in Eph. 5:22-33; Heb. 13:4; 1 Cor. 7:3-5; and 1 Thess. 4:1-8.

The New Testament, like the Old, assumes that such sexual expressions as enhance the nuptial joy between spouses are permitted. Restrictions on this count are not mentioned by either Jesus or the apostles. The marital privileges which husbands and wives give to one another include embracing, fondling, caressing, and other expressions of intimate affection. The sharing of sex is so important that the apostle advises against prolonged periods of abstinence and reminds spouses that their bodies are really subject to their partners. (1 Cor. 7:3-5)

Sex Discussion Not Frowned Upon

When the apostle says, "for it is a shame even to speak of those things that they do in secret" (Eph. 5:12 RSV), does he thereby forbid all discussion of sex? Hardly. He does condemn those "unfruitful works of darkness" (v. 11) which involve the misuse of sex (immorality and impurity, v. 3), and he wants no filthy jokes to be told about them. But he voices no objection

---

[9] Derrick Sherwin Bailey, *Sexual Relation in Christian Thought* (New York: Harper & Bros., 1959), p. 2.

[10] Ibid., p. 5.

to a sanctified discussion of sex whose purpose is to give young people the information which is essential to their normal sex development. Writing to young Timothy on another occasion, he urges him to flee youthful lusts and to keep himself pure (2 Tim. 2:22; 1 Tim. 5:22). This advice surely implies that such youthful lusts are known or have been explained to Timothy and that he has been given adequate information and directives for overcoming them.

THE NEW TESTAMENT CONDEMNS PROMISCUOUS OR DISTORTED USE OF SEX

Double Standard Not Tolerated

The apparent tolerance of a double standard of sex morality in the Old Testament (cf. ch. 2) is rejected in the New Testament. It may be true that at Paul's time the woman was forbidden by civil law to have more than one husband, while no such prohibition was specified for the man (Rom. 7:2, 3). It may also be true that a man who married a divorced woman was condemned by Jesus as being an adulterer, while no such specific charge was made against a woman who married a divorced man (Matt. 5:32; 19:9; Luke 16:18). But the argument from silence in both of these cases is quite tenuous. In the account of the second Gospel Jesus condemned both the woman and the man who divorced their spouses and took other partners (Mark 10:12). The apostle Paul also placed man and woman under equal moral obligations. As the wife has no power over her own body, so the husband has no power over his own body. There is no difference between male and female in the area of sexual responsibility; each is subject to the other. (1 Cor. 7:4)

There is thus good reason for stating that the New Testament has overcome the popular tradition which gave the man greater liberty than the woman in sexual relations.[11] A single standard prevails. The man is obligated to be faithful to his wife. As the Mosaic marriage legislation was tolerant of divorce because of the hardness of people's hearts (Matt. 19:8), so the double stand-

---

[11] Friedrich Hauck, "*moicheuō*," in *Theologisches Wörterbuch zum Neuen Testament*, ed. Gerhard Kittel, IV (Stuttgart: W. Kohlhammer Verlag, 1942), 741.

ard in sex responsibilities may well belong to those things which
Paul referred to when he told the people of Athens that God
had winked at the times of ignorance. (Acts 17:30)

Immorality, Adultery, Harlotry

For the promiscuous use of sex the New Testament has two
distinctive words: immorality *(porneia)* and adultery *(moicheia)*.
In its original sense the word that is translated immorality refers
to the practice of harlotry. But in the New Testament it is the
most general word for sexual abuses, including aberrations among
both married and unmarried people.[12] The word that is translated adultery is much more restricted and is used only of unfaithfulness on the part of married people.

In Paul's warning against sins of the flesh he seldom touches
on the word adultery.[13] The reason apparently is that he slots
almost all of what he has to say about sexual abuses under the
more general label of immorality (1 Thess. 4:3).[14] Repeatedly
Paul places immorality side by side with uncleanness. (2 Cor.
12:21; Gal. 5:19; Eph. 5:3; Col. 3:5)[15]

By contrast Jesus preaches against adultery (Matt. 5:27;
14:3, 4; John 4:18). But our Lord does not have much to say
about immorality in general. When He does use the word (Matt.
5:32 and 19:9), it is almost always in the context of marital
unfaithfulness and therefore really means adultery.[16] This difference in emphasis between Paul and Jesus may well be attributed
to the fact that the impact of Hellenism exposed Paul's readers
to graver and more extensive sexual excesses than the earlier
church had had to contend with.

Whether it be immorality among the unmarried or adultery
among the married, the New Testament makes it abundantly
clear that such promiscuity is incompatible with the kingdom of

---

[12] William F. Arndt and F. Wilbur Gingrich, *A Greek-English Lexicon
of the New Testament* (London: Cambridge University Press, 1957),
pp. 699, 700.

[13] But see Rom. 2:22; 13:9.

[14] Hauck, IV, op. cit., fn. 35.

[15] Friedrich Hauck and Siegfried Schulz, *"porne," Theologisches Wörterbuch zum Neuen Testament*, ed. Gerhard Friedrich, VI (Stuttgart:
W. Kohlhammer, 1959), 593.

[16] Ibid., VI, 591, 592.

God. In his listing of sins that will deprive one of entrance into the Kingdom Paul places immorality on one side and adultery on the other side of the cardinal sin of idolatry (1 Cor. 6: 9, 10; cf. also Heb. 13: 4; Rev. 2: 21, 22). Sexual aberrations are an expression of the sinful flesh and are therefore opposed to the activity of the Spirit (Gal. 5: 19, 22). All of these abuses of sex are of this world, but the follower of Christ is bidden to seek the things that are above. (Col. 3: 1-7; cf. also James 4: 4) [17]

Finally, our Lord was aware of the seriousness of sexual offenses, but He was also willing and ready to forgive. The adulteress who was caught in the act deserved death according to the then prevailing Jewish justice (John 8: 4 ff.). Yet Jesus set aside this penalty on the basis of theological and ethical considerations. He not only forgave the guilty woman when she gave evidence of repentance, but He also maintained the validity of God's moral requirements by warning her to sin no more.[18]

Like immorality and adultery the activity of harlots is vigorously opposed and condemned in the New Testament. Harlots engage in a business that is opposed to the righteousness of the Kingdom which God requires (Matt. 21: 31 ff.; Luke 15: 30). While the church of God is pictured in the New Testament as the pure and spotless bride of Christ (Rev. 21: 9 f.), the unchristian forces of the world are likened to a great whore who misleads the nations and their kings. (Rev. 17: 1, 2)

Harlotry is denounced not only regarding the prostitute but also regarding the client. The Greek word *pornos* may mean both the immoral person in general (as noted above) and also the client of the harlot or the one who sponsors and promotes her business. Men who patronize harlots are described as being excluded from the kingdom of God (Eph. 5: 5; 1 Tim. 1: 10; Heb. 13: 4; Rev. 21: 8; 22: 15). In his appeal to the Corinthians Paul says that a Christian who is a temple of the Holy Ghost, whose body is a member of Christ, cannot give his members to a harlot. (1 Cor. 6: 15-20; cf. *Theol. Wörterbuch*) [19]

---

[17] Ibid., VI, 593.

[18] John 7: 53—8: 11 is not found in the best ancient mss, but it is regarded as a well-attested or historically correct Agraphon. Hauck, IV, 742.

[19] Hauck and Schulz, VI, 593.

Other Sexual Irregularities

In the New Testament there are frequent references to homo-sexuality, the offense so characteristic of the Greco-Roman world. Homosexuality, both male and female, is mentioned and denounced. Paul noted that God gave the Gentiles up "to dis-honor their own bodies between themselves" (Rom. 1:24), that "even their women did change the natural use into that which is against nature; and likewise also the men, leaving the natural use of the woman, burned in their lust one toward another, men with men working that which is unseemly [RSV: men committing shameless acts with men]." (Rom. 1:26, 27)

Paul said that the Law was given to curb males who had relations with males [20] and that such would not inherit the king-dom of God (1 Tim. 1:10; 1 Cor. 6:9). Jude added that eternal damnation was the lot of the people of Sodom and Gomorrha who indulged in unnatural lust. (Jude 7)

Incest is also reproved in the New Testament. The apostle Paul demanded that the man who had taken his father's wife be excluded from the Christian congregation (1 Cor. 5:1-5). It is not certain exactly what relationship is meant here or on what basis the objection to it was raised. It seems unlikely, however, that the father's wife was actually the man's mother. She was probably his stepmother. It is also unlikely that the apostle Paul, in writing to a congregation that was largely Gentile, was basing his objections on Jewish law (Lev. 18:8). His objection was probably based on the fact that this type of relationship was obnoxious also to most heathen, since he says it is "not so much as named among the Gentiles."

The New Testament, like the Old, is silent on the matter of autoerotic practices such as masturbation. The same must be said of the automatic or unconscious processes of sexual activity, such as nocturnal seminal emissions. It should also be mentioned that the New Testament passage which is held by some to refer to masturbation actually refers only to homosexuality. (1 Cor. 6:9; see above)

---

[20] Greek: *arsenokoitai.*

Misdirected or Excessive Desire

In its condemnation of sexual abuses the New Testament includes not only immoral acts but also immorality in such areas as speaking, thinking, looking, and desiring. When the apostle mentioned filthiness, foolish talking, or jesting in connection with the things that should not even be named among the Ephesians, he was no doubt including any kind of speaking that would make light of the sacredness of sex or would belittle the fearful evils associated with a misuse or perversion of it (Eph. 5:3, 4). This would include any kind of indecent songs and jokes and stories. The Christian's speech should rather be "always . . . with grace, seasoned with salt." (Col. 4:6)

Our Lord named the heart as the source of unclean thoughts (Matt. 15:19; Mark 7:21). He made clear that anyone who looked at a woman to lust after her had committed adultery with her already in his heart (Matt. 5:28). Peter also felt constrained to mention those who had eyes filled with adultery. (2 Peter 2:14)

But is the desire for the opposite sex not something which God Himself put into man and which therefore must be good? Certainly! According to the order of creation in Genesis 1 and 2, which our Lord approved (Matt. 19:8), sex is a gift of God that is good (cf. ch. 2). At what point, then, or in what connection does such a God-implanted sex impulse become a sin? The New Testament answers: When it becomes lust *(epithymia)*, that is, when it is a desire that is either misdirected or excessive.

Epithymia is usually translated in the King James Version as "concupiscence." [21] The Revised Standard Version has been consistent and translated the word with "lust" all the way through. Apparently all translators have felt, however, that the word as most often used in the New Testament has an evil connotation, suggesting either misdirected or excessive desire. The latter interpretation is indicated, for example, in Col. 3:5, where the word *pathos* immediately precedes it; or in 1 Thess. 4:3-5, where the same word is used as a parallel. The King James Version

---

[21] The Greek *epithymia* means "desire, longing." It includes legitimate longing, for instance, for food. Jesus uses it so in Luke 22:15 "I have earnestly desired to eat this passover with you." Later it came to be restricted more to evil longing, such as desire for the neighbor's house or wife. Paul uses it thus in Rom. 7:7: "I had not known lust, except the law had said: Thou shalt not covet." Cf. Hauck, op. cit., IV, 742.

translates *pathos* with "inordinate affection," whereas the Revised Standard Version translates it with "passion." Both translations indicate excess. In another instance the idea is rendered by the word "burn" (KJV), or "be aflame with passion" (RSV).

Sex is misdirected when it is permitted to focus on or cling to a person of the opposite sex whom one cannot rightfully possess. For the unmarried this means desire for sexual satisfaction with a person to whom one is not yet married. For the married it means desire for sexual satisfaction with a partner other than the one to whom one is married. Sex desire is excessive when it is carried to such extremes that it distracts a person from other purposes of life and from spiritual pursuits. This is likely to happen particularly to the unmarried if the unsatisfied sex urge is permitted to hamper a person in his work, in his studies, in his other normal pursuits. But it may also happen within marriage, as is indicated by Paul's advice to the Thessalonians. Husbands are bidden to possess their vessels ("take a wife," RSV) in sanctification and honor, not in the passion of lust (1 Thess. 4:4, 5). The urge for sexual satisfaction within marriage should never reach the point where consideration for the partner is overlooked. Neither the married nor the unmarried person is to burn with inordinate affection, to be aflame with uncontrolled passion. (Col. 3:5)

There are also some references in the New Testament to the shame of being unclothed or improperly clothed. Nakedness is spoken of as a definite shame (Rev. 3:18; 16:15). Reference is also made to the evil of looking on something which incites misdirected or excessive desire (Matt. 5:28; 2 Peter 2:14). This could easily include a person indecently clothed.

Paul's Statements on the Works of the Flesh

A passage which has given rise to many misinterpretations is Gal. 5:16-24 (the conflict between the flesh and the spirit). The word "flesh" has been interpreted in terms of Hellenistic and Manichaean teaching, that the body is evil and only the soul is good. The conclusions drawn were that anything that has to do with the body is sinful, including all sexual relations. This, however, is a misreading of the passage and an oversimplification of the term "flesh" as used in the New Testament. Here *sarx* (flesh) has an ethical sense and means "the earthly nature of man apart from divine influence and therefore prone to sin and opposed to God." [22] Luther in his preface to the Epistle to the Romans says, "Thou must not understand 'flesh,' therefore, as though that only were 'flesh' which is connected with unchastity, but St. Paul uses 'flesh' of the whole man, body and soul, reason and all his faculties included, because all that is in him longs and strives after the 'flesh.'" Melanchthon defined it as the entire nature of man "without the Holy Spirit." [23]

In this passage fifteen sins are enumerated (against six commandments), including anger, idolatry, selfishness, envy, drunkenness, strife. Only three of them have sexual connotations: immorality, impurity, licentiousness. All of these stirrings of the sinful self are to be restrained and kept in check because they repress rather than express the new life in Christ. "Those who belong to Christ Jesus have crucified the flesh with its passions and desires." Galatians 5:24 has likewise been falsely interpreted to mean that the virgin state (or abstinence in marriage) is a holy and desirable thing. However, this verse refers to the disciplining of all sinful strivings of the heart, such as selfishness and anger as well as immorality and impurity. This mortification, however, does not refer to the quenching and repressing of normal and wholesome sexual desires in marriage, which are neither immoral nor impure but holy and God-given and to be satisfied in marriage. (1 Cor. 7:3-5)

THE NEW TESTAMENT AND HUMAN SEXUALITY

There is no comprehensive or systematic treatment of sexual matters in the New Testament, just as there is no systematization of other doctrines. Even 1 Cor. 7 is not a rounded out and complete coverage of the subject. It is rather a collection of answers to submitted questions concerning problems of sex in a certain place. Bailey summarizes Paul's position briefly in these words:

> "He chose a middle way, commending celibacy without condemning marriage, and approving continence in those who possessed the gift while recalling husbands and wives to the

---

[22] The word *sarx* is used in a number of ways in the New Testament. Thus it means the physical body in Eph. 5:29. See Arndt-Gingrich, s. v. *sarx*, pp. 750—752.

[23] Quoted in J. H. Thayer, *A Greek-English Lexicon of the New Testament* (New York: American Book Co., 1889), s. v. *sarx*.

obligations of their state, and bluntly telling the 'highly-sexed': It is better to marry than to burn." [24]

Nevertheless, the New Testament says something very significant and far-reaching on human sexuality. Our Lord taught that every breach of fidelity in marriage is sin and in this way elevated also the sexual relation of man and wife. In His sayings, parables, and miracles He taught the infinite value of every soul and the dignity of every person under God. His whole ministry was an expression of love and forgiveness — which is to be our pattern for all human relationships, especially the relationships between the sexes. Jesus applied the rule of chastity to both sexes without partiality. In the Gospel He gave the world the transforming power that has raised man's regard for man and lifted to new heights the institution of marriage and the family. Asceticism regarding sex is wholly absent from Jesus' teaching.

The apostle Paul expounds the one-flesh principle from Gen. 2 and sees in the nuptial union spiritual significance. It is a symbol of the unity of Christ and His church, and, like the latter, somewhat of a mystery that may never be fully comprehended by finite man (Eph. 5: 25-32; 1 Cor. 7: 3-5; 6: 12-20). Paul sees an equality between man and woman regarding sexual rights (1 Cor. 7:4). Above all Paul has given the world a concept of Christian love which transforms marriages (1 Cor. 13; Eph. 5) and which condemns all exploitation of personality. He gives a profound and realistic treatment of intercourse in the context of the Christian's total commitment to God, including his body (1 Cor. 6: 12-20). Bailey gives this insight into Paul's meaning:

> 1 Cor. 6: "The apostle denies that coitus is, as the Corinthians would have it, merely a detached and peripheral venereal function involving no more than an appropriate exercise of the genital organs. On the contrary, he insists that it is an act which, by reason of its very nature, engages and expresses the whole personality in such a way as to constitute a unique mode of self-disclosure and self-commitment." [25]

While Paul's statements have been the point of departure for many misinterpretations and distortions, his treatment of sex

---

[24] Bailey, p. 13.

[25] Bailey, p. 10. See also his book: *The Mystery of Love and Marriage* (New York: Harper & Bros., 1952), pp. 50—54.

in 1 Cor. 7 should be viewed in the light of his total teaching on the life "in Christ."

In a context which includes the concepts both of marriage and of abstinence from food the apostle states that those who believe and know the truth receive marriage with thanksgiving as a gift of God to be consecrated by the Word of God and prayer. (1 Tim. 4:1-5)

The New Testament teaches Christian consideration of one spouse for the other. While wives are to be submissive to their husbands (Eph. 5:22; Col. 3:18; 1 Peter 3:1), husbands are to love their wives as their own bodies (Eph. 5:28; Col. 3:19) and live with wives "considerately . . . bestowing honor on the woman as the weaker sex, since you are joint heirs of the grace of life, in order that your prayers may not be hindered" (1 Peter 3:7). Consideration of the partner also in sex matters is never to be overlooked. To force intercourse on a wife otherwise willing and co-operative also in matters of sex, is immoral and reprehensible.[26] Thus the New Testament teaches mutuality in conjugal relations. With sexual intercourse in marriage, as with abstention, there should be mutual agreement (1 Cor. 7:5). In their marriage relations Christian husband and wife are to live together as mutual partakers of divine grace, equally entitled to the blessings of God and sharing the privileges, duties, and responsibilities of their marriage.

The New Testament's central teaching that Christ's redemptive suffering and death on the cross atones for all sins, also human aberrations in the realm of sex, affects the Christian's attitude toward the sexual transgressor more than any other Biblical truth.

SUMMARY

1. The attitude toward sex expressed in the New Testament is in general identical with that expressed in the Old Testament. This is obvious and is expected by those who acknowledge the same Lord as the Author of both divisions of Scripture.

2. The New Testament reinforces Old Testament conclusions with regard to the purpose of sex and its proper use only within the marriage relationship. The New Testament, ad-

---

26 Sometimes called by scholastic theologians "rape within marriage."

dressed to the Greek and Roman world, emphasizes morality in thought and desire.

3. The New Testament knows no double standard of morality. It deals not only with sexual transgressions but also with the motives and desires of the heart. Sexual impulses which are either misdirected toward a person specifically forbidden by God or excessive to the extent that they exclude other proper Christian behavior are called lust and are looked upon as adultery in the heart.

4. The New Testament condemns all immorality, adultery, fornication, harlotry, not only in acts but also in words and thoughts. Those who persist in such sins in stubborn resistance to the will of God and in impenitence cannot inherit the kingdom of heaven. Living an immoral life is incompatible with the Christian profession. Various sexual perversions are severely condemned, especially homosexuality.

5. The apostle Paul, though misinterpreted by those who have torn some of his statements out of context (particularly 1 Cor. 7 and his references to the works of the flesh), sets forth some basic teachings concerning sex, conjugal rights, love and respect of husband and wife, and the management of sex as a gift of God in sanctification and honor.

6. Like the Old Testament the New emphasizes that sex is a wonderful gift of God. Like all other blessings, it is to be received with thanksgiving (1 Tim. 4:3, 4) and sanctified by the Word of God and prayer. (1 Tim. 4:5)

CHAPTER 4

Sex Attitudes of the Apostolic and Postapostolic Fathers

HISTORIANS DETECT a distinct difference between Judeo-Christian concepts of marriage and sex and the concepts developed in the first four centuries among the ante-Nicene and the post-Nicene fathers. Why this change? How account for this difference?

In the Old Testament marriage is the accepted pattern of life, and celibacy and asceticism are practically nonexistent. Sex is accepted as part of life and as a God-designed arrangement for man and woman. This has been called the naturalism of the Old Testament.

No appreciable change is noticed in the teachings of Christ. Going back to Genesis, He taught that in marriage man and wife become one flesh in a union that is to endure for life. He uses the bride-bridegroom relationship as a symbol of the union of the church with Himself. Jesus consistently emphasizes right motives. This is His frame of reference for such statements as: "Whosoever looketh on a woman to lust after her hath committed adultery with her already in his heart." (Matt. 5:28)

The apostle Paul makes the forthright statement: "If you marry you do not sin" (1 Cor. 7:28). He urges husbands and wives to give each other their conjugal rights and cautions against any prolonged continence (1 Cor. 7:3-5). He insists on the right to marry and be accompanied by a wife (1 Cor. 9:5). In the classic passage in Eph. 5 he presents a sublime conception of conjugal love and marriage. This does not sound like a man who is convinced that "sex is evil in and of itself." Yet his statement, "It is well for a man not to touch a woman" (1 Cor.

7:1), has caused much debate and has been classified by some as the entering wedge of monasticism.

A full consideration of the context reveals that Paul wrote in answer to specific questions from Corinthian Christians, in view of definite social circumstances and deeply conscious of the imminence of the Lord's return. An eschatological and apocalyptic note runs all the way through 1 Cor. 7 (for instance, vv. 29-31). While he counsels caution in view of the prevailing circumstances (7:38), he not only recognizes the place of marriage in God's order but also encourages faithfulness in marriage. (7:10, 13, 14, 16, 27)

Some students accuse Paul of being the victim of Hellenistic dualism,[1] but others hold that Paul's strongly ascetic note, e. g., in 1 Cor. 7:8, 9, 32-35, is purely incidental and was influenced by the immoral atmosphere of the times, as well as by the belief in the nearness of great political and social transformations through the expected second coming of Christ. (1 Cor. 7:28-32)[2]

A reaction on the part of Christians against the moral corruption of the pagan world could be expected. Sacred prostitution in pagan temples was rife, and ordinary fornication was common. Various forms of sexual perversion are strongly condemned in the first chapter of the Epistle to the Romans. Corinth was notorious for its moral laxities.[3]

> In the Graeco-Roman world prior to the rise of Christianity stringent laws were enacted against adultery on the part of a wife, but men continued to be allowed to cohabit with mistresses and concubines with restrictions limiting the choice to approved sections of the community. A concubine, however, was recognized by law as a quasi wife in the absence of a legal partner *(uxor),* and differed only from her by being of a lower social status, and the union less binding.[4]

---

[1] William Graham Cole, *Sex in Christianity and Psychoanalysis* (New York: Oxford University Press, 1955), pp. 40, 41.

[2] Philip Vollmer, *New Testament Sociology* (New York: Fleming H. Revell Co., 1923), pp. 139, 140.

[3] Ernest C. Messenger, *The Mystery of Sex and Marriage in Catholic Theology,* Vol. II in *Two in One Flesh,* 2d ed. (Westminster, Md.: The Newman Press, 1950), pp. 107, 108; Messenger gives as references Augustine's *De civitate Dei,* lib. III, cap. 80; lib. VII, capp. 21, 26, etc.

[4] Edwin Oliver James, *Marriage and Society* (New York: Hutchinson's University Library, 1952), p. 155. See also Hans Licht, *Sexual Life in Ancient Greece,* 7th print. (London: Routledge & Kegan Paul Ltd., 1953), chs. i, p. 6; ii, pp. 4, 7; and Otto Kiefer, *Sexual Life in Ancient Rome,* 6th print. (London: Routledge & Kegan Paul Ltd., 1953), chs. i, iii, vii, Conclusion.

Secular writers have attributed the attitude of the post-apostolic church to three factors: "(1) survival of primitive taboos on sex in the life and teaching of the Hebrews; (2) ascetic cults which practiced rigid denial of the demands of the body; (3) the philosophical dualism of Greek thought, which drew a sharp distinction between the soul and body, making the former akin to the divine and the latter the source of all evil." [5]

William Graham Cole, in *Sex in Christianity and Psychoanalysis*, writes:

> The prevailing dualistic thought about the flesh and spirit produced two types of reaction. The first was asceticism, which regarded all sexual activity, even among married persons, as evil. The second went to the other extreme and regarded all things bodily as matters of complete indifference. These antinomians demonstrated their contempt for the flesh by indulging in sexual orgies. . . . He [Paul] was too good a Jew to adopt either of these positions, asserting the essential goodness of sex and marriage and recognizing the psychosomatic unity of body and soul, so that whatever occurs in one realm inevitably affects the other. Yet, he was enough a child of the Hellenistic age to rate celibacy as superior to marriage.[6]

Mervin Monroe Deems, writing on the sources of Christian asceticism, traces certain sex attitudes to the mystery religions, the cults of Pythia, Athene, and Demeter, which held that before man can approach God he must be pure and that sexual intercourse robbed one of this necessary purity. This was early and generally accepted in the first century of the Christian era. The majority of the Essenes forbade marriage.[7]

Nor was this teaching confined to the Graeco-Roman world. It was also found in Buddhism and Islam. All the cult religions required abstinence from sexual relations as a precondition for the exercise of holy acts. Old taboos were still operative, holding that sexual relations always make the participants unclean, even in marriage. "He who has relations with a wife renders himself unclean, since in procreation dangerous demons are at

---

[5] Andrew G. Truxal and Francis E. Merrill, *Marriage and the Family in American Culture* (New York: Prentice-Hall, Inc., 1953), p. 61. See also E. O. James, pp. 150, 157.

[6] Pp. 38, 39.

[7] Mervin Monroe Deems, "The Sources of Christian Asceticism," in *Environmental Factors in Christian History*, eds. John Thomas McNeill, Matthew Spinka, Harold R. Willoughby (Chicago: University of Chicago Press, 1939), pp. 150, 152, 153.

play, while the continent gathers physical and psychic powers
and secret energies which lift him into the suprarational, holy
world." [8]

Philo (30 B. C. to A. D. 50) had high admiration for the contemplative ascetic life and held the soul to be "a fragment of
divinity" and that the body was "a heavy burden." Pleasure and
appetites were "keepers of the prison, the body," and Philo
would flee them. "His asceticism arose from the dualism in
Greek philosophy, and his goal was control of the body in order
that the soul might contemplate God." [9]

Hellenism, paganism, and asceticism helped to set the tone
for postapostolic writings. The literature of this time does not
restrict itself to the express statements of the Scriptures but
deals largely with speculations about those things on which the
Scriptures are more or less silent. Questions like these are asked:
Even though the Bible permits marriage, is it really right for
the Christian? Is sex, as such, basically good or basically evil?
Has the Christian any right to the "enjoyments of the body"?
Such questions occupy the theological leaders down to the time
of the Reformation.

THE ANTE-NICENE CHURCH FATHERS (A. D. 170—325)

The attitudes toward sex in the early church seem to pass
through a rather definite cycle. The earliest church fathers, in
common with the apostles, apparently had a high regard for
marriage and sex. This position declined until virginity and
celibacy were practically always rated far more God-pleasing
than marriage, and all sex activity even within a legitimate union
was stigmatized as inherently evil.

The Greek Fathers

The early Greek fathers, Messenger writes, "tended to hold
the balance more fairly between marriage and virginity, and to
avoid exaggeration in either direction." [10] Clement of Alexan-
dria (d. A. D. 217) spoke of marriage as "a sacred image to

---

[8] Friedrich Heiler, *Der Katholizismus: Seine Idee und seine Erschei-
nung* (München, Germany: Verlag Ernst Reinhardt, 1923), pp. 104, 446.
Rudolf Hirzel, *Zur heutigen Ehenot* (St. Gallen, Switzerland: Vadian
Verlag, 1949), p. 21.

[9] Deems, pp. 152, 153.

[10] Messenger, II, 139.

be kept pure from those things which defile it." He spoke of the "crime" of despising matrimony, instituted by God and sanctified by Christ.[11] "Not to rear up children," he said, "is to dissolve states and society and is an unmanly evasion of responsibility." [12]

Justin Martyr (A. D. 100—166) asserted that Christians married only for the sake of procreation and that many, including men, kept themselves as virgins. Marriage, he taught, becomes for the Christian a matter of self-control. In this position he was supported by Athenagoras and Tatian. Minucius Felix says that Christians are "temperate and chaste and marry only once, if at all." Montanism in the last half of the second century, while permitting marriage, discouraged it and designated second marriage adultery.[13]

Writing of the period of the Roman Empire, Bainton says in effect: Life in the flesh, specifically in marriage, was increasingly disparaged by the Gnostics in the second century. The followers of Marcion (ca. 100) demanded either celibacy or continence within marriage for all Christians. The Gnostic Satornilus branded marriage and the begetting of children as the work of Satan. Tatian (A. D. 110—172) held that marriage is corruption and fornication and that Paul's reluctant concession of marriage was tantamount to condemnation. This period was marked by a tendency to regard every measure of self-denial as meritorious, including the withdrawal of married couples from marital relationship.[14]

Origen (A. D. 185—254) claimed that Adam definitely did not have sexual knowledge of his wife until after the fall and

---

[11] Johann C. W. Augusti, "Von der Ehe," in *Handbuch der christlichen Archaeologie* (Leipzig: Dyk'schen Buchhandlung, 1836), III, 131.

[12] Quoted by Roland H. Bainton in *What Christianity Says About Sex, Love, and Marriage* (New York: Association Press, 1957), p. 33; see also Clement, "Stromata," II, c. 23, in *Ante-Nicene Fathers*, eds. Alexander Roberts and James Donaldson, American Reprint of the Edinburgh Edition, rev. and chronologically arr. by A. Cleveland Coxe (New York: Christian Literature Co., 1896), photolithoprinted (Grand Rapids, Mich.: Wm. B. Eerdmans Publ. Co., 1953), II, 378. Hereafter cited as *ANF*.

[13] Deems, pp. 159, 160.

[14] Bainton, pp. 25—31, with a reference to Karl Müller, *Die Forderung der Ehelosigkeit aller Getauften in der Alten Kirche,* Sammlung gemeinverständlicher Vorträge und Schriften aus dem Gebiet der Theologie und Religionsgeschichte, No. 126 (Tübingen: J. C. B. Mohr [Paul Siebeck], 1927), p. 25.

tended to agree with an ancient Jewish theory that without sin
our first parents would have propagated their kind, not by sexual
union but in some "mysterious angelic manner." [15] Gregory of
Nyssa, while approving Origen's idea, maintained that man in
the state of innocence possessed a body as well as a soul and
therefore must at least have had the sex organs.[16]

Messenger asserts that some early heretics "insisted too
strongly upon marriage and despised virginity," [17] then cites
the apocryphal Acts of Paul, Acts of Peter, and the Acts of John,
Thomas, and Andrew as glorifying virginity, possibly by way of
reaction. He mentions one fragment of the Acts of John, where
the apostle, invited to a wedding, explains to the bridal pair
that the conjugal act is a crime and a sin. In the same book
a certain Drusiana refuses to allow her husband to perform the
conjugal act even though threatened by death. When she is
killed, her husband, Adronicus, is consoled for the death of his
wife by being told about all the cares and troubles which come
with having a family. Messenger points out that all these stories
are "tainted with Ebionite and Gnostic ideas" and show a beginning of a deformation of the Christian tradition.[18]

Significant is this quotation from the Acts of Paul (ii, 5, 6):

Blessed are the pure in heart for they shall see God. . . .
Blessed are they that keep the flesh chaste. . . .
Blessed are they that abstain [or: the continent]. . . .
Blessed are they that have renounced the world. . . .
Blessed are they that possess their wives as though they
     had them not. . . .
Blessed are they that have kept their baptism *pure*. . . .
Blessed are they that for love of God have departed from the
     fashion of the world. . . .
Blessed are the bodies of the virgins. . . .[19]

The Roman Fathers

In the Western, or Roman, world before the Council of Nicea
we find, as Messenger puts it, "a tendency to depreciate mar-

---

[15] Origen took such a literal view of Matt. 19:12 that he castrated himself
before being ordained. Cf. Messenger, II, 15, 141.

[16] Messenger, II, 15.

[17] Ibid., II, 141, 142. See *The Clementine Homilies* III. 68, in *ANF*,
VIII, 250.

[18] Messenger, II, 142.

[19] Deems, p. 163.

riage and to use exaggerated [derogatory] language concerning the female sex in general, and the marriage state in particular." [20]

In the *Shepherd of Hermas,* written about A. D. 140, we find this statement: ". . . To your [Hermas'] wife, who is to be *your sister.*" [21] Cyprian (A. D. 200—258) wrote: "Chastity is the dignity of the body, the ornament of morality, the sacredness of the sexes, the bond of modesty, the source of purity, the peacefulness of home, the crown of concord. . . . What else is virginity than the glorious preparation for the future life? . . . Virginity is the continuance of infancy. Virginity is the triumph over pleasure." [22]

Tertullian

It was Tertullian (born ca. A. D. 150), however, who brought to a climax the extremely rigorist views of some of the leaders of the early church against all sexual matters. Although the doctrine of celibacy for the clergy, the advantages of the celibate state for all, the glorification of virginity developed at a gradual pace throughout the succeeding centuries, the writings of Tertullian [*Ad uxorem, De exhortatione castitatis, De monogamia*] seemed to have reached a peak from which there was a sort of reaction among succeeding church fathers.

It is interesting to note that this very same Tertullian wrote one of the finest passages in praise of marriage, defending his own point of view as opposed to that of Marcion, who forbade marriage altogether. He said:

> Meat and drinks are not on this account to be condemned, because, when served up with too exquisite a daintiness, they conduce to gluttony. . . . So, on the same principle, the state of matrimony is not to be refused, because, when enjoyed without moderation, it is fanned into a voluptuous flame.[23]

He paints this word picture of a Christian man and his wife:

> . . . together they pray . . . together perform their fasts; mutually teaching, mutually exhorting, mutually sustaining. Equally they are both in the church of God; equally at the banquet of God; equally in straits, in persecutions, in refreshments. Neither hides anything from the other; neither shuns

---

20 Messenger, II, 146.

21 *Shepherd of Hermas,* Vision second, ch. II, in *ANF,* II, 11.

22 Cyprian, "Of the Discipline and Advantage of Chastity," in *ANF,* V, 588, 589.

23 Tertullian, "Against Marcion," I, ch. 29, in *ANF,* III, 294.

the other; neither is troublesome to the other. The sick is
visited, the indigent relieved with freedom. . . . Between
the two echo psalms and hymns; and they mutually challenge
each other which shall better chant to the Lord." [24]

However, it was this same Tertullian who wrote: "The Lord
Himself said, 'Whoever has seen a woman with a view to concupiscence has already violated her in his heart.' But has he
who has seen her with a view to marriage done less or more? . . .
Accordingly the best thing for a man is not to touch a woman;
and accordingly the virgin's is the principal sanctity, because it
is free from affinity with fornication." [25]

Writing what he calls a sort of last will and testament to his
wife, he says that marriage may be good, but celibacy definitely
is preferable. He interprets "It is better to marry than to burn"
(1 Cor. 7:9) with the comment: "Nay, but how far better it
is neither to marry nor to burn!" [26]

Taking up the arguments usually advanced in favor of a second marriage, Tertullian writes:

> I am aware of the excuses by which we color our insatiable
> carnal appetite. Our pretexts are: . . . a house to be managed;
> a family to be governed; chests and keys to be guarded;
> the wool-spinning to be dispensed; food to be attended to;
> cares to be generally lessened. . . . "In my present (widowed)
> state, too, a consort in domestic works is necessary." (Then)
> take some spiritual wife. Take to yourself from among the
> widows one fair in faith, dowered with poverty, sealed with
> age. You will (thus) make a good marriage. A plurality of
> *such* wives is pleasing to God.[27]

Tertullian restricted the term monogamy to that institution
which prohibits second marriages (even after the death of the
spouse). He states that even the heathen have such high regard
for single marriages that virgins at their weddings will have no
one as a brideswoman who has been married more than once.[28]

Eusebius of Caesarea [A. D. 280—339] in the days of Con-
stantine well formulated the previous development when he
posited two grades of Christian conduct: the first for the laity,

---

[24] Tertullian, "To His Wife," II, ch. 8, in *ANF*, IV, 48.
[25] Tertullian, "Exhortation to Chastity," ch. 9, in *ANF*, IV, 55.
[26] Tertullian, "To His Wife," I, ch. 3, in ANF, IV, 40.
[27] Tertullian, "Exhortation to Chastity," ch. 12, in *ANF*, IV, 56. For
a fuller description of "spiritual wife" see D. S. Bailey, *Sexual Relation in
Christian Thought* (New York: Harper & Brothers, 1959), pp. 33—35.
[28] Tertullian, "Exhortation to Chastity," ch. 13, in *ANF*, IV, 57.

who might participate in pure marriages, just wars, and in farming, trade, and civic pursuits; and the second for the clergy, requiring celibacy, poverty, aloofness from the world, and complete dedication to God. The only new element in this formulation is the equation of the distinction between the levels of conduct with that between the clergy and the laity.[29]

All of this, of course, coincided with the monastic movement, where the self-denial went even farther — not merely getting away from women but getting away from mankind.[30]

In this era of the church there were three "unforgivable" sins: fornication, apostasy, and bloodshed. The commission of any of these excluded from fellowship in the church. Later, of course, this severe position was challenged and modified.

In his chapter on "Marriage and Morals," E. O. James, an Anglican church historian, speaks of the postapostolic period as a time when nuptial intercourse, while not regarded as sinful, was represented as "little more than a lawful substitute for fornication," and celibacy was extolled "as the counsel of perfection, while marriage was a secondary alternative for those who could not aspire to the ideal." Efforts were made to restrict more and more the conjugal life of the clergy, forbidding altogether a second marriage. At the Council of Elvira (ca. 295) conjugal abstinence was enjoined on all persons in the major religious orders. In his footnotes James cites as the basis for this thinking both Scriptural passages (1 Cor. 7:8, 40; Heb. 13:4; 1 Cor. 7:2, 5, 9, 20, 38; Gal. 5:16-24; Rev. 14:4) and the church fathers (Origen, Cyprian, Eusebius, Ambrose, Jerome, Athenagoras, Hippolytus). [31]

THE POST-NICENE FATHERS (A. D. 325—590)

Greek Fathers

Among the Greek fathers of the post-Nicene period, St. John Chrysostom (A. D. 345—407) is probably the most interesting. He apparently modified the extreme views expressed by some earlier writers, although he, too, held that in the original state Adam and Eve could not have had sexual relations. He wrote, "When sin had entered through disobedience . . . as a result

---

[29] Bainton, pp. 27, 28; Cecil John Cadoux, *The Early Church and the World* (Edinburgh: T. & T. Clark, 1925), p. 469.

[30] Bainton, p. 28.

[31] E. O. James, p. 149.

Almighty God, according to His wisdom, provided for the propagation of the human race and granted that our race should be increased through sexual union." [32] While in one of his sermons on Colossians Chrysostom expresses the point of view that marriage is something honorable and holy,[33] he counseled a young friend against marriage "because having once affianced himself to Christ, to contract thereafter a human marriage would be adultery." [34]

Chrysostom maintained that marriage is no obstacle to salvation, that it was established for procreation but since the fall its chief end is to be a remedy for concupiscence, that it is established by God and honored by Jesus; but even so it is not the perfect state — marriage is good, but virginity is better.[35]

Latin Fathers

Among the Latin fathers, Jerome (A. D. 331—420) says that since St. Paul declared it is good for a man not to touch a woman, therefore it is bad to do so, for there is no contrary to good other than bad; that marriage cannot possibly be good, since it renders prayer difficult; that though there may have been some saints among married people, these have always kept a virginal life even in marriage.[36]

Bainton says that Jerome went as far as anyone could go in disparaging marriage on four counts: first, marriage rates only 60-fold reward in comparison with virginity, which is reckoned at 100; second, the Creator Himself refrained from pronouncing a blessing upon the second day of creation because the number *two* prefigured marriage; third, only the unclean animals went into the ark two by two; and fourth, marriage distracted thoughts from the religious life. He quotes Jerome as saying that the only good of marriage is that it produces virgins.[37]

Ambrose (A. D. 340—397) in his *Apology for David* writes:

---

[32] Messenger, II, 143.

[33] Ibid., II, 144.

[34] Bainton, pp. 31, 32; *Nicene and Post-Nicene Fathers of the Christian Church*, ed. Philip Schaff (New York: Chas. Scribner's Sons, 1886), photolithoprinted (Grand Rapids, Mich.: Wm. B. Eerdmans Publ. Co., 1956), First Series, IX, 113. Hereafter cited as *NPNF (1)*.

[35] Messenger, II, 143.

[36] Ibid., II, 146.

[37] Bainton, pp. 29, 30.

"Marriage is indeed good, and the copula holy. Nevertheless, as St. Paul says, let those who have wives be as those who have not. The marriage bed is undefiled, and no one is to defraud the other party, except for a time, that they may give themselves to prayer. Even so, according to the apostle, a man does not give himself to prayer while he is exercising the use of the bodily contract." [38]

Augustine

Among all the early Christian writers Augustine (A. D. 354 to 430) has most to say on the subject of sex and marriage. He was the father of Latin theology and laid the foundation of the classical Catholic doctrine on marriage still held today.[39]

Before his conversion Augustine was for nine years a follower of Manichaeism, which believed in a rigid asceticism and disciplining of the flesh. It identified the body with evil and the soul with good. When Manichaeism no longer satisfied him, Augustine turned to Neo-Platonism, which taught that "pure goodness is pure Being; pure evil is absolute non-being." [40] These two influences, antedating his conversion to Christianity (in A. D. 386), Augustine carried with him into his speculative theological writings. This helps to account for his thinking.[41]

Having lived many years with a concubine, he knew the strength of the human sex drive and after the transformation of conversion longed to live without "the degrading necessity of sex." He set himself the task of reconciling this subduing of the flesh with the conjugal relations of husband and wife in marriage.[42]

Augustine regarded both marriage and virginity as good but held that neither marriage nor virginity is commanded by God. The individual is left a choice in the matter. Marriage, he said, was honorable and good but exists chiefly for those who cannot contain themselves. Virginity is more God-pleasing because it demands more self-discipline.[43]

---

[38] Messenger, II, 147.

[39] Messenger, II, 147.

[40] Cole, pp. 44, 46.

[41] Heiler, p. 104.

[42] Cole, p. 44.

[43] Ibid., pp. 57, 64. Cf. "Of Holy Virginity," in *NPNF (1)*, III, 419, 420; Messenger, II, 149.

But Augustine never gave "a clean bill of health" to marriage. It was always to be hedged about with conditions and modifications. Roland H. Bainton summarizes Augustine's thinking as follows:

> Since procreation is definitely approved, the sexual act as such cannot be wrong. Nevertheless, it is never without wrongful accompaniments. There is never an exercise of sex without passion, and passion is wrong. If we could have children any other way, we would refrain entirely from sex. Since we cannot, we indulge regretfully. Augustine almost voices the wish that the Creator had contrived some other device. If we are to fulfill His will, we are inevitably placed in the position of being constrained to sin. This sin, however, is covered by the sacrament of marriage to the degree that that which outside of marriage would be a mortal offense, within marriage is only venial. The same point applies to relationships within the marriage bond for satisfaction rather than progeny. The practice is condemned, yet no married couple will profess to have confined itself to the needs of procreation. The offense is again covered by the sacrament.[44]

In a lengthy treatise Augustine attempts to explain how it is that, if marriage is something evil, Christ performed a miracle at a wedding and forbade men to put away their wives except for fornication. He recognized that procreation could not be considered the sole purpose of marriage, for in that case, whenever no children are possible (as in the case of barrenness or old age), there would be no marriage. He then concludes that marriage can be a good thing even without begetting children, since it gives a couple an opportunity to resist temptation, namely, to have sex relations for other purposes than procreation. He says, "It should be a matter of praise to have been unwilling at the first to do what they have power to do." [45] This was "increasing merit by augmenting temptation." [46]

Derrick Sherwin Bailey, in his carefully documented work, *Sexual Relation in Christian Thought*, summarizes and evaluates Augustine's thinking on the subject of sexuality:

> Augustine held that the sexual consequences of this original transgression still persist in us, and are shown by the inability of the will to govern the genitals, and by the shame generally

---

[44] Bainton, pp. 42, 43.
[45] Augustine, "On the Good of Marriage," in *NPNF (1)*, III, 400.
[46] Bainton, p. 23.

aroused by coitus — so that the act is always veiled in secrecy,[3] and even parents blush to think of what they have done together.[4] Concupiscence reveals itself continually in the unbidden motions of the organs;[5] at one time tumescence occurs involuntarily, while at another impotence defies the prompting of the mind and 'lust has to be waited.'[6] But above all concupiscence is displayed through the sexual impulses themselves, which are stronger than the other passions and less tractable to the sway of the will, and can only be satisfied in an orgasm which engulfs the rational faculties in violent sensual excitement. This led Augustine to a virtual equation of original sin, concupiscence, and venereal emotion,[7] from which he drew the inference that while coitus in theory is good, every concrete act of coitus performed by fallen man is intrinsically evil — so that every child can be said literally to have been conceived in the "sin" of its parents.[8] Venereal desire as implanted by God for the promotion of the increase of mankind is blameless, but the same desire, corrupted by concupiscence, is shameful and sinful;[9] and since generation cannot occur unless the carnal union of husband and wife is motivated and aided by the seductive stimulus of fleshly lust, neither can it ever occur without at least material fault.

[Bailey's footnotes:] [3] Cf. *de civ. Dei*, xiv. 18 [The City of God, in *NPNF (1)*, II, 277]; *de grat. Chr. et de pecc. orig.*, ii. 39 [34] [On the Grace of Christ and on Original Sin, *NPNF (1)*, V, 251]; *de nupt. et concup.*, ii. 36 [21] [On Marriage and Concupiscence, *NPNF (1)*, V, 297]. [4] *De nupt. et concup.*, i. 6 [5] [*NPNF (1)*, V, 265]. [5] Cf. *de Trin.*, xiii. 18 [23] [On the Trinity, *NPNF (1)*, III, 180]; *de nupt. et concup.*, i. 30 [*NPNF (1)*, V, 276]. [6] *De nupt. et concup.*, i. 7 [6] [*NPNF (1)*, V, 266]; cf. *de civ. Dei*, xiv. 16 [*NPNF (1)*, II, 275]. [7] See N. P. Williams, op. cit., pp. 366, 367 [N. P. Williams, *The Ideas of the Fall and of Original Sin* (London, 1927)]. [8] *De pecc. merit. et remiss.* i. 57 [29] [On the Merits and Remission of Sins, *NPNF (1)*, V, 37]. [9] Cf. *c. duas epist. Pelag.*, i. 31 [15] [Against Two Letters of the Pelagians, *NPNF (1)*, V, 386][47]

This, of course, left unanswered the question: Can marriage itself then be defended as an honorable, God-ordained, and God-pleasing state? Bailey summarizes Augustine's answer thus:

As concupiscence cannot take away the good of marriage,[2] neither can marriage mitigate the evil of concupiscence [3] — but it can serve to moderate venereal desire, and to divert it harmlessly and usefully to the task of procreation. Wedded chastity,

---

[47] Derrick Sherwin Bailey, *Sexual Relation in Christian Thought* (New York: Harper & Bros., 1959), pp. 55, 56; also Bailey's footnotes, to which the editor has added the English titles, volume, and page numbers in *NPNF (1)*.

in fact, consists in transforming coitus from a satisfaction of
lust to a necessary duty,[4] and when the act is employed for
generation it is excused of its inherent sinfulness [5] — though
it remains none the less the channel by which concupiscence
and the concomitant guilt are transmitted from parents to
their children. Hence arises the need for baptismal regeneration, by which the guilt (*reatus*) of lust is washed away —
though the impulse (*actus*) of lust remains, and with it the
sense of sexual shame.[6]

[Bailey's footnotes:] [2] *De grat. Chr. et de pecc. orig.*, ii. 38 [33],
42 [37] [*NPNF (1)*, V, 250—252]. [3] *De nupt. et concup.*,
i. 8 [7]: "We ought not to condemn marriage because of the
evil of lust, nor must we praise lust because of the good of
marriage." This proposition Augustine illustrates by the
example of the lame man limping to do good; the evil of the
limp does not affect the good object, nor does the latter alter
the evil of the limp. [*NPNF (1)*, V, 266, 267]. [4] Ibid., i. 9 [8],
[*NPNF (1)*, V, 267]. [5] Cf. *de bono conj.*, x [On the Good of
Marriage, *NPNF (1)*, III, 304]. [6] Cf. *c. duas epist. Pelag.*, i. 27
[13], 30 [15] [*NPNF (1)*, V, 385, 386]; also *de nupt. et concup.*,
i. 19, 25, 26 [*NPNF (1)*, V, 271, 274].[48]

Bailey reaches the conclusion that Augustine's theory of
human sexuality rests on no more substantial basis than his
own speculative thought:

The practical consequence of this teaching could only be to
establish the assumption that almost all coitus is in some
degree culpable, since the act excused of its intrinsic sin by
a premeditated purpose of generation, and undisfigured by
sensual feelings, is really a grotesque and somewhat repulsive
abstraction — not to say a physiological absurdity. Augustine
must bear no small measure of responsibility for the insinua-
tion into our culture of the idea, still widely current, that
Christianity regards sexuality as something peculiarly tainted
with evil.[49]

Augustine's chief thrust is against concupiscence:

Since concupiscence entered into the whole of the life of
fallen man, and especially in his sexual activity, no sexual
union takes place without its corrupting effect. . . . All children are born out of the workings of concupiscence, and they
inherit both the reality and the guilt of this lust. . . . They are
not evil because they are human; their humanity as such is
the creation of God and therefore good. The evil lies rather

[48] Ibid., p. 56.
[49] Ibid., pp. 58, 59.

in their concupiscence, which is a pollution, a degradation, a loss of being.[50]

Augustine says: It is particularly appropriate that the generative organs should be especially affected, for it is through them that the results of the original sin are passed on from generation to generation.[51]

As we review the moral-philosophical-theological thought of the bishop of Hippo we note that Augustine held many opinions *without Biblical support;* for instance, that before the fall the sexual urge was controlled entirely by reason and the will and not by emotions; that this urge was wholly in the service of and with the purpose of procreation; that polygamy was permitted to people the earth and in order to procreate more people for God's chosen race; that the heavenly "mansions" reserved for those possessing virginity will have greater glory than those for the married; that virginity is of such value that not even the desire to raise up children for Christ can compensate for its loss.[52]

Augustine tends to *rationalize;* for instance: that polygamy was never for the satisfaction of the flesh; that the evil of concupiscence does no harm if the will does not agree to the promptings of the instinct.[53]

Augustine appears also to be *inconsistent,* for instance: when he classifies both marriage and virginity as good yet exalts the latter; when he counsels the Christian man and wife to make a mutual vow of celibacy, following the example of Mary and Joseph, who, he asserts, lived in such celibacy, that is, companionship which does not depend on physical intercourse at all.[54]

Augustine shows his inconsistency further when he presents the second purpose of marriage: fidelity, i. e., the purpose of putting out the flames of passion within lawful bonds. But even while he purports to allow this purpose of marriage, he actually nullifies it by restricting its use and by insisting that its exercise is in any case a sin, even though a venial one.[55]

To understand Augustine it must be remembered that he

---

50 Cole, pp. 50, 51.
51 Augustine, *City of God* xiv. 16, in *NPNF (1),* II, 275, 276.
52 Cole, pp. 51—55.
53 Ibid., pp. 52, 55, 57.
54 Ibid., pp. 51, 57.
55 Ibid., pp. 58, 59.

regarded fasting and virginity as pathways to God and self-denial as a meritorious work.[56]

Cole suggests that Augustine had a scale of values in which he places virginity *first*, celibacy on the part of those who once had sex experiences *second*, marriage for procreation *third*, and sexual relations out of love and pleasure in marriage *fourth*.[57] The key offense was concupiscence, which he identified with sexual desire whether in marriage or outside marriage.[58]

Sex and the Postapostolic Age

The abnormal ascetic view of sex and marriage was a mark of the entire postapostolic age. It was influenced more or less by a number of cultic-theological-cultural movements: Encratism, Essenism, Ebionism, Gnosticism, Montanism, and Novatianism.[59]

Sex was viewed (almost morbidly) with distaste, suspicion, and antipathy. It was deplored that God ever created sex and ordained it as a means of procreation. Everything about sex was considered unseemly, unclean, shameful, and a hindrance to the holy life. This appears not only from the writings of the theological leaders and from apocryphal literature of the time but also from such sources as canons, decrees, conciliar and synodal enactments, and regulations concerning marriage, priestly celibacy, and virginity.[60]

While it is true that a negative view of sex represented by men like Tertullian, Augustine, and Jerome (leaving their writings to influence subsequent centuries) carried the field, yet they were extremists, and the rank and file of the church held to a saner interpretation of sex and marriage. Most of the fathers held that wedlock was "relatively a good and not necessarily a hindrance to the devout life, provided it was used with moderation." The saner views were expressed in such documents as *The Apostolic Tradition,* the *Didascalia,* the *Sahidic Heptateuch, The Statutes of the Apostles,* the *Canons of Hippolytus.* The extreme views were opposed, for instance, by Synesius of Cyrene, Helvidius, Jovinian, and Vigilantius. This opposition

---

[56] Ibid., pp. 59, 60, 65.
[57] Ibid., p. 62.
[58] Ibid., pp. 49, 50, 55.
[59] Bailey, pp. 36—39.
[60] Ibid., pp. 39, 69—75.

was, however, not very effective. Bailey in his extended treatment of the patristic age concludes: "The fact that they [the extreme ascetic views] were tolerated at all, and that they passed without ecclesiastical censure, is in itself a significant comment upon the early church's ethical and theological view of the family." [61]

Seward Hiltner evaluates this period of the church's history as follows:

> By the fourth century of our era, the suppression of any sex life was considered by many Christians to be a positive good in itself, better pleasing to God than the married state. Although marriage was not held to be contrary to God's will, it was felt to be inferior to celibacy. Many church leaders after the third and fourth century, unlike those of the New Testament, held or implied that abstinence from sexual expression was itself a kind of road to salvation. This was, as the Protestant Reformers later pointed out bluntly, attempting to achieve salvation by a form of "works." [62]

SUMMARY

1. As the first century of the Christian era came to a close, a marked change was apparent in the teachings of the church regarding sex and marriage. This change was a departure from the naturalism of the Old Testament. Scholars attribute this change to a number of factors: (1) the dualism of Greek thought; (2) the asceticism common to many religions of that day; (3) the pagan licentiousness of the Graeco-Roman world; (4) the statement of St. Paul: "It is well for a man not to touch a woman."

2. In the Ante-Nicene period the shift of emphasis passed through three stages: from a high regard for marriage to an equally high regard for virginity and marriage, and then to a higher regard for virginity than for marriage. Instead of being accepted as a gift of God for the good of man, sex was viewed with distaste, suspicion, and antipathy. Justin Martyr asserted that Christians married for procreation only and that many married couples "kept themselves as virgins." By A. D. 295 a council could decide that all who were in religious orders should maintain conjugal abstinence.

---

61 *Ibid.*, pp. 46, 99, 25, 26.

62 Seward Hiltner, *Sex and the Christian Life* (New York: Association Press, 1957), p. 56.

3. It is significant that this concept of a "pure life" and a "perfect life" developed by the church fathers is closely related to monasticism and its false ideal of withdrawal from the world. Connubial intercourse was considered one of the "works of the flesh." Those who did not regard it as sinful viewed it as "little more than a lawful substitute for fornication." This is a period in which nonbiblical asceticism entered the church's thinking and colored its views of the place of sex in human life.

4. In the Post-Nicene period Augustine further confused the situation with his unbiblical speculations and scholastic rationalizations. He virtually equated original sin, concupiscence, and sexual emotion so that every concrete act of coitus performed by fallen man (also in Christian marriage) was regarded as intrinsically evil. Augustine placed virginity first, celibacy second, sexual union for procreation third, and coition for pleasure fourth in his scale of values. The suppression of any sex life was considered a positive good. Virginity and self-denial were regarded as meritorious works and pathways to God.

5. Some historians hold that the extremely ascetic views of the church fathers were not practiced by the rank and file of the church. Bailey contends that these views are distinctive of the whole post-Apostolic period and holds it to be significant that they passed without ecclesiastical censure. One thing is certain: the warped thinking of this period shaped Christian thought for centuries to come.

CHAPTER 5

The Church of the Middle Ages

THE PEOPLE of any age are never completely divorced from the past. Perhaps more than we are ready to admit, the moral teachings of the Middle Ages have carried over into our thought patterns. This is true also in the realm of sex.

Four movements may be discerned in this period: (1) the influence of secular society,[1] particularly the moral standards of the Germanic and Celtic societies; (2) the extremes developed from the church's drive for a celibate clergy; (3) the influence of the cult of courtly love; (4) the thinking of the scholastics and the systematization of morals by Thomas Aquinas.

Monastic Communities

From the time of St. Benedict (A. D. 480—543) monastic communities sprang up everywhere, binding members together not in families but in celibate societies for devotion, study, and manual labor. Men and women were no longer viewed primarily as founders of families.

Something similar took place in secular society. Feudal lords set up joint households in their castles with common meals and with servants, chaplains, soldiers, and entertainers living in close quarters. Even the manor house in the village offered only a little more privacy than the castle.

The crusades and foreign wars removed father and husband from the patriarchal family and contributed to the rise of chivalric and romantic love with its inroads on sex and marriage.

---

[1] *Secular* is used in the sense of nonecclesiastic, nonmonastic.

Even the revival of pagan classical culture in the Renaissance contributed to certain sexual liberties and license.[2]

The Sex Mores of Secular Society

One contributing factor to the sex mores of the Middle Ages was the invasion of the Roman Empire by the pagan Goths and Celts. Some historians believe they contributed to the double standard of morality with a vulgar approach to sex and regarded woman as little more than property; while others consider them less offensive than the Romans.

Roland Bainton in discussing this period of the church's history makes the comment that "the Western world of the Middle Ages served in many respects to demean marriage."[3] Although there is some evidence that the Germans were more restrained in their sexual behavior (the Roman historian Tacitus declaring that barbarians behaved better in this respect than Romans), abundant evidence shows that among the Celts premarital chastity was not the rule, and sexual hospitality was long practiced. If the Germans were more rigid in their standards of sex conduct, they made light of marriage by their concept of male domination over the property and person of the woman.

The Church and Celibacy

Another factor which served to minimize regard for sex and marriage was the emphasis of the church on virginity and clerical celibacy.[4] Bainton mentions highly popular tales like that of St. Alexius, who at the very altar forsook his bride to go on a pilgrimage to the Holy Land and did not let her see him again until his death. He also tells the story of a priest who kept his wife at a distance. When he was on his deathbed, she came to say farewell, but he forbade her with the words, "Depart, woman, take away the straw, for there is yet fire here." Priestly celibacy was not fully established until about the end of the Middle Ages.

---

[2] Edwin Oliver James, *Marriage and Society* (New York: Hutchinson's University Library, 1952), pp. 118—120.

[3] Roland Bainton, *What Christianity Says About Sex, Love, and Marriage* (New York: Association Press, 1957), pp. 45 ff. See also Karl Weinhold, *Die Deutschen Frauen in dem Mittelalter*, 2d ed., I (Wien: Druck und Verlag von Carl Geroldts Sohn, 1882).

[4] The term *virgin* is used in its general sense of a woman or man who has not had sexual intercourse. The term *celibate* is used of a person who has taken a vow to remain unmarried.

Obviously the persistent attempt to force celibacy on the priests tended at the same time to depreciate marriage. Virginity was constantly held up as the ideal; antifeminine literature was widely distributed. Bainton quotes Abel Lefranc as saying that "on the eve of the Reformation marriage appeared to be an institution in disrepute. . . . Marriage was sacramental, lifelong, primarily for progeny, unromantic, and rating below virginity." [5]

Extreme Views

Modern Catholic writers blame the attitude of the Middle Ages on "the Henricians, Cathari, Albigenses, and other 'heretics,' who carried on the Manichaean tradition, definitely condemned the institution of marriage, and regarded the marriage act itself as essentially sinful." [6] The Cathari, for example, avoided sex so completely that they would not even eat anything connected with processes of sex: no eggs, cheese, butter, or milk. Bainton comments: "Luckily they did not know that fish and vegetables have sex." [7] Catholic writers admit that during the Middle Ages the church itself went to great extremes in attempting to belittle the sexual side of marriage. Complete abstinence from sex relations had to be maintained on no less than five days out of seven, on Thursdays in memory of the arrest of our Lord, on Fridays in commemoration of His death, on Saturdays in honor of the Blessed Virgin, on Sundays in honor of the resurrection, and on Mondays in honor of the faithful departed. However, they insist that "more reasonable theologians such as Petrus Cantor and Robert de Courson, pointed out that this very rigorous attitude constituted an indirect attack on the institution of marriage itself." [8]

Archbishop Egbert, writing during this same period, said that when a man took his legitimate wife home, they should observe continence the first three days. On the third day their mass should be celebrated. After that they should conduct their marriage before God and world "as necessity compels them."

---

[5] Bainton, p. 56.

[6] Ernest C. Messenger, *The Mystery of Sex and Marriage in Catholic Theology,* Vol. II in *Two in One Flesh,* 2d ed. (Westminster, Md.: The Newman Press, 1950), p. 152.

[7] Bainton, p. 58.

[8] Messenger, II, 153.

All families should maintain continence forty days and nights before Easter and the entire Holy Week, also on Sunday, Wednesday, and Friday. Wives should preserve their purity three months before delivery of a child and 60 days and nights thereafter, no matter whether it be a boy or a girl.[9]

There was some debate as to what the sin in the sex relationship might be. "Hugo of St. Victor (1097—1141) thought that it lay in the pleasure concomitant with the act; Peter Lombard (died 1164), that it was connected with sexual desire; Albertus Magnus, that it was to be found in the weakness of man's reason, whereby he cannot enjoy pleasure without losing sight of the First Good." [10]

In summarizing the influence of the asceticism of the early church on the later Middle Ages, the Schaff-Herzog *Encyclopedia* says: "Thus the estimate of matrimony in comparison with the sanctity of the monastical and priestly states remained low. The unchastity [incontinence] of many monastics and celibates and the low valuation of marriage induced in the laity a moral degeneracy which was intensified toward the end of the Middle Ages by the coarseness which literature took on, by habitual slander of woman, and by the humanistic renascence of pagan lasciviousness and contempt of matrimony." [11]

The Struggle for Celibacy

As a part of the spirit of asceticism which pervaded the post-apostolic church down through the Middle Ages, regulations against the marriage of priests or any dedicated church workers were to be expected. The clergy, however, did not give up the right to normal family life without considerable struggle, and celibacy was not definitely established in the church until the Fourth Lateran Council in 1215, and the Council of Trent, about 1570. The struggle was more prolonged in the Eastern Church, where the asceticism of the West never did take such a firm hold.

---

[9] *S. Egberti Eboracensis Archiepiscopi Poenitentiale,* lib. II, caput XXI, in J. P. Migne, *Patrologiae cursus completus* (Paris: D'Amboise, 1844, and Garnier Fratres, 1878 seq.), series secunda, LXXXIX, 419.

[10] Derrick Sherwin Bailey, *The Mystery of Love and Marriage* (New York: Harper & Bros., 1952), pp. 56, 57.

[11] *The New Schaff-Herzog Encyclopedia of Religious Knowledge,* ed. S. M. Jackson (Grand Rapids, Mich.: Baker Book House, 1949—53), VII, 194.

The Eastern Orthodox Churches have never embraced clerical celibacy, and even in the Roman Church to this day the Uniate Greek clergy is permitted to marry.

It is generally agreed that by the time of Pope Leo the Great (d. A. D. 461) celibacy for the clergy was widely favored. However, in succeeding years church laws were often disregarded by the clergy, and many and serious abuses crept in. Priests would take wives without the benefit of wedlock, have children by them, and then just before death be legally married in order that they might pass on their property to their children. In this way church property and church offices became in many cases matters of inheritance. In the eleventh century Pope Gregory VII took vigorous and determined steps to wipe out all marriage of priests and to prevent the ministrations of those who would not give up their wives and families. It was largely his influence and the influence of his successors which eventually won the day for celibacy.[12] Bainton says, however, that in many areas "clerical marriage was simply succeeded by clerical concubinage and in the age of Renaissance popes made no secret of concubines and bastards." [13]

The Cult of Courtly Love

A third factor which tended to make light of marriage during the Middle Ages, according to Bainton, was what he calls "The Cult of Romantic or Courtly Love," [14] the forerunner of our modern American "romantic fallacy." [15] The three conditions of this love are that "love ennobles," "the beloved must be superior to the lover," and "love must be a quest ever uncertain." This type of love was held to be impossible within marriage, because the legal character of marriage makes it possible to take love for granted. Also in marriage the woman is the equal if not the inferior of man, and in marriage there is "no exhilarating

---

12 For a complete discussion of clerical celibacy see *The Catholic Encyclopedia* (New York: Robert Appleton Company, 1908), III, 483—487.

13 Bainton, pp. 54, 55. Also see Henry Charles Lea, *History of Sacerdotal Celibacy in the Christian Church,* 4th rev. ed. (London: Watts & Co., 1932).

14 Ibid., pp. 58—63.

15 See, for example, Andrew G. Truxal and Francis E. Merrill, *Marriage and the Family in American Culture* (New York: Prentice-Hall, 1953), pp. 129 ff.

quest, no furtive fulfillment." Says Bainton: "The conditions of
courtly love are best realized if the lover address himself to
a married woman on whom he has less than a claim and whom
he cannot enjoy without stealth and adventure. Hence courtly
love became the cult of adultery." [16]

There is some question, however, as to whether the romantic
view of marriage actually involved sex relations (as pictured in
Arabian Nights) or whether it was an outgrowth of the mystical
eroticism of St. Bernard and the so-called "cults of the Virgin."
One writer even contends that the cult of romantic love was an
outgrowth of the Catharian repudiation of all life in the flesh.[17]
Possibly both theories are correct, since some transition was
needed before the romantic idea could be combined with the
Christian view of marriage. "The cult of the virgin, the lyrical
rhapsodies of St. Francis toward *La Donna Poverta*, Dante's devotion to the etherealized Beatrice may so have contributed to
the refinement of romance as to make possible its attachment
to the sacrament of marriage." [18] The more mystical type of
romance always involved the concept of love unfulfilled and is
best illustrated by such stories as that of Abelard and Eloise or
Tristan and Isolde, where "fulfillment is forever deferred in
order to prolong the delights of languishing." [19]

Platonic Love Revived

E. O. James sees in the period of romantic love (12th to 14th
centuries) a throwback to Platonic love, which regarded the love
relationship a response to physical beauty. This was, however,
fundamentally a philosophical concept in which conjugal love

[16] Bainton, p. 60; Clive S. Lewis, *The Allegory of Love* (London: Oxford University Press, 1936 [1953 print.]), pp. 12, 13, 36; Alexander J. Denomy, "An Inquiry into the Origins of Courtly Love," in *Medieval Studies* VI (1944), 175—260. Charles George Crump and Ernest Fraser Jacob, eds., *Legacy of the Middle Ages* (New York: Oxford University Press, 1926), pp. 403—405.

[17] Denis de Rougemont, *Love in the Western World*, trans. Montgomery Belgion (New York: Harcourt, Brace and Co., 1940), referred to by Bainton, pp. 62, 63.

[18] Bainton, pp. 66, 67.

[19] Bainton, pp. 60—62; cf. also, "The love concept of the troubadors," the "cult of the Virgin," or the "cult of the lady," mentioned in Crump and Jacob, pp. 403—405; Johan Huizinga, *Herfstty der Middeleeuwen* (Haarlem: H. D. Tjeenk Willink en Zoon, 1928), pp. 148—158; 166—176; William James, *The Varieties of Religious Experience* (London: Longmans, Green and Co., 1902), p. 318.

had little or no place and was sublimated in a search for goodness and truth. "Love of wisdom, not of wife and children, was the foundation on which a sound and harmonious personal and social life alone could be established. Yet Plato did bring into prominence the psychological and intellectual factors which raise human love to its unique level and make it distinct from non-rational instinct, though he failed to place them in the natural context in the institution of marriage." [20]

Our Western concept of romantic love is the outgrowth of this period of history. What it came to be eventually is summed up well by Herbert Spencer in 1890:

Round the physical feeling forming the nucleus of the whole, are gathered the feelings produced by personal beauty, that constituting simple attachment, those of reverence, of love, of approbation, of self-esteem, of poverty, of love of freedom, of sympathy. These, all greatly exalted, and severally tending to reflect their excitements on one another, unite to form the mental state we call *love*. And as each of them is itself comprehensive of multitudinous states of consciousness, we may say that this passion fuses into one immense aggregate most of the elementary excitations of which we are capable; and that hence results its irresistible power.[21]

Toward the end of the Middle Ages, Bainton points out, Albrecht von Eyb in his *Ehebüchlein* of 1472 presents a more balanced picture of love and marriage as "joyous, delightful, and sweet," with love tying man and wife to each other and parents to children and lessening the ills of life while multiplying the joys. [22]

The Scholastics

The fourth and most influential factor of the Middle Ages in determining the church's teaching on sexuality was the thinking of the Scholastics, especially the moral philosophy systematized by Thomas Aquinas.

Among the Scholastics there was much debate as to what actually constitutes marriage: consent only, coitus only, or consent and coitus. Gratian, a Benedictine writer of the 12th century, held that only a union in which coitus has taken place,

---

20 James, p. 198.
21 Quoted by James, p. 196.
22 Bainton, pp. 69, 70.

which he termed *conjugium ratum* [valid union], is indissoluble. Peter Lombard (d. 1164) claimed that both consent and coitus symbolized the intimate relationship of Christ and the church. Gandulph suggested that this symbolism obtained only if procreation or payment of the conjugal debt is the intention of coitus. Vacarius maintained that only the one-flesh relation makes a union valid. The ecclesiastical courts, which had gained full jurisdiction over marriage, followed Roman jurisprudence and held consent to be decisive. Marriage was viewed more as an institution and less as a personal relationship.

There is much evidence that the Scholastics found references to sex embarrassing, and pleasurable emotions connected with it reprehensible. Peter Lombard, though rejecting the idea that coitus is sinful, still held it contained an element of evil.[23]

Thomas Aquinas

Although Thomas Aquinas (1224—1274) stands on the threshold of the Renaissance, or Reformation, period, his thinking is quite definitely an outgrowth of the Middle Ages, and a treatment of this period in European history would hardly be complete without some comment from the "Angelic Doctor," as he was called, "the master theologian of medieval Christendom," "who gave scholasticism of the Middle Ages its great synthesis." [24] In the mind of Aquinas, says Cole, "was acted out one of the most exciting events in intellectual history — the administration of the Christian sacraments to Aristotle, who was baptized a believer and married to Augustine" [25] By this Cole means to say that the philosophy of Aristotle and the writings of St. Augustine were, through the clever mind of Aquinas, made to say the same thing, and from this type of synthesis was derived the very foundation of what was to be the theological system of Roman Catholicism.

Passion Versus Reason

The main premise of all the theology of Aquinas regarding sex and marriage lies in his assumption that, since reason is

---

[23] See Bailey's fuller description in his *Sexual Relation in Christian Thought* (New York: Harper & Bros., 1959), pp. 125—134.

[24] William Graham Cole, *Sex in Christianity and Psychoanalysis* (New York: Oxford University Press, 1955), p. 67.

[25] Ibid.

man's distinctive characteristic over against all other forms of creation, to live in accordance with "right reason" is to live the good life. In order to guide the conscience in its decisions as to what is reasonable behavior, man must look to "natural law." This is simply the eternal law of God projected into the created world, or that much of the divine law which is discernible by reason, unaided by revelation. "In his quest for the good life, then, the Christian uses his reason to discover what the natural law requires, looking always to the divine law as a corrective, as a guide which directs him to the proper interpretation." [26]

Of the attitude of Aquinas regarding sex, Cole writes:

> Sex as a fact of creation was, for Thomas, good, but a secondary good, because in the animal kingdom, including man, the male is not found in continuous union with the female, as among plants, but only at the time of coition. By this means, the two became "one flesh," but man has a destiny far higher than sex — the use of his reason. Here Thomas was following Aristotle but without any conflict with Augustine, for all three men placed great stress on the life of reason, the realm of the mind. This emphasis is derived from the classical tradition, not from the Bible.
>
> The stress on communion with God through the reason found in both Aquinas and Augustine explains their suspicion of sex as an intense physical drive which interferes with the placid, contemplative life. Both of them were naturalistic enough to recognize the good of the body and its sexual functions, but they clearly preferred a life above the weary necessities of the flesh. They could never have derived such a point of view from the Bible, nor could they have found there the notion that the reason should control the bodily impulses.[27]

Sex in the Garden of Eden

Thomas Aquinas held that sex was a gift of God, because it was necessary for procreation, the only means for bringing souls into life. Aquinas agreed with Augustine, however, that "a certain deformity of excessive concupiscence," which, he said, characterizes all sex relations, did not exist in the Garden of Eden, where "the lower powers were entirely subject to reason." [28] Both Aquinas and Augustine taught that the fall had occurred

---

26 Ibid., pp. 69—71.
27 Ibid., pp. 72, 73.
28 Quoted by Cole, p. 73.

before the marriage of Adam and Eve had been consummated. Yet they spent a great deal of time speculating on what the never-realized sexual relations would have been like if the parents of the race had not fallen into sin. Aquinas was sure that without sin man and woman had such complete control of sex in all its form that they could have determined the sex of their children by a mere act of will.[29] He differed from Augustine in that he was willing to allow for intensity of pleasure even in the state of innocence. "Rather, indeed, would sensible delight have been the greater in proportion to the greater purity of nature and the greater sensibility of the body."[30]

Thomas Aquinas was not opposed to all passion in the exercise of the sex function; he distinguished on the one hand between passion which precedes an act and diminishes its voluntary character and therefore diminishes its moral goodness, and on the other hand, the concomitant and consequent passion which accompanies or follows the act. This latter, he held, increases its voluntary character and its moral goodness. "Right reason" was to him and other scholastics the determining factor for good.[31]

Aquinas was willing to allow that pleasure was a part of God's purpose for sex both in Paradise and for sinful man as well. The only trouble was that original sin intervened and brought the ravages of concupiscence, or pleasure without reason. This concupiscence, Aquinas said, "is transmitted from generation to generation through the sexual act, or . . . 'the seminal power' . . . because it is the sexual act which is the carrier of original sin, not the flesh itself."[32]

Monogamy and Polygamy

Aquinas argued for monogamy in the marriage relationship, not on the basis of Scripture but on the basis of natural law, demonstrated (in the manner of Aristotle) on the basis of the animal kingdom. "The Bible nowhere condemns polygamy," says Cole, but Aquinas argued that "where the father's care is

---

[29] Cole, p. 73.

[30] Thomas Aquinas, *Summa theologica* (London: Burns, Oates, and Washbourne, Ltd., 1932), Part I, Ques. 98, Art. 1.

[31] Messenger, II, 178, 179.

[32] Cole, p. 75.

needed for the protection and training of the young there is what he called 'determinate union,' that is, the joining of only one male with one female. But where the mother's care is sufficient . . . there is 'indeterminate union' — males and females coupling indiscriminately. Obviously, man falls into the former group." Cole remarks that "one could quibble with Thomas, asking why man should not do as some of the 'determinate' animals, shift mates after the young leave the nest, but that would be captious." [33] Aquinas went along with Augustine in stating the three goods of marriage as (1) the procreation of children, (2) the promotion of family harmony, and (3) the reception of sacramental grace. He then said that polygamy might serve the first of these purposes, but it could hardly serve the second, and it is ruled out by the third. He excused the patriarchs on the ground that their polygamy was commanded by God.

In spite of his approval of marriage and its purposes, Aquinas still advocated virginity as the higher and holier way of life. "The word virgin, he said, comes from the Latin *viror,* meaning 'fresh,' unparched by the heat of the sun. So the virgin is determined to keep free from the heat of venereal passion." [34] Those who say that marriage is better than virginity are refuted by the example of Christ Himself, who both chose a virgin for His mother and remained unmarried in His own life, and by the authority of the apostle Paul, who wished that all might be unmarried as he was. Aquinas agreed that the thoughts of the heart were most important and a married person might actually be better than a virgin if his inner attitude toward sex were holier.[35]

Sins of Sex Classified

Aquinas also classified sexual sins in the order of their severity. The worst sins were the "unnatural vices," bestiality, sodomy, pederasty, masturbation, etc. He considered masturbation "the least grievous of all the unnatural vices," since there is no connection with another, and incest, though listed as "unnatural," was considered less serious, "violating prudential con-

---

[33] Ibid., p. 76.
[34] Ibid., p. 78.
[35] Ibid., p. 77.

siderations rather than physiological ones." [36] The sexual sins
which are not "unnatural" were, in the order of their seriousness, "rape of a wife, adultery, rape of a virgin, seduction of
a virgin, and simple fornication." Cole writes: "Aquinas regarded seduction of a virgin as less serious than adultery,
remarking that it is a 'greater injustice to have intercourse with
a woman who is subject to another's authority.' . . .

"Thomas seemed far more concerned over the injury done the
husband of an adulteress and the father of a seduced virgin than
over any harm done to the women." [37]

In line with his repeated emphasis on the inner motive rather
than the outward act, Aquinas saw no evil as such in the automatic release of sexual desire through nocturnal emissions or
"wet dreams." What occurs in sleep, he said, is not under the
control of reason and therefore cannot be sin. However, if emissions were the result of a visitation of the devil or lustful thoughts
before retiring, sin might be involved previously but not in the
physiological process itself.[38]

Regarding sex relations within marriage Aquinas believed that
whatever of evil there might be in the passion and intensity of
marital coitus was a punishment for original sin and altogether
excused by the marriage blessing. "While the orgasm may over-
whelm the husband's reason for the moment, nonetheless his
reason directed him into the marriage in the first place, and therefore no sin is incurred." [39] The marriage act could be considered
virtuous under two conditions only: if performed for the begetting of children or if performed as a "debt" to the other
partner, who might otherwise be driven to fornication. The
partner for whom the motive for sex is lust is sinning just the
same, although the sin is a venial one.[40] Cole says that the whole
discussion of the "marriage debt" (1 Cor. 7) "elaborates a small
bit of practical advice from the apostle Paul into a complex
array of legalism." Though Aquinas believed, in common with
medical science of that day, that intercourse during the menstrual
period might damage future offspring, yet he advised that the

---

[36] Ibid., p. 84.
[37] Ibid.
[38] Ibid., p. 86.
[39] Ibid.
[40] Ibid., p. 87.

woman must render the debt to her husband if he asks for it, lest he fall into sin through her refusal.[41]

Polygamy, Thomas Aquinas held, was a "condescension" on the part of God to the customs of surrounding pagan nations; permissible because it infringes mainly against a "secondary end" of marriage (peace and harmony) but not against the "primary end," the procreation of children. The need for the "multiplication" of children for God's people no longer obtains now.[42]

Regarding concubines he distinguishes between temporary concubinage (for the pleasure attached to it), equivalent to fornication, and permanent concubinage (distinguished only socially from marriage), which he did not regard a mortal sin.[43]

Aquinas gave three reasons for the institution of circumcision: to symbolize a profession of faith, to lessen the heat of concupiscence in the male, to both mock and correct phallic worship.[44]

Shame and Modesty

The scholastic philosophers concerned themselves with every aspect of sex. Thus Aquinas makes many distinctions between various forms of shame (*verecundia*) and modesty (*modestas*), attempting to determine whether these are evils or virtues, natural or acquired, and trying to penetrate into the guilt aspects of these phenomena. There are extensive treatments on the term "less honorable" (1 Cor. 12:23) parts of the body, translated *inhonesta* in the Vulgate.[45] He differentiated between chastity, modesty, and sense of shame. Though modesty and sense of shame are considered by him as "natural," both have been extended and widened through the sin of man.[46]

---

41 Ibid., p. 88.

42 Messenger, II, 68, 70, 71.

43 Ibid., II, 70, 71.

44 Ibid., II, 73. Messenger had already stated (p. 72): "The Book of Genesis says that circumcision was to be a sign of the covenant which God made with Abraham, the founder of the Jewish race [Genesis 17:11]." Now (p. 73) he adds: "A rite widely used in pagan religions, but given also by God to the Jewish race, with a definite meaning," Gen. 17:11, as an equivalent to Baptism; and "a sacramental rite which formed the remedy for original sin at that time." Aquinas explained the Old Testament rite of circumcision thus: Symbolically, circumcision foreshadowed the removal of original sin by the death of Christ. Practically, it "weakens the concupiscence of the penis and serves as a remedy against original sin, which is contracted through the act of generation."

45 See Messenger, II, 191; 137, 138.

46 See Messenger, II, ch. 25, ch. 26.

Aquinas regarded the "virtue" of modesty as "fundamentally present" in the state of innocence, though no clothes were then worn. It was "the custom" sanctioned by the moral law, and in accordance with right reason, for man then to be naked. He did not then suffer from extremes of heat or cold, and he was not then subject to the rebellion of sex appetites and organs.[47] Aquinas recognized the function of accepted standards of modesty (as he defined it) and dealt precisely with departures from those standards (which vary in different societies) as immodesty.[48]

Perhaps these summary references have been sufficient to show that the streams of dualism and naturalism which had been flowing down through the centuries since the beginning of Christianity were finally in the writings of Thomas Aquinas brought together in one well-reasoned philosophy of sex and marriage. That this was a philosophy utterly foreign to the Bible was scarcely disturbing to Aquinas or to the church of his time.

SUMMARY

1. The medieval church exalted virginity, refused marriage to the clergy, insinuated that coitus defiled and hindered service to God, and emphasized that marriage serves as a remedy for lust. This left the general impression that the physical relationship of the sexes is inherently unworthy, if not shameless and obscene. In this period marriage was viewed more as an institution and less as a unique personal relationship.

2. Historical factors in establishing the sex mores of the Middle Ages were the rise of monasticism, the manorial and feudal systems with their common households, the crusades, the revival of classical culture, the invasion of southern Europe by the Germanic tribes, and the rise of the romantic and courtly love with its extramarital excesses.

3. The church, though accepting marriage as God's order because of its "sacramental" character, nevertheless considered it only a *secondary good,* and many theologians regarded it as essentially sinful. This was a throwback to Greek dualism and ascetic cultism.

4. The celibacy of the priesthood strongly advocated in the post-

---

[47] Messenger, II, 13, 204.
[48] Ibid., II, 205.

apostolic period now became established, but only after centuries of struggle and formulations of canon laws, with many a revolt.

5. Thomas Aquinas made reason determinative and entered into a maze of "rational" refinements and fine distinctions to codify actions. He made moral judgments on polygamy, concubinage, circumcision, chastity, modesty, and the sense of shame.

CHAPTER 6

The Reformation Period

The Council of Trent

BETWEEN THE TIME of Thomas Aquinas and the Council of Trent the position of Roman Catholicism on matters of sex and marriage was subjected to a severe crisis through the revolutionary changes wrought by the Protestant Reformation. These changes had a perceptible influence on the statements on marriage in the *Canons and Decrees of the Council of Trent.* In its 24th session on Nov. 11, 1563, the Council decreed vigorous and severe sanctions *against* all who questioned the sacramental character of marriage, who approved of polygamy, who argued that adultery is a ground for divorce and that the innocent party in a divorce process is free to marry again, who gave those pledged to celibacy the right to marry if they found that they lacked the gift of chastity, who said that the estate of marriage is more honorable than the unmarried state, who maintained that marriage problems have a place in civil courts, but not before judges of the church.[1] Each of these decrees was intended to denounce a basic position on sex and marriage that had been taken by the Protestant reformers. The following discussion of the Reformation period will therefore take up these basic new positions in the order mentioned above.

The Catechism of the Council of Trent, on the other hand, shows that the position of the Roman Church was not without benefit from the labors of the reformers. Conceding that marriage is not only a sacrament but also a natural union, the Catechism ascribes the same three divine purposes to this natural

---

[1] H. J. Schroeder, *Canons and Decrees of the Council of Trent* (St. Louis: B. Herder Book Co., 1941; 3d print., 1955), pp. 180 ff.

union which are found in the program of the reformers: spouses are to be helpers and companions one to another; they are to have children and give them religious training; they are to use marriage as an antidote against immorality. The Catechism of Trent maintained that it was God's grace imparted *through the sacrament of marriage* which made the sex act honorable. The reformers had held that it was God's grace imparted *through His Word* which sanctified sexual relations within marriage.[2]

Marriage as Companionship

If, as Bainton holds, the sacramental view of marriage was contrasted chiefly with the romantic view at the time of the reformers, it remained for the Protestant Reformation to develop most completely what Bainton calls the third type or third view of marriage, namely, that of companionability. Bainton believes that the greatest progress in this direction was made by the more radical Protestant sects, since Luther tended to emphasize the sexual side of marriage in contrast to the Roman Catholic exaltation of virginity. This may be debated, however, on the ground that Calvinism and Puritanism, for example, often reverted to St. Augustine's definition of marriage as being primarily for procreation, although they added also the matter of child training and the care and management of the household. Wherever the credit lies, it may be said that the Reformation did tend to bring a new point of view and to restore the Biblical view of marriage as both a useful and an enjoyable gift of God.[3]

Luther's Views of Sex and Marriage

It may be questioned at the very outset whether Luther's views on sex and marriage are relevant for us today. Some have argued that there is so much inconsistency in Luther's statements on this subject that it is almost impossible to draw up a summary of them or to generalize about them.[4] But if it is noted that Luther's literary activity extended over a period of thirty years, that his initial writings were influenced very strongly

---

[2] William Graham Cole, *Sex in Christianity and Psychoanalysis* (New York: Oxford University Press, 1955), pp. 96, 97.

[3] Roland Bainton, "Marriage and Love in Christian History," *Religion in Life*, XVII, 3 (Summer, 1948), 399, 400.

[4] Olavi Lähteenmäki, *Sexus und Ehe bei Luther* (Turku: Luther-Agricola-Gesellschaft, 1955), p. 172.

by his Roman Catholic background, and that the mature Luther stressed the spiritual aspect of marriage much more than the physical, some of his divergent views will not be so disconcerting.[5] And even if Luther's disposition of some practical cases seems to leave much to be desired from our ethical point of view today, his starting point was a deep conviction based on the Gospel. This conviction in turn produced a radically new approach to sex and marriage which still has much to commend it today.

Early Development

Some of the early writings of Luther show a serious lack of understanding of sex and marriage. In 1513—1515 he does not hesitate to use pure allegory in referring house, wife, father, and children in Psalms 127 and 128 to the church, to Christ, and to the believers.[6] During this time he also defends the traditional attitude of the church that celibacy is better than marriage. In the well-known first sermon on marriage of the year 1519 he still maintains the church's position that marriage is a sacrament.[7]

In 1520 a radical change took place in Luther's concept of marriage. It is interesting to note that this change came after his sojourn in the Wartburg. There the true nature of marriage became clear to him. The shift in Luther's thinking is reflected in his treatise On the Babylonian Captivity of the Church. Marriage is no longer a sacrament; it cannot be because it is not based on Christ's words and does not bring grace. It is, however, a divine ordinance and a blessed one. This full-fledged Reformation view of marriage is also expressed in the Treatise on Married Life in 1522 and the Seventh Chapter of First Corinthians of 1523.[8]

The Reason for the Change

How is this radical change in Luther's view of marriage to be explained? It derives from his intense preoccupation with the justification of the sinner by faith in Christ alone. Luther's

---

[5] Gerhard E. Lenski, *Marriage in the Lutheran Church* (Columbus, Ohio: Lutheran Book Concern, 1936), pp. 76, 77.

[6] Ibid., p. 125.

[7] Lähteenmäki, p. 22.

[8] Ibid., pp. 25—27; cf. Lenski, p. 126.

contemporaries in the church had an erroneous concept of sin
and redemption with which he felt constrained to break. They
held that sin started when the human soul came to reside in
a material body and that redemption consisted in releasing the
soul from that sinful body by abstinence and self-denial.[9]

Luther countered that man was redeemed from sin and from
the devil but not from corporeality. The body was made as
something good. Our Lord was sinless even though He had
a body, and the devil is sinful even though he is without a body.
It was, moreover, the devil who spoiled the beautiful sex instinct
which God made. Through the fall pure love was changed into
rampant lust, childbirth became painful, nakedness was associated with shame. Since the fall sex and marriage repeatedly
remind man that he cannot sanctify himself.[10]

Therefore man's hope of sanctifying marriage lies solely in
hearkening to the saving Word of the Gospel of Christ. While
sins are committed in thought, word, and deed within marriage,
this is no reason to avoid marriage; rather it is a reason to repent
and to combat lust with the Spirit's power. Through Christ,
the incarnate Word, God sanctified the lowliness and filth that
had replaced the innocence of sex. He still heals the sin which
inevitably is involved in marriage. Therefore Luther concluded
that in matters of sex and marriage the only factors that are
to determine people's activities are faith, love, and the neighbor.
He put sex and marriage under God's grace and pointed spouses
to Christ. Faith regards even the worldly, the material, the
physical as holy because the holy God's hands made these.
On the other hand anything moral or spiritual that is based
on the merits of man is unholy.[11]

Ordinance of God

In addition to this redemptive approach to marriage Luther
also held out strongly for marriage as a divine ordinance. As
such it is acceptable to God. Man is indeed obliged to marry
for the simple reason that in creation God commanded him to

---

9 Cole, pp. 102, 103; Lähteenmäki, pp. 43—45.

10 Lähteenmäki, pp. 48, 49; Cole, pp. 106, 107.

11 Lähteenmäki, pp. 173, 175, 51, 53, 174, 67, 68. See also Ernst Troeltsch,
The Social Teaching of the Christian Churches (London: Allen and Unwin,
1949), II, 546, 547.

do so. God created man with such a strong sexual urge that
man is left with no choice. His desire for gratification with
the opposite sex is as natural as the flame that consumes straw
when it is kindled by fire. Sexual desire is as necessary and as
important as hunger and thirst. Luther honored marriage as
a miracle of God, as a great treasure received from Him, as
worthy of the same esteem that is due every creative act of
God. He did not feel obliged to explain or justify the mysterious power of sex; it was implanted by the Creator and was
therefore His responsibility. He argued that because God made
us this way, we ought to leave it this way.[12]

Polygamy and Divorce Are Special Concessions

In his early writings Luther was of the opinion that polygamy was not clearly forbidden in Scripture. In 1531 he advised
Henry VIII to take Anne Boleyn as a second wife in addition
to Catherine of Aragon; yet in 1536 he declared that the marriage with Catherine was invalid because the Pope had set
aside God's Word to make it possible. In 1527 he also gave
assent to Hans Behm's taking an additional wife.[13]

Luther regarded polygamy as a legitimate form of marriage
during the patriarchal period, but it was a special dispensation
for great people. This privilege could also be stretched, the
early Luther held, to the great people of his day, including
Philip of Hesse. In this case Luther acted in the role of confessor whose secret advice to Philip to engage in bigamy was
not intended to be made known. Still it cannot be denied that
in counseling in favor of bigamy, Luther the priestly confessor
somehow contrived to triumph over Luther the Reformer.[14]

Later Luther modified his views on polygamy. When Jacob
took both Leah and Rachel, he acted like a hero with a special
dispensation from God. But we have no right to follow the example of such heroes. Polygamy may have been a suitable
arrangement for the patriarchal heroes, but monogamy is the
best marital arrangement for us.[15]

---

[12] Cole, p. 108; Troeltsch, pp. 546—547; Lenski, p. 169; Lähteenmäki,
pp. 66, 173, 49, 52, 54, 60.

[13] Lenski, p. 111; Cole, p. 116; Lähteenmäki, p. 72.

[14] Lähteenmäki, pp. 87, 89, 90.

[15] Ibid., pp. 94, 97.

For Luther adultery was not merely a ground for divorce; rather, adultery actually constituted the dissolution of marriage. If the marriage were to continue after one party committed adultery, that would call for love and forgiveness. But such gifts were held to be so rare that in most cases the marriage needed to be terminated. In 1522 Luther felt that a person who committed adultery deserved the death penalty. In 1530 he was more moderate in pointing out that the adulterer was spiritually dead. If, moreover, adultery fractured a marriage to such an extent that the guilty party was as good as dead, then the innocent partner certainly was free to marry again, even though the Gospel made no general provision for this. Thus the privilege that Paul gave the Christian in mixed marriage with an unbeliever in 1 Cor. 7 was extended by Luther to anyone who was deserted by a marital partner.[16]

Luther contended that refusal to participate in sex relations was another form of adultery and therefore might make separation advisable. In such circumstances it would be better to end a marriage that did not work out than to endure the wrong patiently. After two or three warnings a sexually recalcitrant or unco-operative wife may be left as Ahasuerus left Vashti for Esther. How shockingly realistic Luther could be in stating, "If the wife refuse, let the maid come!" Impotence or sexual incompetence could also be regarded as a reason for terminating marriage. Luther made bold to suggest that if a woman had an impotent husband, she should desert him and marry another in some other part of the country.[17]

When two wretched and sinful mortals enter marriage, such abuses may develop, according to Luther's view, that divorce is finally the only way out. Luther could condemn one divorce unequivocally and approve another just as unequivocally. Now a directive to release and liberate may be called for, then a directive to bind and hold may be just as necessary. Each case must be decided for itself; concessions may need to be made in order to meet the demands of love, to help an oppressed spouse, and to avoid greater evil.[18]

---

16 Ibid., pp. 70, 71; Cole, p. 115.

17 Lenski, pp. 107—109; Cole, p. 115; cf. Lähteenmäki, p. 72.

18 Lähteenmäki, pp. 80, 84, 86, 83.

Celibates Not Bound by Vows

In Luther's day the state of virginity was held to be better than that of married persons. Luther opposed this view and argued that such an emphasis on celibacy with its accompanying antimarital attitude was at variance with the divine order of creation.[19] He did not go so far as Karlstadt, who made the ordination of priests contingent on marriage, but he did seriously question the right of the church to demand unconditional vows of celibacy of its servants. The vow of celibacy could not be binding, because it lacked any precedent in early Christianity, it was a relatively late church law, and it called for superhuman powers of continence. For almost all people to vow to be chaste was to vow the impossible; it was like vowing to create stars or to move mountains or to grow to be as old as Methuselah.[20]

> It is not continence that Luther declares impossible, but simply that it is not possible for the physically constituted man to pretend he is not subject to natural impulses. After all, a man is a man and a heathen is no different from a saint so far as bodily functions are concerned. Vows do not unsex, neither do they make a man into something other than what he normally is.[21]

Luther himself experienced great temptations in his days of sexual continence and advised a friend to marry because his body required and needed it and God sanctioned and demanded it. At first Luther condemned only compulsory vows of celibacy, but finally he rejected even the voluntary ones because they conflicted with nature and with man's conscience. He was willing to recognize voluntary celibacy if a person had the God-given capacity for it. But in such a case no vow was needed, because such continence was God's special gift.[22]

Thus Luther's struggle against the vow of celibacy was comparable to Paul's struggle against circumcision among the Galatians. He labeled celibacy as false piety because it was based on human merit and thus falsified man's relations with God. He rejected it because it served as an escape from the respon-

---

[19] His two main works against celibacy were: Of Monastic Vows, 1521, and the Seventh Chapter of Saint Paul to the Corinthians, 1523.

[20] Lähteenmäki, pp. 20, 28, 29, 30, 31, 33.

[21] Wilhelm Walther (*Für Luther wider Rom* [Halle: Niemayer, 1906], pp. 671 ff.) as paraphrased by Lenski, p. 114.

[22] Cole, p. 112; Lähteenmäki, pp. 32, 39, 36.

sibilities of domestic life and was more comfortable and convenient. He considered it unrealistic because women would be used by men either as wives or as prostitutes.[23]

Marriage as the Better Way

Luther was of the opinion that when the world says it is foolish to marry, this is true, because the world looks for no life beyond the grave and therefore promiscuous sexual satisfaction will serve to make the evil days on earth somewhat more tolerable. When, on the other hand, the Spirit says it is wise to marry, this is true, too, because the Christian hopes for a future life and therefore he wisely chooses to have restricted pleasures now, so that he may be eternally happy then.[24]

Luther makes a strong case for the view that marriage is the better way. The very fact that the Word of God has so much to say about the blessings and rules that pertain to marriage serves to justify and grant approval to this institution. What makes marriage holy and lifts it out of the area of the purely carnal is the Christian's faith in Christ. If reason argues that marriage is not of God because of all of its miseries, faith overcomes these imperfections and argues that marriage is a good divine ordinance. Faith transforms the trials of pregnancy, the ordeal of childbirth, and the vexing chores that need to be done in caring for babies. The fruit of such faith is in turn the love that moves a man to serve his neighbor. Husbands and wives learn to make concessions and to grant each other pardon amidst the toil and tedium of daily marital life. The trials of married life serve to break down pride and to make men humble and patient.[25]

God has a unique way of bestowing His grace upon people: He disguises Himself as their neighbor and then moves them to love that neighbor. In marriage He disguises Himself as a husband or wife and then moves the other to love the spouse. Thus marriage becomes a stage or an arena in which the highest and finest type of love for the neighbor finds expression. It is

---

23 Lähteenmäki, pp. 40, 41; Cole, pp. 112, 113.

24 *Dr. Martin Luthers Sämtliche Schriften,* ed. J. G. Walch (St. Louis: Concordia Publishing House, 1881—1910), VIII, 1028.

25 Lähteenmäki, pp. 168, 169; 163, 164; 131, 132; 135; Lenski, pp. 117—119; Cole, p. 108.

an ideal setting for social service in which the Christian makes
a noble contribution toward the welfare of his fellow men. Christian marriage has two sides in Luther's thinking: On the one
hand it keeps Christian spouses mindful of the sorrows that
resulted from the fall and enables them to learn to bear their
cross. On the other hand it teaches them to be thankful for
the pardon and peace that are accorded them by God and thus
enables them to rejoice in His wonderful gifts and blessings.
Marriage may be a life full of hardship, but still it is the
best life.[26]

Natural Law and Civil Courts

During the Middle Ages the church had claimed exclusive
jurisdiction in marital matters. Luther challenged this claim
and insisted that the regulation of marriage was a right that
belonged to the civil branch of the government. He based his
argument on the fact that while marriage is ordained by God,
it is still a secular institution that varies considerably from one
people to another and therefore should be controlled by the
respective state authorities.[27]

Luther also held that as an ordinance of creation marriage
comes under the jurisdiction of natural law. There are heathen
people who know neither Moses nor Christ and yet act according
to the law that God has written in their hearts. It was not
Luther's intent, however, to give natural law priority over the
Bible. He did emphasize that in certain areas of marriage problems natural law provides the answer and the Bible does not.
For example, because the commandment on adultery in the
Decalog makes no explicit reference to the sex life of unmarried people, it is narrower in scope than the natural law. Luther
therefore broadened the Sixth Commandment by exhorting married and unmarried to "lead a chaste and decent life in word
and deed." He clarified the natural law by urging every married
person to "love and honor his spouse." [28]

Finally, Christian husbands and wives hold citizenship in

---

[26] Lähteenmäki, pp. 139, 137, 141, 166; Troeltsch, pp. 546, 547; Lenski,
p. 119.

[27] Roland H. Bainton, "Christianity and Sex," in *Sex and Religion
Today*, ed. Simon Doniger (New York: Association Press, 1953), pp. 70, 71;
cf. Cole, p. 109.

[28] Lähteenmäki, pp. 142, 159, 147.

two kingdoms: that of the Lord Jesus Christ and that of the world. In the first kingdom they are guided by faith in the Lord Jesus Christ; in the second they are subject to human ordinances. Righteousness is the objective of both kingdoms, but it is of a radically different nature in each. Through faith the Gospel makes a husband and wife righteous in the sight of God; through ordinances the state can make them righteous only in the sight of men. The Gospel operates with gentleness to comfort consciences; the marriage courts use strict justice to regulate human affairs. Thus Gospel and Law have their respective places also in marital matters: If the church's program for making men righteous before God through the Gospel does not succeed, then the state must intervene with laws and attempt to make them righteous before the world.[29]

The Early and the Later Luther

Considerable variation has been noted between the views of sex and marriage which were held by Luther during his early years and in his later years. It must be acknowledged that in his early writings there was a strong accent on erotic love, while in his later works he stressed marital love as a mighty power for good. In his sermon on marriage of 1519 he describes conjugal love as a love that admires the beauty of the opposite sex, that is intensely emotional, and that desires to possess the other entirely. But it must be remembered that already in the years 1519—1523 Luther compared marriage to a hospital in which men are healed of their sinful lusts and to which every man who has a strong sexual drive needs to be admitted. In his Genesis lectures (1535—45), on the other hand, he ascribes a threefold task to marriage: to help people avoid fornication, to enable them to bear children, and to afford them an opportunity to bring up children. Here Luther also expresses his mature view that monogamy is the better way and that divorce has serious disadvantages.[30]

Recent Luther research, moreover, has shown that both in his early years and later Luther regarded man as one personality, who is responsible to God in both his physical and his

---

29 Ibid., pp. 151, 154, 155—157, 158—160.
30 Lenski, pp. 104, 105; 182; Lähteenmäki, pp. 55—58.

spiritual life. As such it is required of him not to suppress the sexual side of love but rather to resist the allurements of Satan and to do this with the only means that is effective — the wonderful tool of faith. The question may be raised in this connection, whether Luther held that Adam and Eve had their first sex relations *before* or *after* the fall? Scholars have reached various conclusions on the basis of Luther's comments in his lectures on Genesis. Cole argues that Luther followed Augustine and Aquinas in believing that the fall took place before Adam and Eve had known each other. According to Lähteenmäki, on the other hand, Luther held that before the fall Adam and Eve enjoyed a complete and unblemished sex life without any shame or sinful lust. There appears to be no evidence that Luther changed his view in this matter between 1519 and 1545.[31]

Luther's Own Marriage

The difference between the young and the older Luther may also be explained in part by the experiences of his own married life. He met Katharine von Bora some seven years (1524) after the theses episode. Marrying at the age of forty-two (Katharine was twenty-seven), he exhibited a "healthy naturalism, an earthy sense of humor" in his own family life: "I am rich, God has given me my nun and three children; what care I if I am in debt, Katie pays the bills. . . . George Karg has taken a rich wife and sold his freedom. I am luckier, for when Katie gets saucy, she gets nothing but a box on the ear." Thus his own marriage reflected his basic conviction that sex was created by God and was inherently good. Of the thirty years of his literary activity more than twenty were spent in the environment of a happy marriage. While it may be true that he married in response to a call to duty rather than on the impulse of love, yet he enjoyed a full measure of marital affection and companionship and the great thrill of happy parenthood. His marriage was by no means a mere attempt to counteract the Roman ideal of an unmarried clergy; it was to be a living sermon like that of Hosea, it was to proclaim the basic truth that sex was a gift of God and therefore a normal and good function.[32]

---

[31] Lähteenmäki, pp. 66, 139, 45; Troeltsch, p. 545; Cole, p. 106.

[32] Bainton, in *Sex and Religion Today*, p. 67; Cole, pp. 105, 106; Lenski, pp. 163, 166, 76, 158, 180; Troeltsch, p. 545.

Realism and Plain Speech

Luther favored frank discussion of matters pertaining to sex. He observed that Moses spoke frequently of sex, but that today there is a strange silence on such matters among people. The human sense of hearing seems to have become more sensitive than the speech of God's own Spirit! Such prudish silence in turn has produced an unwholesome sense of shame and a biased attitude toward marriage itself. Therefore it is high time to speak to youth plainly about sex.[33]

Luther's own realism with regard to sex is reflected in his response to one form of penance that was required in the church of that day. This penance prescribed sleeping with one's spouse, but having no sexual relations. To this Luther responded, "They put dry wood on a fire and say, 'Don't burn!'" Luther saw an urgency and a compulsion in sex that simply could not be denied in normal persons. This is why he expressed himself so freely in matters of sex. His realism has proved to be a source of offense to some but has been welcomed by others as a very sincere approach to a difficult problem.[34]

It should be noted, moreover, that Luther not only refused to condemn sex and marriage but that he also insisted on bringing both under divine grace by directing man's look at Christ. You cannot sanctify sex by abstinence, he argued, nor can you sanctify marriage by making it a sacrament. Both can be sanctified only by God's grace.[35]

Calvin on Sex and Marriage

A number of significant points of difference stand out between Luther's views on sex and marriage and those of John Calvin. According to Luther, Christian husbands and wives respond to their Lord in love; Calvin bases this response rather on obedience. Luther, especially in earlier years, made sexual satisfaction primary in marriage, but Calvin saw the element of companionship as primary and sex as only secondary. Luther called marriage a remedy for curing sin, Calvin added the picture of

---

[33] Lähteenmäki, pp. 29, 30.
[34] Cole, p. 114; Lenski, pp. 107, 110.
[35] Lähteenmäki, pp. 67, 68.

marriage as a veil that covered sin. Although Luther condoned
the polygamy of the patriarchs, Calvin censured it.[36]

If Luther was a pessimist in sexual matters, Calvin could
be quite prudish. Luther held that in marriage a child of God
could and should enjoy the full pleasure of sexual relations.
Calvin, however, advised a husband to approach his wife "with
delicacy and propriety" and held that it was inexcusable for
a wife to touch or even look at her husband's genitals. As a matter of fact, Calvin seemed to be afraid that enjoying one's self
too much in marriage was wrong.[37]

The Lutheran Confessions

Especially in the Apology to the Augsburg Confession Melanchthon ably defended the new view on marriage which Luther
had advanced. He maintained that no human law could change
the fact that God gave man the natural right to marry and
use the gifts of sex. The Apology spoke of the terrible lewdness, fornication, and adultery among priests and monks which
people saw and talked about throughout the world. Therefore
it maintained that marriage was a necessary institution, not only
to produce children but also as a remedy against sin. The law
did not forbid marriage, it forbade only sinful lust. Therefore
a married man might be more pure in heart than a celibate
with all of his outward continence. The child of God, moreover, would know how to be charitable and moderate in the
use of all marital privileges.[38]

In the Appendix to the Smalcald Articles Melanchthon also
outlined a classic program for the removal of the control of
marriage from the church and for its transfer to the civil authorities. Divorce was conceded a place, and the innocent party
was given the privilege to remarry.[39]

The subject of marriage was not in controversy at the time
of the adoption of the Formula of Concord. This explains why
the Formula had so little to say about marriage. One point,
however, was made very clear: Diversity of faith either between

---

[36] Cole, pp. 118, 120, 124, 131.

[37] Cole, pp. 131, 128, 124.

[38] Lenski, pp. 224—226. Cf. *Triglot Concordia: The Symbolical Books
of the Ev. Lutheran Church* (St. Louis: Concordia Publishing House,
1921), pp. 367, 363—365, 373, 375.

[39] Lenski, pp. 230—232; *Triglot*, p. 527.

a Lutheran and a Roman Catholic or between a Lutheran and an Anabaptist was not to be recognized as a ground for divorce. And the government, not the church, was acknowledged as authoritative in this matter.[40]

Melanchthon's Defense of Sex and Marriage

In the Reformation period celibacy was a subject of severe controversy. This problem is dealt with at length in the Apology of the Augsburg Confession (1530, 1531) by Melanchthon, who refers to the inhibition of sex through mandatory celibacy in the Roman clergy as being in conflict with divine and natural law and at variance with the canons of the Councils.[41]

Celibacy, as established for priests, monks, and nuns, the Apology declares to be a human law contrary to God's will for man. "Just as by human laws the nature of the earth cannot be changed, so, without a special work of God, the nature of a human being can be changed neither by vows nor by human law (that a woman should not desire a man, or a man a woman). . . . The union of male and female belongs to natural right. . . . Moreover a natural right is truly a divine right because it is an ordinance divinely impressed upon nature." [42]

Distinguishing between physical love (which would have existed between man and woman even though their nature had remained pure) and concupiscence, which came with the fall, the Apology says: "These two things concur, namely, natural appetite and concupiscence, which inflames the natural appetite, so that now there is more need of marriage than in nature in its integrity" (1 Cor. 7:9).[43] The Apology cites Ambrose to the effect that virginity can be recommended but not commanded.[44] It also points out that the continence of the married Levites was only temporary and is not applicable to celibacy.[45]

SUMMARY

1. The Reformation period saw a radical change in the view of sex and marriage as distinguished from views held by Thomas Aquinas. The Roman Church took cognizance of this change in its decrees and Catechism of the Council of Trent.

---

[40] Lenski, pp. 233, 234.
[41] *Triglot,* p. 365.
[42] Ibid., p. 367.

[43] Ibid., p. 369.
[44] Ibid., p. 369.
[45] Ibid., p. 371.

2. Luther scholars find considerable variation between the Reformer's views on sex and marriage in his early ministry and those held in his later years. As a monk he still regarded marriage as a sacrament and held to Augustinian views regarding sex. Luther's earlier decisions on polygamy would leave much to be desired from our ethical point of view today. As the full Biblical view of sin, redemption, and justification by faith dominated his theology, Luther greatly modified his views.

3. Luther broke with the widely held view of his day that redemption takes place when the soul is released from the sinful body by abstinence and self-denial. He taught that the body as such is not sinful but that the devil spoiled the beautiful instinct of sex. The sex drive and desire is sanctified not by making marriage a sacrament but by letting God's grace in Christ hallow all acts and transform them into deeds of faith, love, and service to the neighbor.

4. The use of sex in marriage Luther called a miracle of God commanded in creation. To him it was as natural and necessary as hunger and thirst. Luther accepted what has been called the natural, or creation, point of view. Luther opposed celibacy because vows cannot unsex the individual.

5. Sex is to be used responsibly in marriage. Although marriage carries with it such burdens as pregnancy, birth, and child care, it is the better way of life for both man and woman. Faith lifts marriage out of the purely physical realm and transforms even the trials, making of marriage an arena for the practice of true Christian love.

6. Luther dealt with the total personality. To him body and soul were two sides of one life. The sexual side is not to be denied or repressed but properly used as God intended within the confines of marriage, not without pleasure but in moderation. Satan's temptations are to be resisted. Luther's own marriage was characterized by happiness and good humor.

7. Luther dealt with the matter of sex realistically, talking freely about it with plainness of speech. Though the accents and emphases differed among the reformers, their basic attitudes were quite similar. The Lutheran Confessions record the final approval to the new approach to sex and marriage.

CHAPTER 7

The Age of Orthodoxy

AFTER THE REFORMATION followed a period (16th—18th Centuries) in which the doctrines of Protestantism were organized into dogmatic systems much as moral philosophy had been systematized by Thomas Aquinas and theology by Augustine.

Chemnitz, Gerhard, Quenstedt, and others produced prodigious works compassing the whole field of theology. Although they also gave attention to the Christian life (Gerhard's *Schola pietatis*, Scriver's *Seelenschatz*, Arndt's *Wahres Christentum*), the emphasis was on Biblical doctrine based on sound exegesis and not on the development of a separate system of Christian ethics.

Marriage and celibacy received ample treatment. So did the Ten Commandments. Sex sins were frankly faced, classified, and analyzed after the pattern of scholastic theology, with traces of Aristotelian philosophy apparent. Fundamentally these writings followed Roman Catholic tradition and held to many medieval concepts, terms, classifications, and minute distinctions.[1]

This kind of literature was a distinctive mark of the age of orthodoxy, but it was not divorced from the central Reformation teaching of justification by faith. The dogmaticians, like Luther, emphasized the Gospel approach to life, asserting that the Christian life is motivated by and proceeds from justifying faith. Forgiveness through Christ's redemptive work alone is the beginning of the new, voluntary obedience. Troeltsch describes the Lutheran ethic, in distinction from the Roman Catholic ethic and the Calvinistic ethic, as consisting primarily in the establishment

---

[1] Ernst Troeltsch, *The Social Teaching of the Christian Churches* (London: George Allen & Unwin, Ltd., 1949), II, 527, 528.

of a religious relation to God which humbly, joyfully, and thank-
fully surrenders self to Him in prayer, in self-discipline, and in
love for the neighbor — an inward impulse which uses to its
fullest extent the overflowing happiness produced by justification.[2]

This response of the man free in Christ carried over into the
treatment of sex and the relationship of husband to wife. We
shall let the leaders of Orthodoxy speak for themselves on marriage, celibacy, sins of sex, chastity, and other problems related
to sex. In the compass of a single chapter only a small part of
the evidence from the Age of Orthodoxy can be given. Much of
the following material has been translated directly from the Latin.

Balduin on First Corinthians Seven

A famous exegete of the post-Reformation period was the
Wittenberg professor Friedrich Balduin (1575—1627). In his
classic interpretation of 1 Cor. 7 Balduin defends the institution
of marriage against Romanist distortions. He says the gift of continence is something to be wished for more than hoped for, Paul
being one of the few who could hold sexual passions in subjec-
tion.[3] The monastic position that every contact with a woman
is evil he calls hypocrisy, since such an interpretation of Paul's
word (1 Cor. 7:1) never occurred to the apostle. In fact, touching a woman is good and laudable by God's ordinance. All of
God's works are full of honor and majesty (Ps. 111:3).[4] Paul
expressly says that both husband and wife owe each other conjugal rights, which the theologians called a *debitum* (debt). The
apostle does not prescribe something that is impure, a work of
the flesh, an impediment to the exercise of piety. Pretending that
the use of a wife is impure is hypocritical.[5]

Balduin, using 1 Tim. 2:15 as proof, denies that fulfilling the
office of a wife or husband is a denial of the Christian vocation
(as Jerome erroneously claimed).[6] The remedy for incontinence

[2] Troeltsch, II, 524, 525. See also Hans Emil Weber, *Reformation, Orthodoxie und Rationalismus* (Gütersloh: C. Bertelsmann Verlag, 1951),
pp. 42—48.

[3] Friedrich Balduin, *Commentarius in omnes epistolas beati apostoli
Pauli* (Francofurti: A. D. Moenum, 1691), p. 364.

[4] Ibid., p. 370.

[5] Ibid., p. 371.

[6] Ibid., p. 371.

is not fasting, maceration of the body, or abstinence, but, as
Paul teaches, marriage.[7]

Martin Chemnitz on Sins of Sex

The most learned Lutheran theologian of his time, Martin
Chemnitz (1522—1586) complains about sexual laxity in the public mind. He contends that "adultery" in the Decalog is used as
a synecdoche (a part for the whole). Chemnitz grants that
naaph (adultery) in general signifies only illicit mingling between a male and a female, one of whom is married, and that
zanah (harlotry) is the Hebrew word that refers to open fornication outside marriage; but he protests against the inference that
harlotry or fornication is therefore not condemned in the Sixth
Commandment, is in fact not sinful, and has under circumstances
even been commanded by God, as for instance to the prophet
Hosea. The Decalog, he continues, must be understood in keeping with the interpretation of the prophets and apostles, and so
it becomes evident that the Sixth Commandment forbids all
commingling outside marriage; and not merely the physical act,
but even "the inner flames of lust." [8]

"In Matthew 5:32," says Chemnitz, "Christ, reciting the commandments of the second table, includes fornication with adultery. Similarly in the other commandments one species is named,
but the other sins are comprehended with it." Chemnitz continues:

> It must be considered, however, why God chose to specify
> by name the crime of adultery in preference to all others in
> the Sixth Commandment. The Son of God Himself shows the
> reason in Matt. 5:28 when He says, "Already he has com-
> mitted adultery in his heart"; obviously God chose this way
> in order to show the seriousness of a sin which, as civil law
> also recognizes, is a terrible disgrace and worthy of the
> severest punishment; likewise before the judgment of God
> also the sinful flames of lust are judged.
>
> And because the old Adam is accustomed to assign to the
> sins of riotous living gentle and mild names, therefore God
> labels all of them with the hideous name of adultery lest we
> delude ourselves by extenuations or excuses; but let us
> acknowledge and deplore our uncleanness, and let us seek

---

[7] Ibid., p. 372.
[8] Martin Chemnitz, "De lege Dei," in *Loci theologici*, ed. Polycarp
Leyser (Frankfurt, Wittenberg: Christian H. Schumacher, 1690), II, 74.

remission through the Mediator and by the Holy Spirit mortify the deeds of the flesh lest they rule us.

There is also another reason why God did not mention any other kind of illegitimate mingling in the Sixth Commandment but used the word which signifies a violation of the marriage union [Hebrew: *naaph*, Greek: *moicheia*, German: *Ehebrechen* — "breaking of marriage"]. For because He forbids this violation, He shows that He sanctifies, approves, and safeguards marriage, its association, its familiarity, and its conjugal copulation. And that pronouncement which forbids breaking lawful marriage, God — by shaking His finger in the Decalog — chose to direct against the devilish teaching which condemns marriage. For He shows that He is not only the Author but also the Defender of marriage.

> . . . an inventory of the sins against the Sixth Commandment needs to be set up. . . . It must be observed that the Holy Spirit did not choose to leave it to our ingenuity to establish the scope of individual sins upon mere definition and their inventory upon our own whims, for human perversity makes a sin of those things which God has permitted to be free and definitely minimizes and excuses, if it does not defend, those things which the judgment of God has condemned.[9]

Chemnitz then puts sins against the Sixth Commandment into five categories: (1) adultery (*moicheia* — fornication, rape, adultery, incest, sodomy); (2) baseness or uncleanness in words (Col. 3:8); (3) lasciviousness (unclean gestures, motions, signs, dress: Jer. 5:8; Prov. 5:20; 7:13; Rom. 13:13; Gal. 5:19; Eph. 4:19; 2 Peter 2:7; shamelessness, 1 Tim. 5:11); (4) lust of the eyes (1 John 2:16; Matt. 5:28; Ezek. 23:16; 1 Peter 2:11; Gen. 39:7); (5) excitements to uncleanness (Eph. 5:18; Rom. 3:14; Prov. 23:30). These sins are considered so vehement that they cannot be resisted and that therefore it is better to marry than to burn. (1 Cor. 7:9)

Chemnitz, with Luther, holds that the conjugal act in marriage is "infected with the leprosy of lust" and that one must distinguish between coition itself and the accompanying concupiscence which came through sin. He asserts that Scripture ascribes to Christian marriage both *akrasia* (want of self-control, incontinence), 1 Cor. 7:5, and purity and sanctity, 1 Cor.

---

[9] Chemnitz, II, 74, 75.

7:14.[10] By the respectability, sanctity, and purity of marriage, however, the *akrasia* which was added is overshadowed and covered so that it is not imputed to believers. Although it must be granted that the conjugal act is not as pure as it was before the fall, for it does not occur without the flames of lust, yet before God and in His sight let it be considered chastity, sanctification, purity, etc., for now after the fall marriage is, as it were, an umbrella under which much silly behavior is covered so that it is not imputed to believers, as Luther beautifully argued in connection with Genesis 26. Pious spouses, therefore, ought to preserve chastity in marriage. They ought to learn to think about the flames, the burning, the ardor, and, as it were, the vile raging of lust, not in order to conclude that it is a good thing and pleasing to God, but to learn that if it [lust] be kept within the limits of marriage, God will not impute the same to believers but will tolerate, overlook, and pardon it, as Luther eloquently says. Chemnitz believes this is what Paul says in 1 Cor. 7:5. He also cites Prov. 5:18 ("Rejoice with the wife of thy youth") and Eccl. 9:9.[11]

Gerhard's Treatment of Sex Life, Celibacy, Adultery

Like most of the orthodox theologians of this period, John Gerhard (1582-1637) dealt with many phases of the man-woman relationship in society within the framework of his times and the Roman Catholic-Protestant encounter. Worth noting are (1) his teaching in regard to sex life in marriage as contrasted to celibacy and (2) his understanding of the commandment against adultery.

Gerhard saw an inconsistency in teaching on the one hand that marriage is a divine ordinance, and on the other that virginity is superior to it. Since marriage is a holy ordinance, we cannot say that any actions within this holy relationship are in

---

10 "In 1 Cor. 7:14 *hagiazesthai* is used in a peculiar sense of those who, although not Christians themselves, are yet, by marriage with a Christian, withdrawn from the contamination of heathen impiety and brought under the saving influence of the Holy Spirit displaying itself among Christians; cf. Neander ad loc." (Joseph H. Thayer, *A Greek-English Lexicon of the New Testament* [New York: American Book Co., 1889], p. 6.) The RSV translates "consecrated."

11 Chemnitz, II, 177.

themselves impure and wicked.[12] The fall into sin has corrupted man's whole nature, but this does not make the conjugal act as such wicked and unclean; it is not in the sight of God impurity and defilement, for since the fall it is also an antidote for libido. Coitus must be kept within a lawful marriage to be right in the sight of God.[13]

Gerhard maintains that citing the prohibitions regarding the intercourse of married Levites establishes no rule proving celibacy, virginity, or abstinence as superior, because nowhere does the Law say that the use of conjugal privileges renders anyone unclean. Even if Moses had called it a legal or ceremonial uncleanness, it would not follow that it is a moral uncleanness. Rather, like the purifications, these special regulations regarding abstinence at certain times (e. g., Ex. 19:15) were part of God's pedagogy, an external discipline, to remind Israel that conception and birth [as indeed all acts of sinful man] since the fall are contaminated by sin. God wanted to teach Israel that He desires purity of the soul. This is the thought also behind 1 Cor. 7:4. The nondefilement referred to in Rev. 14:4 concerns spiritual virginity. It does not say what Romanists have interpreted it to mean: that "impurity is connected with every act through which a virgin ceases to be a virgin." Furthermore marriage is called "undefiled" in Hebrews 13; how then can it be called impure? [14]

To the question, If there is nothing wicked in the conjugal act, why are men ashamed and restrict this act to extreme privacy? Gerhard replies: "We must distinguish between civil decency [modesty] and moral turpitude. The *usus conjugii* seeks privacy, not because it is impure and morally wicked in the sight of God, but because civil decency requires it, just as relief of the bladder is sought privately, and yet it is not impure or evil in the sight of God." [15]

Like the early church fathers, Gerhard has much to say about concupiscence and believes that though it adheres to all persons

---

[12] John Gerhard, *Loci theologici*, ed. Ed. Preuss (Berlin: Gust. Schlawitz, 1869), locus 25, De conjugio, VII, par. 27, p. 18.

[13] Ibid., VII, par. 27, p. 18.

[14] Ibid., VII, par. 28, pp. 18, 19.

[15] Ibid., VII, par. 28, p. 19.

since the fall, this by no means implies that the conjugal act as such is sinful.

God has implanted the inclination in human nature that one sex should desire the other, and shows that husband and wife take God's place in the procreation and education of children. Gerhard points to the dignity, usefulness, and loveliness of the Christian family.[16]

Marriage and Celibacy

Gerhard develops the following principles regarding celibacy: (1) Pure and chaste celibacy is never to be condemned in persons suited for it.[17] (2) Celibacy is not absolutely and of itself a good work but is a state in which good works are done and it contributes to good works.[18] (3) Celibacy is to be approved and praised only in people suited for it.[19] (4) Celibacy must not be praised by affronting marriage.[20] (5) Celibacy, when preferred to marriage, is not to be defined by our own judgment but from Sacred Scriptures and deduced from the proper *sedis* [source passage] of this doctrine.[21] (6) In preferring the celibate life to marriage the proper intention, an exploration of the individual's gifts, and diligent consideration of all circumstances ought to prevail.[22] (7) No celibate, even though he lives chastely, should place himself on a higher plane than that occupied by pious spouses, even if, before God, he may be in greater grace on account of his celibacy.[23]

The Meaning of One Flesh

Gerhard lists the following sequence of reasons why husband and wife are called one flesh: (1) the agreement of will and affection; (2) the indissoluble bond between them; (3) the inseparable association of their lives; (4) the duty of conjugal intercourse; (5) the fruit of their conjugal cohabitation.[24] In their

---

16 Ibid., VII, par. 13, p. 7.
17 Ibid., VII, par. 490, p. 299.
18 Ibid., VII, par. 492, p. 301 f.
19 Ibid., VII, par. 494, p. 304.
20 Ibid., VII, par. 496, p. 305.
21 Ibid., VII, par. 499, p. 309.
22 Ibid., VII, par. 503, p. 315 f.
23 Ibid., VII, par. 504, p. 317 f.
24 Ibid., VII, par. 46, pp. 35, 36.

use of sex Christian couples should be aware of the ravages of original sin in this area also.[25]

Thou Shalt Not Commit Adultery

It is well established that "adultery" in its strict sense and in the context of the Old Testament meant extramarital relations of a husband or wife with another betrothed or married person and is to be distinguished from fornication.[26]

In the teaching of the Ten Commandments throughout the ages the principle of *pars pro toto* has been applied to the word *adultery*. This is also the position taken by Gerhard.

He teaches that the Sixth Commandment forbids not only adultery but also fornication, illicit sexual desire, and all internal and external departures from moral purity. Any violation of marriage is prohibited. From the negative the affirmative must be deduced, namely, that God in this commandment protects the institution of marriage and wishes to preserve true chastity, before marriage and within marriage.[27] God desires cleanness of mind and body proceeding from true fear, love, and trust of God. The man-woman relationship should be one of "holiness" (1 Thess. 4:4), of "self-control" (Gal. 5:23), and of a "clean heart." (Psalm 51:10)

Gerhard spoke of a twofold chastity: chastity in the unmarried state and in marriage. While in the premarital state it means "continence," within marriage it means "preserving the body chaste and holy for one legitimate spouse." [28]

The heart should strive continuously against the "flames" of lust and corrupt thoughts and should develop wholesome attitudes toward sex (Matt. 15:19). Filthy talk, impudent gestures, lasciviousness of the eyes, and all obscenity are to be avoided. Chastity should be demonstrated in deeds, that the body may be preserved pure and unpolluted.

To avoid sin the temptations to sin must also be avoided. The commandment therefore warns against intemperance, drunken-

---

[25] Martin Chemnitz, Polycarp Leyser, Johann Gerhard, *Harmonia Evangelistarum* (Geneva: Chouet, 1645), II, 190 f.

[26] See chapter two of this study or any theological encyclopedia; also Frederick D. Kramer, "Elementary Pupils and the Sixth Commandment," *Lutheran Education*, XCIV (June 1959), 499, 500.

[27] Gerhard, *Loci theologici*, III (1865), par. 159, p. 73.

[28] Ibid., III, par. 160, p. 73.

ness, voluptuousness, levity in dress, improper dance, leisure, carnal security, impure speech, love prattle, establishment or toleration of a brothel. Finally, since in this commandment marriage is sanctified, likewise censuring of marriage and of the feminine sex, rash divorces, pretended chastity outside marriage, prohibition of marriage for suitable persons, and neglect of the duties which Scripture prescribes for spouses are a sin against this commandment.[29]

Some Distinctions of Koenig and Quenstedt

The Rostock (Germany) professor J. F. Koenig (1619—64) distinguishes between the moral and natural bases and purposes of marriage and sex.

Marriage is not a natural union, because we are not born married, but a moral union which is founded on divine institution and natural instinct, by which people of both sexes are attracted to each other. Marriage is necessary because it is apparent that without marriage the human race cannot be propagated, nor mutual assistance given, nor promiscuous libido [lust] avoided. Marriage also fosters good society and cultivates various virtues.[30]

In his comprehensive work on systematic theology Johann Andreas Quenstedt (1617—85) deals with concupiscence under the doctrine of sin. Significant is his distinction between physical and natural concupiscence and theological and moral concupiscence. When God created man He built into man's nature a potency and appetite for sexual union which is in itself good and is concerned with the conservation of nature, "which surely no one will affirm to be a fault or a sin." On the other hand, there exists a "depraved concupiscence which breaks this natural potency" and is the origin of all lawlessness.[31]

He makes "the glory of God" the ultimate and highest end of marriage, classifying the subordinate ends in the following order: (1) propagation and preservation of the human race and of the church through the generation and education of chil-

---

[29] Ibid., III, par. 161, pp. 73, 74.

[30] John F. Koenig, "De conjugio" in *Theologia positivo-acroamatica* (Vitembergae et Servestae: Sam. G. Zimmermann, 1755), pars. 996, 997.

[31] Johann Andreas Quenstedt, *Theologia didactico-polemica* (Wittenberg: John Ludolph Quenstedt, 1701), bk. 2, ch. 2, sec. 2, 138—140.

dren (Gen. 1:28); (2) mutual and faithful help which marriage
partners ought to offer to each other in civil life and in the spiritual life; (3) "avoiding fornication, or a remedy against wan-
dering or unsettled lusts." This aim, however, he considered
"incidental and accessory" in accordance with 1 Cor. 7:2. He
adds: "What before the fall was instituted as an office is after
the fall made into a remedy." [32]

Baier's Interpretation of Chastity

John William Baier (1647—95) another of the well-known
theologians of orthodoxy, while expanding in great detail on the
Levitical law of forbidden degrees in marriage, states the causes
of marriage as natural attraction between the sexes, the desire for
companionship, social customs, the desire for children, and the
avoidance of fornication.[33]

Both marriage partners, one man and one woman, must be
capable of discharging the conjugal obligation, both as to age
and especially as to the natural power itself to procreate or to
extinguish for the other person the flames of desire. (1 Cor. 7:3) [34]

In his discussion of the Law (Sixth Commandment) he defines
chastity both in and outside wedlock. "There is a conjugal chastity, not only of virgins and of widows but also of married people.
With regard to virgins the commandment implies abstinence from
carnal copulation and related indulgences. In the case of widows
it implies an abstaining from a former [sexual] practice [*usu
priori*]. And in the case of married people it implies a moderate
and holy use of conjugal privileges." [35]

Baier regards carnal copulation as consequence and effect
rather than a cause of marriage and quotes Musaeus to show
that the conjugal bond continues even if coitus ceases.[36]

Hollaz on the One-Flesh Relationship

David Hollaz (1648—1713), in his *Examen theologicum acroamaticum* takes for granted normal sex relations in marriage

---

[32] Quenstedt, pp. 453, 454.

[33] John Wm. Baier, *Compendium theologiae positivae*, ed. C. F. W.
Walther (St. Louis: Concordia Publishing House, 1879), ch. 16, secs. 2—6,
III, 746—749.

[34] Ibid., ch. 16, par. 8, III, 754—756.

[35] Ibid., ch. 7, sec. 12 g, III, 357.

[36] Ibid., ch. 16, par. 31 e, III, 773.

when he says: "From the nature of marriage, adultery of itself directly conflicts with unity of flesh and therefore also with the substance of marriage, through which two become one flesh (Gen. 2:24). For he which is joined to a harlot is one body with the harlot (1 Cor. 6:16) and therefore no longer one flesh with his wife. . . . Whatever immediately interferes with conjugal fidelity itself and the *usus tori* [use of the marriage bed] dissolves the marriage bond and therefore, by its own right, opens the doors of a second marriage to the innocent party." [37]

Other Statements of the Dogmaticians

Those acquainted with the patristic and the medieval theological treatment of concupiscence will not be surprised to find the dogmaticians of this period asserting that sexual feelings in themselves are evil. Masturbation is definitely condemned as sinful [38] and a greater offense in God's sight than fornication or adultery. [39]

Gerhard, in speaking of involuntary seminal emissions, [40] says that since they are rarely if ever possible without accompanying sex fantasies, they are sinful, and they are one of the things for which God provided marriage as a remedy. [41] The Jena theological

---

[37] David Hollaz, *Examen theologicum acroamaticum* (Leipzig: Godfrey Kiesewetter, 1741), trans. Heinrich Schmid, quoted by G. E. Lenski in *Marriage in the Lutheran Church* (Columbus, Ohio: Lutheran Book Concern, 1936), p. 242.

[38] John C. Dannhauer, *Theologia casualis* (Greifswald: John W. Fickweiler, 1706), pp. 415, 416. Dannhauer, following the rule of *De vita contemplativa* (inaccurately ascribed to St. Prosper of Aquitaine instead of to its rightful author, Julianus Pomerius), says: "In general the rule which is set down in St. Prosper's *On the Contemplative Life* (1.3.c.6) should be noted: 'It is an emission of the body in sleep, but in waking hours it is an act of sin; to stimulate such an emission is a serious sin. But if one prays for chastity and the reasons for the irritation are removed, then that emission of the body, since it befalls at night, is — materially at least, though not formally — a sin in the service of Moloch; for whoredom's devil is honored with the hope of child sacrifice if the act takes place through stimulation in broad daylight.'"

[39] For a discussion of the Jewish and Roman Catholic attitudes toward masturbation, particularly in this period, cf. Alfred Kinsey et al., *Sexual Behavior in the Human Male* (Philadelphia: W. B. Saunders Co., 1948), pp. 473—476.

[40] Gerhard, III, par. 161, p. 73, where he quotes Thomas Aquinas from Hom. XXXII in the *Opus imperfectum*, falsely ascribed to St. John Chrysostom in *Summa theologica* (Vol. 19), Third Part (Supplement), QQ. XXXIV to LXVII, literally translated by Fathers of the English Dominican Province (London: Burns, Oates and Washbourne Ltd., Publishers to the Holy See, 1932). See also Gerhard, VII, par. 612, p. 411.

[41] Ibid., III, par. 165, p. 75.

faculty described *coitus interruptus,* after the example of Onan, as a sin against the First (Ps. 128:4), Fourth (1 Cor. 7:3), Fifth, and Sixth (1 Cor. 6:9) Commandments, graver than fornication and adultery. The assent of the wife to the practice, far from excusing the husband, makes her a partaker of his sin.[42] Any type of sexual fantasy or thinking on sexual matters is also condemned as evil.[43]

The Consistory of Electoral Saxony held that panderers, whether on behalf of their own wives or other women, and persons who make any facility available for fornication or prostitution, are punishable as adulterers.[44]

Sex relations, it is said, are primarily for conception. Other incidental aspects, insofar as they are discussed, are not stressed. However, the dogmaticians do acknowledge that sex relations within marriage are not intrinsically sinful, and intercourse for the sake of procreation is not the only licit and decent kind. (Prov. 5:18; 1 Cor. 7:2, 5, 7) [45]

In discussing the use of sex, Gerhard repeats the injunctions of 1 Cor. 7, 1 Thess. 4, and 1 Peter 3:8 and applies 1 John 2:27. He quotes Aristotle to the effect that excessive use of sex destroys the body and shortens life, since 100 drops of blood hardly equal one drop of semen. He quotes the "medical profession" to the effect that a single *coitus* exhausts the body more than if forty times as much blood had been lost. [46] He also quotes the councils of the scholastics on not having intercourse with a pregnant spouse or one still nursing a child, before solemn feasts (Ex. 19:15), before receiving Holy Communion, in old age (Genesis 18), or in the daytime, but warns that counsels like this must not be allowed to become snares of conscience.[47] Dunte holds that it is not wrong for old people to have sex relations

---

[42] George Dedekennus, *Thesaurus consiliorum et decisionum,* ed. John Ernst Gerhard (Jena: Hertel, 1671), III, 366; Christian August Crusius, *Kurzer Begriff der Moral Theologie* (Leipzig: Saalbach, 1773), II, 1179.

[43] Chemnitz-Leyser-Gerhard, *Harmonia Evangelistarum,* I, 446; John Francis Buddeus, *Institutiones theologiae moralis* (Leipzig: Fritsch, 1715), p. 491.

[44] Dedekennus-Gerhard, III, 371.

[45] Gerhard, pars. 432, 433, 441, VII, 254—257, 263, 264.

[46] Gerhard, par. 437, VII, 260; Louis Dunte, *Decisiones mille et sex casuum conscientiae,* 3d. ed. (Lübeck: Wetstein, 1664), pp. 838—840.

[47] Gerhard, pars. 438, 439, VII, 260, 261.

nor for a young spouse to have relations with an aged marital partner.[48]

Intercourse with a menstruating woman is considered wrong (Lev. 15:24; 18:19; 20:18; Ezek. 18:6; 22:10).[49] It is not wrong for a husband to have intercourse with his pregnant wife unless there is danger of miscarriage.[50] A couple may not vow perpetual continence by mutual consent.[51] Impotence resulting from the malice of men, accident, or illness is to be borne as a visitation from God. (Is. 56:4, 5; Ecclus. 30:21; Matt. 10:29)[52]

Very little is said on the subject of premarital sex education, and whatever instruction was given was apparently restricted to the periodic reading of prohibited degrees of marriage in the church service, remarks made at weddings, sermons and instructions concerned expressly or incidentally with marriage, works on moral theology, and a limited and rather sentimental *Erbauungsliteratur*.[53] One of the *Kirchenordnungen* of 1544 states that the pastor should make certain before marriage that young people are familiar with the Ten Commandments, the Creed, the Lord's Prayer, and other parts of the Catechism, especially if they have been poor churchgoers.[54] Another order says that the servants of the Gospel of Christ shall not go deeper into marriage affairs than as far as "conscience and copulation [marriage ceremony] are concerned."[55] Pastors are, however, urged to "spread more information about the holy estate of marriage."[56]

Traces of Asceticism and Scholasticism

The dogmaticians of the 17th and 18 centuries seem to be on the road back to the asceticism of the Middle Ages. In explanation of this return Bainton writes:

---

[48] Dunte, p. 804.

[49] Gerhard, par. 438, VII, 260, 261. His argument reflects the ignorance of the medical profession of that day, which taught that children conceived at the time of the menstrual flow will be monstrous births and prone to epilepsy and elephantiasis.

[50] Koenig, pp. 802—807.

[51] Gerhard, pars. 442, 443, VII, 264, 266.

[52] Dieterich in Dunte, pp. 842, 843.

[53] Such as Abraham Hosemann, *Verus amor conjugalis, Das ist: Eheliche Liebe Zweyer Ehegatten usw.* (Brunswick: Zilligern, 1682).

[54] Aemilius L. Richter, *Die evangelischen Kirchenordnungen des sechszehnten Jahrhunderts* (Weimar: Landes-Industrie Comptoirs, 1846), II, 70.

[55] Ibid., II, 79.

[56] Ibid., II, 276, 277.

At one point the Reformation and the Counter-Reformation were agreed. Both so revolted against license as to land in prudery. Luther at the very end of his life was in such a panic over the low necks worn by the girls of Wittenberg that on a journey he wrote declaring his intention never to return (*Briefwechsel,* No. 4158, Weimar Edition). The Council of Trent at its 25th session decreed: "Figures shall not be painted exciting to lust . . . and no image shall be placed in the church without the approval of the bishop." In the spirit of these injunctions Paul IV commissioned the painter Daniel de Volterra to clothe some of the nudes in Michelangelo's Last Judgment in the Sistine Chapel. . . .

Clement VIII proposed to obliterate the entire fresco of the Last Judgment and was deterred only by remonstrances. Innocent X was shocked by the nudity of the baby Jesus and had Him provided with a shirt. . . . Such prudery, commonly associated with Puritanism, was indeed not absent from the movement, yet was not peculiar to it, but rather characterized the Anglicanism of the period. The Geneva Bible of 1582 was popularly called the *Breeches Bible* because in it Genesis 3:7 was so rendered that Adam and Eve after the fall clothed themselves in breeches. This spirit continued well into the Victorian era.[57]

The Christian Ethic of Sex

After the Age of Orthodoxy more attention was given to the field of Christian ethics. This helped to bring the whole area of sex into better focus within the framework of evangelical doctrine. One of the chief works was written by Adolph von Harless (1806—1879). It sweeps away the fogs of monkish asceticism and pietistic prudery with telling effect. "Where the attraction between two persons of opposite sex is purely a matter of mind (*geistig*) and not an attraction of both body and mind (*geistig-leiblich*), there is no motive for contracting a marriage." [58] But Christian marriage is much more. It is the flowing together of two lives and the surrender of the whole person, one to the other. This personal attraction and personal trust is the precondition of marriage and its one-flesh union. It forms the true foundation for monogamy.[59] He points out that where the sensuous sex drive

---

[57] Roland H. Bainton, "Christianity and Sex," in *Sex and Religion Today,* ed. Simon Doniger (New York: Association Press, 1953), pp. 72—74.

[58] G. Chr. Adolph von Harless, *Christliche Ethik* (Gütersloh: C. Bertelsmann, 1875), p. 503.

[59] Ibid., p. 505.

and personal sex love are properly balanced in the sexual union the former diminishes and the latter increases as the social-spiritual-personal relationships of the spouses develop and mature. Christian virtue is manifested in marriage, not in ignoring sexual attraction but in this, that the sex motive is never dominant, but subordinated to personal love for the spouse.[60]

Body and Soul Are to Serve God

Christian piety which grows out of gratitude for God's redeeming love is the response of the total person, both body and soul. The activities of body and spirit or mind are inseparable. Also the body is included and committed in the Christian vocation. In the life of the body there are God-ordained natural gifts and drives; there are also (since the fall) tempting lusts and desires. The Christian experiences a reign of the converted heart over all members of the body. The soul seeks the health and welfare of the body on the one hand, and the mortification of sinful lusts in moderation, sobriety, and chastity — thus the Christ life within makes also the life of the body a part of the Christian calling.

Harless makes a good case for this position, showing that the Christian cannot accept the pagan notion that body (flesh) and matter are evil while mind and things of the spirit alone are good. God does not order killing the life of the body, but sin. In fact, God wants us to love the body of this flesh (Eph. 5:29). The battle is not against flesh but against sin — so that the reborn man may glorify God in body as well as spirit (Rom. 6:12, 13). The Christian who follows his vocation in Christ through the power of the new birth preserves and nourishes the body in the service of the soul for the glory of God. In Christian thinking the body is neither despised nor idolized (as among the heathen), but it is held to be holy, consecrated to God as His temple. (1 Cor. 6:15, 19, 20)[61]

Christ is both a gift and an example to the believer. Faith never stands alone. It is always united with love. Justification issues in sanctification. In faith itself the new obedience begins, an obedience to Christ which is not compatible with sin in any

---

60 Ibid., p. 503.
61 Ibid., pp. 418—421.

form. The converted sinner lives out of the forgiveness he has received. Justification not only wipes out the debt of past sins but is at the same time the beginning of a new life, the fulfilling of the Christian calling. The Gospel contains the motive power and drives for new potentials in the new relation to God and man. Justification leads to finding the way of life that accords with God's will. It leads to proper self-discipline. It puts sin in its place. It certifies and proves faith with works. It mortifies the flesh, that is, the sinful stirrings in the body. While the Christian lives "out of the Gospel," he needs also the Law to regulate his life.

SUMMARY

1. Orthodoxy followed in the footsteps of the reformers. It made a strong defense of sex as a gift of God and of marriage as God's ordinance — an arrangement in accordance with nature — which no man-made asceticism or church-made doctrines of virginity and celibacy can overthrow. Sex within marriage is honorable and not impure.

2. At the same time the dogmaticians did not mitigate sins related to sex but identified them, frankly examined them, classified them, and traced them back to concupiscence, which pollutes what in creation was pure. Chastity was prescribed for all, married as well as unmarried, being a cleanliness of mind and heart which the Christian earnestly cultivates.

3. There is noticeable, however, a swing back to asceticism and Aristotelian moral philosophy so closely combined in the scholastics. This no doubt led to prudery and was not fully consistent with a Biblical view of sex. Some scholars note that Lutheran dogmaticians dealt with virtues related to sex, not as preparation for grace (Romanist view) but as expressions of obedience in the state of grace.[62]

4. The dawn of the 19th century found attitudes toward sex still very confused, with Augustinian concepts prevailing. The study of Christian ethics later placed sex into better Christian focus, as part of the order of creation and under the Gospel of Christ, which supplies the motive for the new obedience.

---

[62] Hans Emil Weber, *Reformation, Orthodoxie und Rationalismus* (Gütersloh: C. Bertelsmann, 1951), pp. 49—63.

CHAPTER 8

The Influence of Puritanism, Pietism, and Rationalism

THE MAIN STREAM of history has many sources and, as it flows along, the characteristics of one age or several ages project themselves into the next. The changing theological and ecclesiastical waters at any one time contain a mixture of many streams.

After the Reformation Protestant ethics in both the Lutheran and Reformed churches developed distinctive features indicative of further reform. Puritanism became characteristic of moral theology primarily within the religious groups of Calvinistic persuasion and before spreading to Holland and America flowered first in England. Pietism, which some have described as a stream of neoasceticism, began in Lutheranism about 1660. Historians have generalized on Pietism in various ways. Albrecht Ritschl thought of it essentially as a revival of medieval monastic and mystical piety on the soil of Protestantism, a piety which was stimulated from Reformed and Puritan sources and alien to the spirit of Lutheranism.[1] Johannes Juengst, on the contrary, regards it as a progressive movement within Lutheranism and a revolt against the formal scholasticism of the Orthodoxists.[2]

A third movement almost coincidental with Puritanism and Pietism was Rationalism. Its roots may be traced back to the

---

[1] John T. McNeill, *Modern Christian Movements* (Philadelphia: Westminster Press, 1954), p. 71.

[2] Juengst, who wrote *Pietisten* (Tübingen: J. C. B. Mohr [P. Siebeck], 1906) is quoted in McNeill, p. 71. See also *The Encyclopedia Americana* (1955 ed.), s. v. "Pietism."

Renaissance and to the school of thought which held that reasonableness of religious beliefs could be taken as proof of their truth.[3]

These three movements influenced the religious thought of the 17th, 18th, and 19th centuries. Their streams of thought and life flowed across the Atlantic to America and became a part of the social, moral, and religious milieu of the American people, touching all denominations in varying times and ways. To understand the attitudes toward sex, modesty, and chastity which came out of Europe to America one needs the following background.

Puritanism and Pietism and John Calvin

The Calvinistic ethos is evident in both Puritanism and Pietism.[4] By temperament and training Calvin inclined toward austere asceticism. Under his leadership the former license and frivolity in Geneva gave way to strict moral severity. The central and controlling concept of Calvinism, which was congenial to both Puritanism and Pietism, may be stated in the form of a question: What must I do for the greater glory of God? It sees in the Bible the sovereign will for man's conduct and belief, for God has given the Bible to direct man's thinking and conduct in the fields of science, culture, business, society, the home, and politics.[5]

Calvinism holds that there is no area of human conduct for which the Bible does not serve as the norm according to which all men are to pattern their conduct for the greater glory of God.[6]

Lutheran theology, on the other hand, asks: What has God done for my salvation? The answer is found in the Scriptural revelation of God's grace. "Lutheran theology emphasizes the

---

[3] *The Lutheran Heritage*, Vol. II of *Christian Social Responsibility*, ed. Harold C. Letts (Philadelphia: Muhlenberg Press, 1957), p. 80.

[4] Taken together, and in all their aspects, Puritanism and Pietism comprise most of the significant phenomena of Protestantism between 1603, when James I came to the English throne, and 1740, when Frederick the Great of Prussia began his reign with favors to the opponents of Pietism. At its origin Pietism was somewhat indebted to Puritanism. Distinct, and never arrayed against each other, both contributed jointly to the formation and nourishment of later movements. The revival that largely recruited the membership of American frontier churches owed something to both. (Cf. McNeill, pp. 9, 10)

[5] John Calvin, *Institutes of the Christian Religion*, trans. John Allen (Grand Rapids: Wm. B. Eerdmans Publishing Co., 1949), III, xxi, 3.

[6] Ibid., I, xviii, 4; Frederick E. Mayer, *The Religious Bodies of America*, 3d ed. (St. Louis: Concordia, 1958), p. 203.

objective character of the means of grace [Word and Sacraments] as the only foundation for faith; Christian assurance is based solely upon the objective promises of the Gospel. . . . Reformed theology professes to be activistic and therefore directs the Christian to seek the assurance of his being in the state of grace in a program of Christian activity rather than in the means of grace." [7] It is evident that Calvinism would emphasize the outward behavior of people and stress the moral law.[8]

Calvin did not exclude sex from God's creative plan, but it is to be kept within the bonds of a monogamous marriage and shall be the means of propagating the race. God's blessing upon sex is restricted to those who cohabit in chaste and holy wedlock. "You may then take it briefly thus," Calvin wrote, "conjugal intercourse is a thing that is pure, honorable, and holy because it is a pure institution of God; the immoderate degree with which persons burn is a fault arising from the corruption of nature; but in the case of believers marriage is a veil by which the fault is covered over so that it no longer appears in the sight of God." [9]

To Calvin, as to Luther, marriage was "a remedy for avoiding fornication." Calvin taught that within marriage there should be due moderation and modesty.[10] His view may be traced to

---

[7] Mayer, p. 194.

[8] Calvin's theology was based on man's obligation of obedience. Repentance, manifest in self-denial and meditation upon the future life, is the ground of assurance that the believer is in the state of grace and thereby in possession of a certain sign of his election. The basis of faith is therefore not, as in Lutheran theology, the universal promise of God contained in the Gospel, but in the Holy Spirit's activity evident in producing self-denial and observance of the rules for Christian living. For Luther the chief response of the believer was the striving of the soul already saved toward sanctification. While the peril of the Lutheran system is quietism (the reaction of Pietism is a case in point), the peril of Calvinism is legalism (the Puritan strictness is a case in point). For a thorough discussion of Calvin's theology and teachings on sex and marriage see William G. Cole, *Sex in Christianity and Psychoanalysis* (New York: Oxford University Press, 1955), pp. 100—132.

[9] Cf. Calvin's *Commentary on Corinthians*, trans. John Pringle (Grand Rapids: Wm. B. Eerdmans Publishing Co., 1948), I, 231; cf. also Ch. xxi of "The Adultero-German Interim" in John Calvin, *In Defense of the Reformed Faith*, Vol. III of *Tracts and Treatises Relating to the Reformation* (Grand Rapids: Wm. B. Eerdmans Publishing Co., 1959), pp. 217—220.

[10] Calvin warned of two extremes: the one, to abhor sexual expression as a thing of evil and to seek celibacy, thus viewing all forms of sexuality as degrading; the other, to regard sex as self-justifying, that is, to say, as he put it, that married persons have license to indulge in whatever sexual activity they please. (Cole, p. 121)

either Hellenistic dualism with its deep suspicion of all bodily pleasure or, better, to his theory of man under God.

The origin of the tendency toward legalism and asceticism existing in the various branches of the Reformed Church may be found in Calvin's writings and teachings. In the 18th century the various philosophical systems — notably deism, naturalism, romanticism, and idealism — greatly modified the position of stark Calvinism, especially in England.[11]

However, Calvin's view of the soul as essentially distinct from the body and the far more glorious part of man had wide influence. That man's goal in this life is to seek liberation from the body and that only when we are liberated from the body can we really enjoy God, was an earlier concept which influenced a great deal of Christian thought.[12]

Puritan Theology and Sex Ethics

Puritanism, which was one of the early offsprings of Calvinism, produced a curious blend of asceticism which had widespread and continuing influence in many religious bodies and sects in both Europe and America.

McNeill, however, holds that Puritanism had no one founder, that its background is seen in the older forms of Christianity, and that it resembles some religious movements other than Christian.[13] And William Haller observes: "Puritanism, so-called, was nothing new or totally unrelated to the past but something old, deep-seated, and English, with roots reaching far back into medieval life." [14] Haller makes the beginning of historic Puritanism contemporaneous with the coming of Elizabeth I to the throne in 1558.[15] McNeill connects Puritanism with continental Protestantism through the influence of Martin Bucer of Strasbourg, Jan Laski, the Polish reformer (both of whom lived for some time in England), Zwingli, and Calvin.[16]

The Puritan movement has been looked at in two ways.

---

[11] Mayer, pp. 200, 201.
[12] Calvin, *Institutes,* I, xv, 1, 2. O. S., 3, 176, 1.
[13] McNeill, p. 21.
[14] William Haller, *The Rise of Puritanism* (New York: Columbia University Press, 1938), p. 5.
[15] Ibid., p. 5.
[16] McNeill, pp. 25, 26.

Some say that the Puritans were religiously motivated in their ethics and attitudes; others, that their life was regulated to conform with the economics of their existence. Neither view may be ignored. The Puritan must be considered in his total situation.

Intensely Calvinistic in theology and worship, the Puritans held the law of the Old Testament in high regard and used it as the basis of their ethical legalism. Allowing only what the Bible expressly warranted, the Puritans generally developed a more rigidly prescribed code of moral behavior than did the Lutherans, who allowed whatever the Bible did not expressly forbid. Puritans stressed Christian sanctification in order to find an a posteriori basis for the assurance of being in the state of grace. They appealed to the Bible as the divinely given code for both doctrine and life.[17] The moral law of the Old Testament, though not considered an agent for salvation, was not set aside by the Puritans; it was regarded as a directive for those who love God and seek to serve Him. They frowned on excessive sexual expression, whether in or out of marriage; they frowned as much, however, on celibacy or unnatural continency.[18]

Thomas Cartwright (1535—1603), described as the most gifted, able, and learned of the 16th-century Puritans, maintained that prayer and piety, mutual admonition and encouragement, love and devotion belonged to the marriage relationship.[19] Robert Browne defines marriage thus: "Marriage is a lawful joining of the husband and wife, as of two in one flesh, by partaking the

---

[17] In the New Haven Colony the laws of Moses were provisionally adopted as a social code. Cf. Arthur Dakin, *Calvinism* (Philadelphia: Westminster Press, 1940), p. 161. Leonard Bacon (1802—1881), *Thirteen Historical Discourses* (New Haven: Durrie and Peck; New York: Gould, Newman and Saxton, 1839), reveals the moral rigor which the New Haven Colony attempted to attain. Leonard Woolsey Bacon in *History of American Christianity* (New York: The Christian Literature Company, 1897), quoting Leonard Bacon, says: "The greatest and boldest improvement which has been made in criminal jurisprudence by any act since the dark ages was that which was made by our fathers when they determined 'that the judicial laws of God, as they were delivered by Moses, and as they are a fence to the moral law, being neither typical nor ceremonial, nor having any reference to Canaan, shall be accounted of moral equity and generally bind all offenders and be a rule to all the courts.'" (P. 113)

[18] Chard Powers Smith, *Yankees and God* (New York: Hermitage House, 1954), p. 122.

[19] *Cartwrightiana*, eds. Albert Peel and Leland H. Carlson (London: George Allen and Unwin Ltd., 1951), pp. 185—191.

use of each other's love, body, and gifts, in one communion of duties, and especially in generation and bringing up of children." [20]

This is in keeping with Calvin's twin rule: first, to make use of all things in this world; second, to use them moderately (Phil. 4: 5). This principle was at the center of the Puritan concept of morality.[21] Nothing in itself but anything in excess was forbidden. The authorities were always ready to "correct" or punish excessive sexual expression, but they were equally opposed to excessive or unhealthy chastity.[22] Premarital fornication and pregnancy were practically condoned, so long as confession and marriage followed, and in most places and periods they left no social stain.[23]

The Puritan austerity involved the exclusion of whatever was deemed a hindrance to the heavenly voyager. The accent may well have been laid too much on these rejections, and Puritans have been criticized for pruning the tree too closely. McNeill defends them by observing that it is only folly to suppose that there should be no pruning and that where discipline is neglected morality deteriorates or may dissolve altogether.[24]

There is historical evidence that the Puritans certainly endeavored to keep sex within the bounds of the decency and dignity for which they strove in general. Beyond this it is difficult to generalize. Many criticisms of prudery have been

---

[20] *The Writings of Robert Harrison and Robert Browne*, eds. Albert Peel and Leland H. Carlson (London: George Allen and Unwin Ltd., 1953), p. 383 (spelling modernized). Emil Oberholzer, Jr., in *Delinquent Saints: Disciplinary Action in the Early Congregational Churches of Massachusetts* (New York: Columbia University Press, 1956), p. 111, says: "The New England Puritans, influenced by Dutch practices, by Hebraic tradition, and by Calvin, considered marriage a civil matter endowed with a sacred character."

[21] Smith, p. 102.

[22] It is reported that in one case a female church member complained to the minister that her husband was neglecting her, not charging adultery or desertion but simply neglect of normal, healthy sexual routine. The minister expostulated with the husband to no effect. Then the wife complained to the whole congregation, and the culprit was excommunicated. (See Smith, p. 11)

[23] Smith, p. 103. It is of note in this matter that Oberholzer, having examined 1,242 cases between 1620 and 1839, concluded that confessions were recorded "in a matter-of-fact manner" and that the majority of offenders were eventually restored. Oberholzer, pp. 150, 151; cf. also pp. 127 to 151.

[24] McNeill, p. 48.

leveled against the Puritans with the very likely undeserved result that almost everything ascetic or moral in America is classified as "puritan" to the present day.[25]

It would be a mistake, however, to think that Puritan austerity meant lack of love. A tender respectfulness and warmth and a peculiar ardor of affection were noticeable in the husband-wife relations of the Puritans and Quakers.[26]

Bainton observes that "the English Puritans did not discountenance marital delights, but did stress that loyalty to God which takes precedence over all that is cherished by man. In consequence marriage becomes under God a joint enterprise." [27]

Haller says the Puritan code was completely free from anything like the ascetic or suspicious attitude toward marriage. "Like all other activities to which men might be called, marriage was an opportunity for spiritual effort, something to be sanctified by the spirit." [28]

Social-economic Aspects of Puritan Life

Though the moralistic and ascetic strain ran deep in Puritanism, historians and sociologists detect other than religious bases and motives in the Puritan movement and identify it with the efforts of the merchant class in England to attain wealth and power.[29] Some observers of the movement see the Puritan revolt

---

[25] Possibly the case is overdrawn, yet descriptions of the Puritans such as the following are frequently drawn: "All that was glad, all that was gay, colors that pleased the eye, songs that caressed the ear, the idle dalliance of love, the wine cup and the kiss, fine raiment and delicate food, the jewels of art, everything that made up the web and woof of the joy of life became sinful and pandering to the lusts of that supreme enemy of the soul, the sadly abused body." (Clarence Meily, *Puritanism* [Chicago: Charles H. Kerr and Co., 1911], pp. 102, 103)

[26] Edmund S. Morgan, *The Puritan Family* (Boston: The Trustees of the Public Library, 1944), p. 26. Cf. also Alfred Neave Brayshaw, *The Quakers: Their Story and Message*, 2d ed. (London: The Swarthmore Press, Ltd., 1927; New York: The Macmillan Co., 1927), p. 131.

[27] Roland Bainton, *What Christianity Says About Sex, Love, and Marriage* (New York: Association Press, 1957), p. 95.

[28] Haller, p. 120.

[29] Folsom is one who holds this view. He says that with the developing and elaborating commercial activity and discovery of new lands across the sea, new roads to opportunity and personal satisfaction appeared. Emigration and the accumulation of personal property became a new cultural drive. People found that by skillful business dealings and thrift a man could raise his economic status and material standard of living. The complicated liaisons of love and pursuit of pleasure did not fit in with the reaching of one's maximum success in business. Folsom rationalizes

as an event marking the rise of the *bourgeoisie* in England and the decline of feudal politics and economy. V. F. Calverton observes: "In understanding the Puritan's attitude toward love or sex, we can understand the social basis of his life. If we would know why his life was ascetic, his family strictly monogamous, his sex impulses religiously repressed, his simplicity severely cultivated, we must turn to the economics of his existence." [30] Calverton further says without qualifications: "Sex carnality, since it was contrary to his ethic, the very economic basis of his life, evoked his [the Puritan's] unmitigated condemnation." [31]

This would seem, on the face of it, to be an oversimplification of the matter. McNeill's is a more realistic explanation. He says: "Here in a nutshell is the Puritan creed for economic life," as he quotes William Perkins' *The Whole Treatise of the Cases of Conscience:* "The end of a man's calling is not to gather riches for himself or his family or the poor, but to serve God in serving of man, and in seeking the good of all men; and to this end men must apply their lives and labors." [32]

Puritanism, springing as it did out of its own particular matrix in history, did in its own time and way leave its mark on the people of America. "Puritanism," says John Morley, "came from the deeps. It flowed from yearnings that made themselves felt in Eastern world and Western; it sprang from

---

that "it was natural to support these economic motives by a religious ideology which was conveniently at hand. The Puritans turned back to a simpler, less ritualized Christianity, and everything from fiddling to whittling would be suspect as a distraction or a waste of precious time." (Joseph K. Folsom, *The Family: Its Sociology and Social Psychiatry* [New York: John Wiley and Sons, Inc., 1934], pp. 150, 151)

[30] *Sex in Civilization,* eds. Victor F. Calverton and Samuel D. Schmalhausen, 7th prtg. (New York: The Macaulay Co., 1929), p. 265.

[31] Ibid., p. 266. Calverton has much to say on this same theme. "The existence of things carnal was relegated to a nether consciousness, unconversant with one's finer personality. Sexual intercourse was regarded only as a procreative function, a clandestine episode taboo to the tongue. In Puritan art, sex expression is seldom discovered. Whenever themes pertaining to sex were approached, description became restricted, evasive and covert. Spiritual pleasures replaced sensual. Religious realities supplanted material" (p. 270). "The sex attitude of the Puritan was but a rationalization of the economics of his existence. It was but a defense mechanism unconsciously designed to protect the private property concept upon which it has thrived." (P. 271)

[32] McNeill, p. 40. Perkins' work was published by T. Pickering, London, 1611.

aspirations that breathe in men and women of many faiths and communions." [33]

Today, now that the old controversies are forgotten and the issues blurred, the word Puritanism means, for many, simply a certain rigorous kind of life, in the main an ethical outlook. The word carries with it ideas of stern self-discipline, simplicity of manners with a scrupulous care of money, concentration on duty, and what is in many quarters regarded as an unduly strict and narrow code of morals. "This attitude of life undoubtedly derives from Calvinism, though of course it could be held along with variations from the strict Calvinistic theology." [34]

The historical evidence shows that the Puritan ethos was dominant in America down to the first World War. It should be added, however, that there was a sharp reaction against it during the last generation.[35]

Puritan Influence on Lutherans

As to the influence of Puritanism on Lutheranism in the nineteenth century Lutheran historian J. L. Neve notes that the Lutheran Church in America, especially the eastern branch of it, was obliged to choose between two extreme tendencies: Puritanism and European indifferentism. He says that during the greater

---

[33] John Morley, *Oliver Cromwell* (London: Macmillan & Co. Ltd., 1901), p. 46.

[34] Dakin, p. 153. In its pure form Calvinism was taken across the Atlantic by the Dutch and by the Scotch, both Presbyterian and Reformed churches being established. The modified Calvinism of the English sects also went with the early settlers and had profound effect in molding both the constitution and life forms of the new country. From the beginning religion played a great part in the development of the new world, and it meant a great deal that this religion was Protestant, and moreover, Protestant of the Calvinistic kind. The general background of thought remained Calvinistic (Dakin, pp. 158, 159). Lewis S. Mudge estimates that at the time of the War of Independence, two million of the three million inhabitants of the 13 states were of Calvinistic stock (*Encyclopaedia Britannica*, 1951, Vol. XVIII, p. 447). Originally Calvinism dominated the American theological scene. The Pilgrims and Puritans brought it to New England, the Dutch Reformed planted it in New York and New Jersey, the German Reformed carried it to Pennsylvania, the Scotch and Scotch-Irish Presbyterians imported it into the Middle and Southern colonies, and the so-called Regular or Particular Baptists scattered it wherever they went in the colonial period. (Clarence Bouma, "Calvinism in American Theology Today," in *Calvinism in Times of Crisis* [Grand Rapids: Baker Book House, 1947], p. 77)

[35] George F. Thomas, *Christian Ethics and Moral Philosophy* (New York: Charles Scribner's Sons, 1955), p. 121.

part of the nineteenth century "a Lutheranism modified by Puritan elements was looked upon as being desirable for America." [36]

This type of Lutheranism came to be referred to as "American Lutheranism." L. P. Qualben calls it "a Lutheranism that had been greatly modified by American Puritanism and American Methodism." [37]

G. F. Bente described American Lutheranism of the first half of the nineteenth century as being "essentially Calvinistic, Methodistic, Puritanic, indifferentistic, and unionistic." [38]

The lasting and impressive influence of Puritanic thought is noted by Paul W. Spaude when he observes: "Although no synod or general body of the Lutheran Church ever made the Puritan legalism its article of faith, nevertheless, its many leaders and spokesmen have abandoned [note the tense of the verb] the true Lutheran conception of Christian ethics in favor of the Reformed conception of Christian ethics." [39]

The American mores reveal the influence of various social, cultural, and religious strains, all of it too complex to be treated as a simple blend. Although it is most difficult to state the definite causes of the prevailing attitudes toward sex in America today, yet one may say that for many years the Puritan influence was felt to a high degree. Undoubtedly even today the roots of many attitudes toward sex, modesty, and chastity reach down into Puritanism.

Sex Attitudes of the Pietists

In protest against the formalism which had become associated with orthodoxy, the Pietists condemned scholastic theology and tended to leave the church and the world to seek purity in isolation. In the late 17th century Philip Jakob Spener, at Frankfurt on the Main, attempted to rally within the Lutheran body devotional circles which should obey the neglected call of piety.

---

[36] Juergen L. Neve, *A Brief History of the Lutheran Church in America*, 2d rev. and enlarged ed. (Burlington, Iowa: The German Literary Board, 1916), pp. 113, 114.

[37] Lars P. Qualben, *A History of the Christian Church* (New York: Thomas Nelson & Sons, 1933), p. 478.

[38] G. Friedrich Bente, *American Lutheranism* (St. Louis: Concordia Publishing House, 1909), II, 89.

[39] Paul W. Spaude, *The Lutheran Church Under American Influence* (Burlington, Iowa: Lutheran Literary Board, 1943), p. 295.

Pietism elevated Christian behavior to a position alongside Christian doctrine. Its chief center was the University of Halle. Later August Hermann Francke became its chief exponent. Pietists did not, as a rule, separate from the established church but attempted to influence it from within toward a greater practice of evangelistic piety. This action led, of course, to conflicts within congregations.

The most obvious characteristic of the kind of life advocated by Lutheran Pietists was its austerity. Only those who avoided the practices and pleasures of the world were regarded as giving proof that they were regenerate.[40] While the Orthodoxists looked upon the Scriptures primarily as a source of doctrines, the Pietists looked upon them primarily as a mirror of holiness.[41]

The influence of Pietism softened the prevailing crudity and vulgarity of the external relationships of its adherents. Obscenity and cursing, especially in the presence of women, were no longer tolerated as they had been before. Intemperance and immorality were reduced noticeably among persons in high station.[42]

Marriage, like the state, was accepted by the Pietists as an institution of God. Since the distinction between the sexes was established by God in creation, it was not considered a consequence of the fall. However, the fall introduced evil lust, and none could claim to be altogether free of this taint of sin. As for the Orthodoxists, so for the Pietists likewise there were three purposes for marriage: procreation, a remedy against sin, and companionship in fidelity and love. But unlike the Orthodoxists, the Pietists were often troubled by qualms and scruples in spite

---

[40] Theodore G. Tappert, "Orthodoxism, Pietism, and Rationalism 1580—1830," in *The Lutheran Heritage*, Vol. II of *Christian Social Responsibility*, ed. Harold C. Letts (Philadelphia: Muhlenberg Press, 1957), pp. 71, 72.

[41] *The Lutheran Heritage*, II, 67. Pietism aimed to develop the subjective experience, the inner life with Christ. Thus the power of the means of grace was deprecated as such, and spiritual exercises were stressed as being more important. The outward Christian life was to be developed by consistency of character and activity of life. Cf. James I. Good, *History of the Reformed Church in America* (Reading, Pa.: Daniel Miller, 1894), p. 307. Pietists thrived upon abstinence and withdrawal from the amusements and pleasures of this present world, thus becoming more congenial in many ways to the Calvinistic ethos than to Lutheranism. In accord with Calvin's dominant motif of the sovereign will and sovereign decree, the Pietists presented a view of man's vocation which led to "asceticism and legalistic pietism." (Cf. F. E. Mayer, p. 207)

[42] *The Lutheran Heritage*, II, 72.

of their acknowledgment that marriage has divine approval.
A few avoided marriage altogether, and couples who were
married sometimes refrained from cohabitation for extended
periods of time because they were persuaded that physical relations were worldly and wicked.[43]

Divorce was frowned on in this age quite as much as in the
previous age, but not all marriages were successful. Impotence
was considered sufficient cause for annulment, and intercourse
apart from purposes of procreation was generally approved in
casuistical manuals of the time. Divorce was allowed on grounds
of adultery and desertion. The sharp cleavage between grace
and nature caused sex to be associated with sin and a bad
conscience.[44]

In some cases an absolute celibacy was adopted, looking
toward the imminent arrival of the Kingdom. In other cases
a kind of sexual communism was practiced, with the breakdown
of monogamous marriage.[45]

The extreme of this "separatism" was manifested for a time
in America in the Oneida Community (New York) and in the
Zoar Settlement (Ohio). The tendency which characterized the
Pietistic movement among the sects was to subordinate the sexual and by way of compensation to center on common endeavors
in the rearing of children and in the work of the Lord.[46]

Pietism's Influence Among American Lutherans

The early German immigrants to Pennsylvania, next to their
strong instincts for property and home, demonstrated a simple-
minded faith and deep-seated piety. They came largely out of
the ranks of the Pietists and Bible-reading Christians in Germany.[47]

The real source and fountainhead of all Lutheran missionary
activity and spiritual care for souls in Pennsylvania and en-

---

[43] Ibid., pp. 76, 77. Zinzendorf taught that there should be no more
enjoyment of sex in marriage than of wine in the sacrament. Cf. Bainton, p. 104.

[44] *The Lutheran Heritage*, II, 77, 78.

[45] Cole, p. 162.

[46] Marianne Weber, *Ehefrau und Mutter in der Rechtsentwicklung
. . .* (Tübingen: J. C. B. Mohr, 1907), pp. 287—290.

[47] Theodore E. Schmauk, *A History of the Lutheran Church in Pennsylvania (1638—1820)* (Philadelphia: General Council Publication House,
1903), I, 1.

virons was that vigorous center of European Lutheran Pietism, Halle University, and its various institutions.[48] Henry Melchior Mühlenberg, a loyal representative and apostle of the Halle school, won the Pennsylvania Germans during the 1740s to a sober, pietistic Lutheranism.[49] It is interesting to note that one of the early missionaries to Pennsylvania was Anthony Jacob Henkel, who became the progenitor of a long line of orthodox Lutheran pastors.[50]

Both Pietism and Puritanism exerted an evident influence on the colonial church. Carl E. Schneider states that the mixture happened naturally. He says: "The ascetic ideals of German Pietism blended easily with the rigorous puritanic conceptions espoused by New England preachers in the Western frontier." [51] The Lutheran Church confessionally opposed a moralism which makes the Christian religion a matter of right living. By the same token it opposed rationalism, which makes religion a matter of understanding. Nor did the Lutherans accept the Puritanic idea of God's Law but rather the Gospel revelation of God's love. Yet for many years the Lutheran Church in America was strongly influenced by Pietism and Puritanism. One

---

[48] Ibid., I, 194, 195.

[49] McNeill, p. 67. It must not be overlooked that William Penn's missionary journey to Germany in 1677 was made just seven years after Philip Spener had inaugurated the *collegia pietatis* in the Lutheran Church, and two years after Spener had written his *Pia Desideria,* which was creating a pietistic ferment throughout the established churches of Protestantism. Penn, in addition to visiting German Quakers and Mennonites, met the ecstatic and theosophic Frankfurt Pietists and occasioned the founding of the Frankfurt Land Company with the subsequent emigration under Pastorius and Falckner. Meanwhile, in 1694, the University of Halle, with its later institutions, was founded and was training the more than 6,000 theologians that up to the death of August Hermann Francke in 1727 were sent forth as teachers of Pietism. Zinzendorf, the reorganizer of the Moravians, and Mühlenberg, the patriarch of the Lutheran Church in America, were enrolled among its students. Pietism was in full bloom during the generation of German emigration to America (cf. Schmauk, I, 2). Halle sent twenty-four missionaries and leaders to the Lutheran Church in America (cf. Schmauk, I, 201). The first Lutheran church founded by this group of pietists was in Falckner's Swamp (shortly after 1700). The stream of Dunkers, Seventh Day Baptists, Schwenckfelders, Mystics, and Moravians that flowed into this far-off wilderness issued in the forming of separatistic communities based on the peculiar cults, religious and social in principle.

[50] *Lutheran Cyclopedia,* ed. Erwin L. Lueker (St. Louis: Concordia Publishing House, 1954), pp. 455, 456.

[51] Carl E. Schneider, *The German Church on the American Frontier* (St. Louis: Eden Publishing House, 1939), p. 215.

can only estimate to what extent the sex attitudes of Lutherans
may be flavored by early American Protestantism or European
Pietism rather than by anything germane to Lutheran doctrine.

One of the consequences of the Pietistic movement, which
placed pious desires and emotions before the pure doctrine, was
an increased amount of rationalizing that finally opened the way
to rationalism.[52] By its unbalanced emphasis on Christian living
at the expense of doctrine and believing, Pietism prepared the
way for the era of the Enlightenment, or rationalism.[53]

The Moral Ethic of Rationalism

By the middle of the 18th century, rationalism began to in-
filtrate Protestant theology in Germany, substituting the dictates
of reason for the authority of God's Word and subjecting all
ethical maxims to the test of practice.[54] With deism in England [55]
and naturalism [56] in France, this period following 1750 has be-

---

[52] *Lutheran Cyclopedia*, ed. Erwin L. Lueker (St. Louis: Concordia,
1954), p. 819. O. W. Heick, "History of Protestant Theology" in Juergen
L. Neve and O. W. Heick, *A History of Christian Thought* (Philadelphia:
Muhlenberg Press, 1946), II, 31, says: "It was a needed reaction to the
intellectualism of the 17th century and a corrective to the orthodoxism
of its day. But in its theology it paved the way for the Rationalism that
was coming." He also observes: "Rationalism, frequently, is the successor
to Pietism. Pietistic Halle, among the German universities, was the first
to yield to Rationalism" (II, 48).

[53] *Lutheran Cyclopedia*, p. 639.

[54] Rationalism has been defined as "the mental attitude which unre-
servedly accepts the supremacy of reason and aims at establishing a system
of philosophy and ethics verifiable by experience independent of all arbi-
trary assumptions or authority." Cf. George Henslow, *Present-Day
Rationalism Examined* (London: Hodder and Stoughton, 1904), p. 17.

[55] Lord Herbert Cherbury (1582—1648) has been named as the father
of English deism. His argumentation follows: "The test of true religion
lies in its universality. True religion has its foundations in the natural
instincts, in the truths which are intuitively perceived." The five truths
common to all religions, according to Cherbury, are: (1) The being of
God; (2) the duty to worship Him; (3) the practical-moral character of
divine worship; (4) the duty to repent of sins and to forsake them;
(5) divine retribution, partly here and partly hereafter. See Heick, II, 57.

[56] The point of view in which no consideration is given to anything
"spiritual" or "supernatural," that is, to anything that goes beyond experience. In ethics, naturalism is the doctrine that nature and natural impulses
are the highest guide in moral conduct. Such a view has been variously
developed in Stoicism as well as by Rousseau, Tolstoy, and Nietzsche and
is always hostile to Christianity, which finds the supreme rule of conduct in
divine revelation. Such a view of life and values may lead to such
extremes as the elevation of every personal desire to a moral law, contempt of marriage, glorification of the nude, avoiding all idealization and
holding only to reality, beautiful or otherwise. See *Lutheran Cyclopedia*,
p. 731.

come known as the Enlightenment. The questions raised by the English deists and the Dutch philosophers — notably concerning natural religion and the relation of reason to revelation — were discussed in Germany. For this reason these questions gained greater influence in the theology and life of the church.[57]

A consequence of the changed attitude toward Scripture, tradition, and philosophy led to confessional indifference in many quarters. The witness of the Bible was reduced to truths of reason and principles of morality. Much of the doctrinal tradition of the church was repudiated.[58] In rationalism and deism, theology and ethics were almost completely divorced.

The rationalistic philosophy of the autonomy of reason has implications for moral conduct.[59] In group morality man's duties are imposed on him by his society; in rational morality they are determined by himself and guide him to a reasonable and therefore moral, happy life. Revelation must prove itself an expansion of natural knowledge, subject to the criteria of reason. Original sin was especially attacked, its guilt was denied, and it was presumed to be merely a limitation of nature. To man was ascribed a capacity to fulfill his moral duties, and all that was left of grace was the function of supporting and acknowledging human virtue.[60]

The hymns during this period were commonplace rhymes which praised reasonable virtues, delights of nature, and care of the body. Sermons were long-winded moral treatises on the utility of things. Catechisms contained natural religion and shallow morality on the happiness of man. The emptiness of all this resulted in the end of rationalism.[61]

---

57 *The Lutheran Heritage*, II, 80.

58 *The Lutheran Heritage*, II, 83.

59 Under the autonomy of reason there is no place for any moral authority but that of reason, and the only moral obligations that are binding on a man are those he as a rational being imposes on himself. For example, a moral law may have originated in a religious "revelation" and may have been transmitted by the church, but if it is accepted by the rationalist at all, it is accepted because it commends itself to his reason. The dignity of man as a rational person requires him to lay down principles to determine his own conduct rather than let others prescribe his duties for him. Cf. Thomas, p. 368.

60 *The New Schaff-Herzog Encyclopedia of Religious Knowledge*, ed. Samuel M. Jackson (Grand Rapids: Baker Book House, 1949—53), IX, 395, 396.

61 *The Lutheran Cyclopedia*, eds. Henry E. Jacobs and J. A. W. Haas (New York: Charles Scribner's Sons, 1905), pp. 401, 402.

Influence of Rationalism on Matters of Sex

The influence of rationalism on marriage was significant.
The few women who began to play a part in the intellectual life
of the time achieved greater status, but it was not uncommon
for these very women to regard marriage as inferior to a suc-
cession of love affairs. Among intellectuals, chastity was often
considered "an artificial habit and quite contrary to nature."
The relaxation of morals was related to loss of the sense of sin
and to an exaggerated notion of freedom. Divorces became more
frequent as a romantic conception of love began to undermine
marital fidelity and domesticity.[62]

Rationalism was the forerunner of modern pragmatism and
the sexual libertinism espoused by men like Havelock Ellis and
the humanistic school of modern social philosophers, who regard
most Christian standards of sex behavior as unnatural and unnecessary taboos.[63]

Rationalism was short-lived. Immanuel Kant pointed out
the limitations of reason, and Frederick Schleiermacher held
that religion is a matter neither of intellectual beliefs nor of
moral conduct but rather of a feeling of absolute dependence
on God. The latter view at once reflected and contributed to
the emergence of romanticism, which came to flower in the
early decades of the 19th century as a reaction against the arid
intellectualism of the rationalists. Beauty, a new appreciation
of the past, and an awareness of the mystery of life — as opposed
to the plain practicality of the rationalists — were restored.[64]

During the period in which the rationalists flourished, the
weight of custom nevertheless caused the inherited conception
of marriage and the family to retain its sway among the great
majority of Protestants.[65]

However, the seeds of rationalism had been planted, and
some of them sprouted and grew. There are people living in
America today who will attest to the validity of the observation

---

[62] *The Lutheran Heritage,* II, 84.

[63] That this influence is still strong is seen, for instance, in the discussion on sex ethics between David R. Mace and Walter R. Stokes, as
reported in "Premarital Sexual Behavior" in *Marriage and Family Living,*
XV (August 1953), 234—249.

[64] *The Lutheran Heritage,* II, 86.

[65] Ibid., p. 46.

"that hardly a community settled by Germans was without its liberal rationalistic elements, for whom the church and religion were an abomination." [66]

Mühlenberg described the spiritual conditions in colonial America in a letter of 1743 thus: "There are not wanting here atheists, deists, naturalists, and free-masons. In short, there is not a sect in the world which is not cherished here. Whatsoever is not tolerated in Europe finds a place here. The most scandalous things are heard freely and publicly spoken against God and His holy Word. In the whole land there are many thousands, who, according to their baptism, education, and confirmation, should be Lutherans, but they are in part scattered. There is such a pitiable condition and ruin among our poor Lutheran people that it cannot be sufficiently wept for with tears of blood. The parents have permitted their children to grow up without baptism, without instruction and knowledge, and to go into heathenism." [67]

The diverse tendencies in the church when it entered the 19th century — inherited orthodoxy, a revived Pietism which was blended with Puritanism, waning rationalism, and visionary romanticism — contributed to the complexity and creativeness of its life for generations to come. [68]

Speaking particularly of the Puritan-Pietistic period, Seward Hiltner says: "The prudishness that made several generations of Protestant theologians discuss marriage with practically no direct reference to sex supports the notion that some aspects of later Protestantism distorted the Biblical and Reformation views of sex." [69]

[66] Schneider, p. 194. Schmauk (I, 143, 144) describes the German settlement at Falckner's Swamp in Pennsylvania as increasing and prosperous. "But in place of a spirit of thankfulness, the lust of the flesh and the pride of life began to be powerful. The sins of drunkenness and luxuriousness particularly began to rule so grossly that the place, on account of its evil deeds, became notorious in the whole land and was called a 'sauf- und mortgrube.'"

[67] Schmauk, I, 225.

[68] *The Lutheran Heritage*, II, 87.

[69] Seward Hiltner, *Sex and the Christian Life* (New York: Association Press, 1957), p. 64. Hendrik van Oyen shows how the prudishness of this period affected marriage: "Durch alle Zeiten hindurch hat man die Genitalien als die unehrbaren Teile des Leibes betrachtet. In alten Abhandlungen kann man von den 'partes inhonestae, turpes, obscaenae' lesen, die Erb- sünde werde namentlich durch den coitus fortgepflanzt (Augustin), die Geschlechtslust sei böse u. soll es nach Ansicht vieler Pietisten des

SUMMARY

1. To a greater or lesser degree, the sex attitudes and practices of the majority of present-day Americans have their source (whether they realize it or not) in the curious blending of the influences of the Puritans, Pietists, and Rationalists. Each of these movements contributed a part to the whole, though the exact mixture and the precise amount at any one time is not easily determined.

2. John Calvin's theology, emphasizing Christian living and moral behavior in obedience to the Moral Law under the activity of the Holy Spirit as evidence and assurance of being in a state of grace, found acceptance among both Puritans and Pietists. Conservative Lutheran theology, however, based Christian assurance solely on the objective promises of the Gospel. Whereas Calvin's view of man's vocation under God led to asceticism and moral legalism and a disparaging view of the functions of the body, Luther's view was that the redeemed believer's chief response was a striving toward sanctification, free from the demands of the Law.

3. The Puritans chose moderation in all things of this world as their key word in behavior and practice. Loyalty to God was their supreme motive, taking precedence over all that is cherished by man. Monogamy and a single standard of sex morality agreed with Puritan goals of honest labor, devotion to duty, and economic success.

4. The Pietists looked upon the Scriptures primarily as a mirror of holiness of life, and only those who avoided the practices and pleasures of the world were regarded as giving proof that they were regenerate. The sharp cleavage between grace and nature caused sex to be associated with sin and a bad conscience, and the Pietists were often troubled by qualms and scruples of conscience in spite of their acknowledgment that marriage has divine approval. Pietism served to soften

---

17. u. 18. Jahrhunderts in der Ehe eines Christen nicht mehr geben. Sie ist für sie gleicherweise zu verurteilen wie die Unzucht. Jugend, die in solchen Einschätzungen des Geschlechtlichen erzogen worden ist, kann wohl nie das rechte Verhältnis zum Geschlechtlichen, zur Ehe u. damit auch zum Lebenspartner finden. Die Krisen der Ehe liegen hier schon keimhaft vor." (Hendrik van Oyen, *Liebe und Ehe* [Basel: Friedrich Reinhardt, A. G., 1957], p. 125)

the prevailing crudity and vulgarity and reduced intemperance and immorality.

5. Rationalism substituted reason for the authority of Scripture and refused to accept any moral standards except those established by nature, reason, and experience. Rationalism advocated a return to natural religion and humanistic morality. It considered chastity artificial and appealed for a relaxation of moral regulations both outside and inside wedlock. It was the forerunner of the sexual libertinism advocated by Havelock Ellis and others and the modern school of pragmatism in the area of sex.

6. Each of these movements affected Protestant teaching and practice in America. For a time they set the pattern of "American Lutheranism." On the one hand, one may see the influences of rationalism on the sex mores of some early German-American communities and in the writings of social scientists and philosophers before and after 1900. On the other hand, the influences of Puritanism and Pietism undoubtedly account for many of the quietistic, legalistic, and prudish sex views and practices (held by many today), which are rooted in moralism, that is, a living under the Law rather than under grace in Christ.

CHAPTER 9

The Lutheran Church
in North America

AT THE TIME of the heaviest influx of population from Northern Europe to America, there were three movements which more or less influenced Lutheran theology and practice: Lutheran Orthodoxy, which flowered from the 16th to the 18th centuries, European Pietism, and rationalism. Coming from a varied cultural background, the first Lutherans in the New World reflected these movements even though they possessed a common doctrinal heritage. Attitudes toward sex and marriage were varied and not clearly defined. It is the purpose of this chapter to survey the available history and writings of the Lutheran Church in North America on the subject of attitudes toward sex.

THE LUTHERAN CHURCH — MISSOURI SYNOD

From its very beginning The Lutheran Church — Missouri Synod showed a strong tendency to follow rather closely the point of view expressed by the theologians of the Age of Orthodoxy in Europe. The influence of German Pietism was also felt, probably more strongly even than the influence of Luther and his contemporaries.

Marriage a Holy Institution

Early writings take a very definite stand against the glorification of celibacy and virginity which existed in the church before the Reformation.[1] Forbidding marriage (enforced cel-

---

[1] *Neunter Synodal-Bericht des Minnesota- und Dakota-Distrikts der deutschen evang.-lutherischen Synode von Missouri, Ohio und anderen*

ibacy) comes under strong condemnation as a "doctrine of devils" (1 Tim. 4:1, 3). Marriage is presented as a holy and God-pleasing estate, and people are urged to marry. Celibacy, it is said, leaves people open to many temptations (1 Cor. 7:2, 9).[2] Reference is made to the flood of unchastity in the church before the Reformation, and it is said that most of this was a result of celibacy.[3]

Answering the objection of some that the apostle Paul advises against marriage (1 Cor. 7:38), the literature makes the usual explanation that these words of the apostle were spoken "on account of the times." The same explanation is given of the words of Christ in Matt. 24:19 concerning the misfortune of those with child in times of great tribulation.[4]

Theological essays state that it is actually a duty of pastors to marry, because only then can they give effective help to families.[5] One article calls the marriage of Luther "a protest against the cursed restriction which compelled those who would serve God in His church to avoid matrimony as a deadly sin." The same article calls Luther "the founder of the evangelical parsonage, from which untold blessings have come to the world and particularly to the church."

Luther Followed

Luther is given credit for showing the world "a view of matrimony which is as rational as it is Scriptural . . . the source of nearly all human happiness, the strongest pillar of the state and

---

Staaten, 1894, p. 48; *Lehre und Wehre,* LII (1906), 402; *Magazin für ev.-lutherische Homiletik,* VI (1882), 337; *Evangelisch-Lutherisches Schulblatt,* XVI (1881), 35; *Der Lutheraner,* XLV (Sept. 24, 1889), 157.

(For additional references to Proceedings and Periodicals see Ernst Eckhardt, *Homiletisches Reallexikon* [St. Louis: Success Printing Co., 1907—1917], II, 609—616.)

2 . . . *Synodal-Bericht des Minnesota,* etc., 1894, pp. 48, 49, 52; 1892, p. 51; *Theological Quarterly,* III (1899), 429.

3 *Lehre und Wehre,* XLVIII (1902), 24, 25; *Theological Quarterly,* VII (1903), 27; . . . *Synodal-Bericht d. Minn.,* etc., 1894, pp. 51, 52; *Der Lutheraner,* LX (Feb. 2, 1904), 39; *Lehre und Wehre,* LII (1906), 369, 370.

4 . . . *Synodal-Bericht d. Minn.,* etc., 1894, p. 49; 1892, p. 37; *Verhandlungen . . . d. Michigan Distrikts,* 1907, p. 30; *Verhandlungen d. . . . Freikirche in Sachsen,* 1894, p. 20.

5 *Lehre und Wehre,* LII (1906), 401, 402; . . . *Synodal-Bericht d. Minn.,* etc., 1894, p. 53; *Verhandlungen . . . d. Michigan,* etc., 1907, p. 31; Martin Guenther, *Populäre Symbolik,* 3d ed. (St. Louis: Concordia Publishing House, 1898), pp. 268, 411—413.

of orderly civilization." And it is said that "if Luther had done
no more than restore marriage to its rightful position in society,
he would deserve the undying gratitude of mankind." [6] A great
number of sermons, particularly those on the story of the wedding at Cana, speak in high praise of the institution of marriage
and the obligation of all Christian people toward it.[7] One article
especially lists what are called the eight "glories" of holy matrimony: (1) that marriage was instituted by God; (2) that it
began in the Garden of Eden; (3) that many heroes of faith
have graced it; (4) that God devoted one commandment to it;
(5) that God encouraged it for the people of Israel; (6) that
Jesus chose to be born of a virgin who was married; (7) that
Christ attended a marriage feast; and (8) that Christ extended
a helping hand to a young married couple at Cana. These, the
article says, "are eight beautiful flowers to excel any other
bridal wreath." [8]

Second Marriages Approved

It is also definitely stated that second marriages for the
widowed are not wrong and that "not the slightest stigma at-
taches to them." It is said that the Old Testament permits second
marriages, that neither Christ nor the apostles forbid them or
regard them dishonorable, that Paul sanctions and even advises
them, and that Scriptural example and the testimony of many
church fathers favor them.[9]

Sexual Relations in Marriage

In common with Luther, the reformers, and the theologians
of the post-Reformation period in Europe, the leaders of the
Missouri Synod did not completely discard the view of St. Augustine that it is the bearing of children which sanctifies the sex
relationship in marriage. Though this view is not strongly ex-

---

[6] *Lutheran Witness*, XLIV (June 16, 1925), 194.

[7] *Der Lutheraner*, XIX (May 1, 1863), 138; *Magazin f. . . . Homiletik*,
I (1877), 16, 17; IV (1880), 21, 22; XII (1888), 28; XIII (1889), 25, 26; XIV
(1890), 14—21; XXIV (1900), 23, 24; XXIX (1905) 26, 27. Cf. also some more
recent writings on marriage, such as Otto A. Geiseman, *Make Yours
a Happy Marriage* (St. Louis: Concordia Publishing House, 1946), and
Walter A. Maier, *For Better Not for Worse* (St. Louis: Concordia Publishing House, 1939).

[8] *Lutheran Witness*, V (Aug. 7, 1886), 44.

[9] *Concordia Theological Monthly*, III (1932), 855.

pressed, there is persistent reference to procreation as the "chief purpose of marriage." Like Luther, Missouri Synod writers refer to marriage as a way of avoiding fornication rather than as a means of enjoying sexual satisfaction.

In the most complete statement on the purpose of marriage, A. L. Graebner lists sexual intercourse first:

> The divine institution of matrimony, which is the status of union for life of one man and one woman, established and sustained by their mutual consent, for legitimate sexual intercourse, the procreation of children, and mutual aid and assistance, serves as a curb not only to the licentiousness of sexual desires, but also to various other depraved inclinations by affording incentives to habits of industry and economy, sobriety, stability, and good fellowship among men.[10]

Usually, however, procreation is listed as the first purpose of marriage. Many articles are also very careful to state that matrimony was never "designed to indulge in the lusts of the flesh wantonly."[11] It is also said that God has restricted the exercise of the sex function, not only to marriage but also "to such conditions therein as are determined by physical condition, health, occupation, age, etc.," that "the sexual desire should be curbed and not excited. An *artificial* sexual appetite should never be created."[12] However, it must be stated that companionability in marriage is also stressed, particularly in later writings.[13]

Sexual Relations Outside of Marriage

Naturally there are warnings in great number against the sins of adultery, fornication, and even prostitution, incest, and homosexuality.[14] The tragic consequences, both personal and

---

10 August L. Graebner, *Doctrinal Theology* (St. Louis: Concordia Publishing House, 1910), p. 94.

11 *Lutheran Witness*, LI (1932), 334, 335, 350, 351, 372, 373; *Theological Quarterly*, III (1899), 184; *Magazin f. . . . Homiletik* XXVIII (1904), 74, 75; XXV (1901), 71, 74, 75.

12 John H. C. Fritz, *Pastoral Theology*, 2d ed. (St. Louis: Concordia Publishing House, 1945), p. 161.

13 *Lehre und Wehre*, LII (1906), 401, 402; Geiseman, pp. 37—56.

14 . . . *Synodal-Bericht d. Minnesota*, etc., 1894, pp. 25, 26; *Verhandlungen . . . Canada Distrikts*, 1906, p. 26; *Lehre und Wehre*, XXIV (1878), 182; *Magazin f. . . . Homiletik*, XI (1887), 265, 266; XXIV (1900), 196, 197; XXVIII (1904), 68, 69; *Der Lutheraner*, XVI (March 6, 1860), 113; XLVII (Apr. 28, 1891), 68; L (Dec. 18, 1894), 221; LVII (Jan. 22, 1901), 18; *Theological Quarterly*, III (1899), 407.

national, which come as the result of sexual sins are repeatedly
stressed.[15] It is also pointed out that in dealing with sexual sins
the pastor should be extremely careful not to instruct the people
in possible vices, but rather to use the positive approach, as
Luther does, in his exposition of the Sixth Commandment and
tell what is to be done rather than what is not to be done.
Nevertheless, frankness should be used even though people may
feel that their sense of decency is outraged. "To the unclean
all things are unclean." [16]

Some very stern attitudes toward sexual sins are evident
in minutes concerning congregational dealings with such sins
and in minutes of pastoral conferences where such sins and
problems connected with them were discussed. A man accused
of rape, even though the accusation was unproved, was kept
from Holy Communion and had to leave the city because of the
possible offense of the accusation against him; after three years
of deliberation the man was finally reinstated as a communicant
member.[17] The sin of prostitution is mentioned as being dealt
with in five congregations.[18] In one instance, where a married
man was suspected of being the father of a young woman's
illegitimate child, the congregation dealt with the man for
a ten-year period before he finally agreed to confess the sin
publicly and was then reinstated.[19] Persons involved in such
sins were to be named (or at least to have their sin announced)
from the pulpit in the Sunday service.[20] A congregation refusing
to abide by this practice was censured by a pastoral conference.[21]

In one congregation, in a period of ten years, eight individual

---

[15] *Der Lutheraner,* XVI (March 6, 1860), 113; *Magazin f. . . . Homiletik,*
XVII (1893), 57; XXV (1901), 69; XXVIII (1904), 73; *Theological Quar-
terly,* III (1899), 181; *Verhandlungen d. . . . Nebraska-Distrikts,* 1900, p. 30;
. . . *Synodal-Bericht d. Illinois Distrikts,* 1906, p. 17.

[16] *Magazin f. . . . Homiletik,* XI (1887), 262; XVII (1893), 56; XXIV
(1900), 193, 197; XXVII (1903), 154; *Der Lutheraner,* XVI (March 6, 1860),
114; LVII (Jan. 22, 1901), 18; . . . *Synodal-Bericht d. Minnesota,* etc.,
1894, p. 54.

[17] Minutes, "Gesamtgemeinde," St. Louis, Nov. 5, 1860, to Nov. 30, 1863,
File, Concordia Historical Institute, St. Louis, Mo. (All references in this
chapter to minutes of congregations or conferences are from the same file.)

[18] Minutes, "Gesamtgemeinde," St. Louis, Jan. 7, 1863; April 20, 1863;
May 18, 1875; Minutes, Trinity, St. Louis, Aug. 30, 1858.

[19] Minutes, Trinity, Thiensville, Wis., Dec. 12, 1897, to June 9, 1907.

[20] Minutes, Trinity, St. Louis, Dec. 9, 1850.

[21] Minutes, S. Indiana Pastoral Conference, April 19, 1858.

cases of sex relations on the part of young people before marriage (usually engaged couples) were publicly confessed before the congregation, and if penitence was indicated, were forgiven.[22] A rather unforgiving attitude was demonstrated toward unmarried mothers and their children.[23] While this somewhat legalistic attitude prevailed in the practice of many pastors, there were also leaders, such as the institutional missionaries, who emphasized the abounding mercy of Christ to "fallen women" and advocated a more evangelical practice toward "sins of sex."

Sexual Temptations

Temptations to sexual sins are frequently discussed and warned against. Most frequently mentioned among these temptations is dancing.[24] Such references are more common toward the end of the 19th and in the beginning of the 20th centuries. Because of the close embrace of the two sexes, dancing is called not only dangerous, but sinful.[25]

Recent Statement on Dancing

In view of the fact that the traditional view on the dance has been repeatedly challenged especially because of constantly changing social conditions, two pastoral conferences made a fresh study of the problem of dancing, which was defined as "an em-

---

22 Minutes, Zion Congregation, Cleveland, Ohio, Sept. 1858 to June 1869.

23 Minutes, Saginaw Special Conference, Aug. 3—4, 1881.

24 Many cases of church discipline throughout the history of The Lutheran Church — Missouri Synod have centered on the matter of dancing. In the file of Concordia Historical Institute at St. Louis the minutes of seven different pastoral conferences advise pastors to take disciplinary measures against dancing, particularly at baptisms and weddings (Saginaw Special Conference, Aug. 6—7, 1879; Aug. 5—6, 1884; April 17—18, 1885; Northern Illinois Pastoral Conference, Aug. 26—28, 1879; Southern Indiana Pastoral Conference, April 19, 1858; May 2, 3, 4, 1862; Arkansas-Tennessee Pastoral Conference, April 3, 1888). The minutes of two congregations (Zion, Cleveland, Ohio, March 2, 1858; Trinity, Thiensville, Wis., June 8 to October 5, 1879) discussed disciplinary action against members who had conducted dances in their homes.

25 *Magazin f. . . . Homiletik*, XI (1887), 267; XXIV (1900), 199; XXV (1901), 70; *Der Lutheraner*, L (Dec. 18, 1894), 222; *Theological Quarterly*, III (1899), 186; . . . *Synodal-Bericht d. Minnesota*, etc., 1894, p. 55. Cf. particularly Theodore Graebner, *The Borderland of Right and Wrong*, 8th ed. (St. Louis: Concordia Publishing House, 1951), pp. 111—135; Eckhardt, s. v. "Tanz," op. cit., p. 829, 4. a; C. F. W. Walther, *Tanz und Theaterbesuch* (St. Louis: Concordia Publishing House, 1885), pp. 3—49.

brace of members of opposite sexes who are not married to each other." The conclusions of one conference are summarized in the following points:

> 1. Our [Missouri] Synod has issued warnings and advised watchfulness without, however, passing *resolutions* laying definite restrictions on each Christian's participation in the dance.
>
> 2. Christians have been called to freedom in Jesus Christ. This is, however, not to be used "as an opportunity for the flesh" (Gal. 5:13) but with a high sense of accountability so that liberty may not become a hindrance to another Christian. (Rom. 14:12, 13)
>
> 3. Christian principles are to be applied also to other threats to chastity and purity (beside the dance), namely, beach parties, hay rides, petting in cars, and other forms of close contact between the sexes.
>
> 4. Where a Christian group finds dancing and similar forms of social recreation in accord with its Christian objectives and interests and not an offense to other Christians nor an impediment to their spiritual growth, it may permit dancing under careful supervision and proper guidance, if this can be done to the glory of God. (1 Cor. 10:31)
>
> 5. Caution should be exercised in condemning individuals for their participation in the dance or in similar types of amusement lest consciences be unnecessarily burdened and fellow Christians slandered.[26]

The Positive Approach

The dating behavior of young people is also discussed, and such things as kissing (also "kissing games"), caressing, petting are warned against. Indecent speech, pictures, posture, and exposure, and immodest clothing are considered temptations to lust.[27] The same references, however, never fail to take also a positive approach toward sexual temptation, suggesting that by means of prayer, work, temperance, the Word of God, and particularly by means of faith in God and love to Him these temptations may be overcome. Some statements are so strongly worded that they tend to suggest that every kind of sex desire

---

[26] *Badger Lutheran* (published by Milwaukee, Wis., Federation of Lutheran Churches), Jan. 22, 1959. *St. Louis Lutheran,* Sept. 20, 1958.

[27] *Magazin* f. . . . *Homiletik,* XI (1887), 262—265; XXIV (1900), 197; XXVIII (1904), 70; XXXI (1907), 206; *Der Lutheraner,* L (Dec. 18, 1894), 222; *Theological Quarterly,* III (1899), 179, 183; . . . *Synodal-Bericht d. Minnesota,* etc., 1894, pp. 19—23.

or every demonstration of affection outside wedlock is sinful.[28] Positive exhortations toward purity and chastity, however, tend to outweigh the negative statements.

Autoerotic Practices

A number of very emphatic references are made to masturbation. The practice is also called "onanism" or "self-pollution." [29] An entire tract by C. M. Zorn deals with the subject and speaks of it as belonging to the "works of darkness," as being "a heathen vice," as "undermining body and soul and ruining health," as "stunting growth," as causing the victim to "lose ambition and initiative," and as converting a person into a "liar whose lying is second nature." The author asserts that many turn insane because of masturbation. He admits that not every part of his description of what he calls "self-abuse" may be accurate, but he says the effect of the "vice" should not be minimized but regarded seriously.[30] In a discussion of the Sixth Commandment another writer says: "The law condemns everyone who carnally knows himself [sic!] or a brute or another person of the same sex." [31] It is not clear, however, what the author means by "knowing oneself."

More recent articles on the subject of masturbation adopt essentially the same views as those expressed earlier. A writer on the subject of child psychology states that masturbation must be condemned as a sin, although it is not an unforgivable sin. He does, however, modify the possible consequences and criticizes the use of fright or condemnation as a remedy.[32] The same

---

28 See particularly Theodore Stolp in *Concordia Pulpit 1950* (St. Louis: Concordia Publishing House, 1949), pp. 275, 277. See also a sermon preached by C. F. W. Walther on the anniversary of a young men's society, where he lists twelve different fearful results of youthful lust. (Carl F. W. Walther, *Lutherische Brosamen* [St. Louis: Concordia Publishing House, 1897], pp. 353—361)

29 *Der Lutheraner*, XVI (March 6, 1860), 113; LVII (Jan. 22, 1901), 18; *Evangelisch-Lutherisches Schulblatt*, II (May 1867), 266—270; III (Oct. 1867), 50—57; XXXIV (Aug. 1899), 225—243.

30 Carl M. Zorn, *Die heimliche Selbstbefleckung* (St. Louis: Concordia Publishing House, undated), Tract 64 (English No. 27). In his book *Questions on Christian Topics* (Milwaukee: Northwestern Publishing House, 1918), p. 164, Zorn calls masturbation "a practice which, if persisted in, means certain ruin of both body and soul."

31 A. L. Graebner, p. 79.

32 Alfred Schmieding, *Understanding the Child* (St. Louis: Concordia Publishing House, 1945), pp. 114—121.

writer in a more recent book on sex education minimizes the
seriousness of masturbation in little children but speaks of it
as a definite evil among adolescent young people. He writes:
"The Christian condemns it as an unclean sinful act (cf. Rom.
1:24; 1 Cor. 6:9)." He says there is a wide difference between
the person who practices masturbation regularly and condones
it and the person who fights it with all the power he has.[33] Speaking of involuntary seminal emissions, the same author suggests
that there may be some moral evil involved in these acts also.[34]

Another recent book, written jointly by a pastor and a medical doctor, has this to say on the subject:

> Teen-age boys often fall into the sinful and ruinous habit of
> self-abuse, using their sexual organs for the lewd and sinful
> satisfaction of their own lust. This is a serious sin, and one
> that cannot but call down the wrath of God upon the offender.
> But apart from the immorality of this act, which tends to
> enslave the person in his own evil lust, there can be no doubt
> that it drains away much energy and strength from the grow-
> ing youth. If this sin has been indulged in, the offender should
> at once go to God in penitent confession and pray God to give
> him strength to break the spell of this evil habit at once.
> Conscious of the will of God that he should lead a holy life,
> every growing boy and young man should give himself to
> prayer and the reading of God's Word and employ his time in
> work, plenty of recreation, and wholesome social activities.[35]

All written opinions definitely condemn autoerotic practices
as sins against the will of God.

Sex Education

Sex education as we know it today is comparatively recent.
In the literature of The Lutheran Church — Missouri Synod
scarcely anything appears until the third decade of the 20th century. One writer makes the comment that the burden of responsibility for sex education rests with the parents, although it is
admitted that it might be well to have a competent Christian
doctor speak to boys of confirmation age.[36] *The Concordia*

---

[33] Alfred Schmieding, *Sex in Childhood and Youth* (St. Louis: Concordia Publishing House, 1953), pp. 27, 72, 73.

[34] Ibid., p. 69.

[35] Carl H. Harman and Edward W. Marquardt, *Vital Facts of Life*
(St. Louis: Concordia Publishing House, 1949), p. 18.

[36] Paul E. Kretzmann, *The Problems of Adolescence and Youth*
(St. Louis: Lutheran Literature Board, 1925), p. 49.

Cyclopedia (1927) says that sex education is the duty of parents and that if it is to be given in any class, boys and girls should be separated, with a Christian doctor speaking to boys and a Christian nurse to girls.[37]

During that same period in the church, however, one book says that "sex education" as the term is commonly understood is not advisable (1) because ignorance is not the cause of sex abuse; (2) because centering attention on sexual matters, as such, awakens unlawful desires in all of us; and (3) because familiarity breaks down the sense of shame and modesty which exists under normal conditions, especially in the immature mind. The author writes: "I consider the various handbooks and guides for the instruction in sexual matters as worse than useless. . . . [They] must tend to create the very condition which they seek to correct." [38]

A somewhat different attitude is expressed by an article in a 1937 church periodical, where it is stated that it is "of immense value for the child, physically, mentally, and morally, to have this type of information [sex education] consistent with his age." The advice of parents and the use of "suitable books" are the methods suggested for communicating such information.[39] A book on marriage appearing about the same time makes the statement that "the church is not opposed to enlightenment on sex questions." Parents are mentioned as the principal source of such education, and the caution is given that "it is entirely unnecessary to indulge in the intricacies which are often explained in much detail and with the aid of diagrams and profane illustrations." [40]

The first book on sex education within the Missouri Synod appeared in 1939. There it is stated quite definitely that "parents and teachers should teach their boys and girls the true facts about sex in due time and not wait until it is too late."

[37] Ludwig Fuerbringer, Theodore Engelder, Paul E. Kretzmann, eds., *The Concordia Cyclopedia* (St. Louis: Concordia Publishing House, 1927), p. 700.

[38] Theodore Graebner, *Pastor and People* (St. Louis: Concordia Publishing House, 1932), pp. 121—124.

[39] Martin H. Coyner, *Central Illinois District Lutheran,* October 1937, p. 22.

[40] Walter A. Maier, *For Better Not for Worse* (St. Louis: Concordia Publishing House, 3d ed., 1939), pp. 526, 528.

Sex instruction in high school is called "advisable and helpful." It is stated, however, that lectures on sex should be given separately to boys and girls and by an experienced physician.[41] A book on sex education written for young people themselves appeared in 1949.[42] A third book designed to assist parents and educators in the problem of sex education was published in 1953.[43] The latter makes the very clear statement that "sex education is not alone the duty of the home or the church or the school or the physician or the nurse. It is the duty of all of them." [44] The fourth and most explicit book to be issued by the publishing house of The Lutheran Church — Missouri Synod appeared in 1959,[45] in which a high school instructor suggests a frank facing of sex problems and a more positive approach to the physiology of sex. Apparently there is no longer the stern objection to discussing matters of sex outside the privacy of the home.

Positive Statements on Sex

As in many church bodies, the negative side of sex was emphasized to the neglect of the positive side; the wrong use of sex was treated almost to the exclusion of the right use of sex. This frequently left the impression that all sex acts are sinful. Only within the last decade have more adequate, positive statements on sex appeared to correct this imbalance.

In a series of articles written by youth leaders of the Missouri Synod, sex and sexual attraction are set forth in a Biblical and positive frame of reference as gifts of God but shrewdly kept from God-pleasing use by the devil, who implies that God is against all sex. "The problem of sex began only with the fall into sin. The solution of the problem lies not in abolition or avoidance of sex but in battle and victory over sin, which corrupts sex and all else in man."

"God builds into the human framework not only the possibil-

---

[41] Edward W. Marquardt, *Why Was I Not Told?* (St. Louis: Concordia Publishing House, 1939), p. 15.

[42] Harman-Marquardt, *Vital Facts of Life.*

[43] Schmieding, *Sex in Childhood and Youth.*

[44] Schmieding, *Sex in Childhood and Youth,* p. 13.

[45] Reuben D. Behlmer, *From Teens to Marriage* (St. Louis: Concordia Publishing House, 1959).

ity, but the desire for sexual life." Redemption by Christ involves not only our souls but also our bodies, "including our desires for health, for food, and for sexual satisfaction within the bounds of God's will." "As we walk in the Spirit we learn to be not 'against' sex but 'for' sex as a precious, satisfying, glorifying gift of a merciful God."

"Sin moved man's focus away from God and centered it on self. Sex, too, became a pleasure to be exploited rather than a gift to be enjoyed to the glory of the Creator. It became necessary for God to correct man and to set up safeguards." "Thou shalt not commit adultery!" (Ex. 20:14). God says: "You shall use the sex drive I have given you for constructive and wholesome purposes and not merely to gratify the lust of selfish pleasure outside the limits I have set up!" [46]

In his essay "The Biblical View of Sex" [47] Martin H. Scharlemann says:

> God might have extended life by a single divine fiat; instead He chose to bestow upon our primordial ancestors the awesome power and mysterious privilege of creating through sex new beings resembling themselves and their Creator. According to the Bible the human body is not something to be despised or belittled. The Scripture revelation stands in contrast to the Greek teaching as reflected, for example, in the Colossian heresy which thought of the body as an impediment to full spiritual development. The body, including sex, is to be the sanctuary of the Holy Spirit (1 Cor. 6:19). The Old Testament differs radically regarding sexual morality from the records we have of the religious practices among the races surrounding Israel, which surrounded sex with a system of taboos. Marriage is regarded as a natural and essential consequence of man's endowment with sex. The Levitical injunctions on the matter of sex only reflect the sacredness of man's creative faculties, which are to be used in the light of his obligation always to do God's will. To be sure, sex has been much perverted and its presence misunderstood, but that is the consequence of man's fall. Our Lord speaks of sex as a natural and wholesome endowment of creation and yet describes it as being a secondary concern under the terms of God's kingdom (Matt. 19:12).

---

[46] *Workers Quarterly* (The Walther League, 875 N. Dearborn, Chicago, Ill.), July 1958, pp. 8, 9, 20.

[47] *The Lutheran Scholar,* XIV, No. 4 (Oct. 1957), 577—584.

This positive point of view is also expressed in a tract which gives guidance in this matter. Its basic principle is set forth in the following excerpt:

> The right use of sex begins with a person's view of his life. If his view is Christian, he will trust God, who created sex, and in faith accept the limits of its use which God has set. By faith the Christian embraces his sexual life as a divinely given part of creation, and he identifies himself with God's plan for human life and well-being, viewing his own life of sex in its light. This means that all things are looked upon spiritually and accepted gratefully in faith.[48]

Thus writers of The Lutheran Church — Missouri Synod show that their church accepted sex as a gift of God, held marriage in high respect, denounced enforced celibacy, adultery, and fornication, warned against the "temptations of the flesh," carried on a rigorous, perhaps pietistic discipline against sex offenders, and roundly condemned masturbation. Recently a more constructive and balanced attitude toward both sexuality and sex education has been expressed.

In dealing now with the teachings on sexuality of other Lutheran bodies this book must restrict itself to recent pronouncements.

THE EVANGELICAL LUTHERAN CHURCH

Lutherans in America with a Norwegian background also reveal some of the pietistic influence of their forebears. Professor G. M. Bruce of Luther Seminary, St. Paul, reports:

> With regard to questions of sex practice and sex education, it may be said that there is no generally formulated teaching except that there is general understanding that any form of sex perversion is sin and detrimental to the health and morals of the persons guilty thereof. . . . Many feel that sex instruction should be given to the children by parents as soon as they are ripe for such instruction; others feel that any dealing with sex at all is taboo.[49]

In his book *Marriage and Divorce* Bruce calls the period after World War I a "sex-mad age." He discusses the theories of sex current at the time, free love, companionate marriage, prostitution, illegitimacy, and adultery, calling them "warped

---

[48] Harry G. Coiner, *The Christian View of Sex* (St. Louis: Concordia Tract Mission, 1960).

[49] In an unpublished research summary, "The Evangelical Lutheran Church and Family Life."

ideas of marriage and family life." His conclusions call for a positive approach to the situation on the part of the church:

> Positive Christianity is at once a powerful preventive and a sure cure for moral diseases. To those who have fallen, the church, like its Head, should extend a saving and helping hand with intelligent and sympathetic love; for the work of rescuing the lost must never be overlooked. But the preventive work is even more important, though it may lack some of the romanticism which often lends color to the work of rescue. The building of Christian family life, surrounding the child with wholesome Christian influences, and sustaining these homes in the highest state of purity and efficiency through spiritual counsel, guidance, and inspiration, will prove the best preventive of sex perversion and social disease and the greatest bulwark against commercialized vice in all its varied forms.[50]

A more recent book from that church's publishing house gives advice from a Christian point of view on the subject of courtship and dating behavior. There the statement is made that "the sex impulse is a gift from God with powerful good if properly used."[51] At least to the extent that it represents the position of the entire church body, that little book shows a constructive approach to the problem of sex within the Evangelical Lutheran Church.

THE AUGUSTANA LUTHERAN CHURCH

Writing from the background of Swedish Lutheranism in America, A. D. Mattson, professor of Christian ethics and sociology at Augustana Seminary, Rock Island, Ill., in his *Christian Ethics* has a single paragraph on the matter of sex attitudes, dealing primarily with sex education. He writes:

> It should be the business of the church to educate for marriage. It is better to try to prevent dissolution of marriage than to try to decide what to do once that dissolution has been effected. This will involve education on matters of sex. All sex education should guard against stimulating sex curiosity in the young in regard to these matters. A good rule to follow is not to try to instruct faster than the spontaneous interest of the child demands. However, the dangers that await in-

---

[50] Gustav M. Bruce, *Marriage and Divorce* (Minneapolis: Augsburg Publishing House, 1930), pp. 37, 38.

[51] Alice Husted, *Strictly Confidential* (Minneapolis: Augsburg Publishing House, 1944), p. 66.

dulgence and the cruelty and brutality of prostitution are
matters that should be carefully and cautiously taught.
If parents can be depended upon to do it, the best teacher
in this matter is the parent. Nature has provided the sex
instinct with a guard in the sense of shame and modesty.
Prudery is no virtue, but modesty is, and should be developed
and emphasized.[52]

On the problem of temptations to sexual sins, the Augustana
Lutheran Church has probably done more than any other Lutheran church body in the form of official resolutions. Mattson
in his book on church polity quotes a number of church resolutions, all the way from 1875 to 1938, deploring the use of alcoholic
beverages, for one thing, because they are a great temptation
to "sexual promiscuity and other licentious practices." [53] In 1950
the church also passed a lengthy resolution on the question of
the dance, stating that the decision to take part or not to take
part in a dance "must remain the responsibility of the individual." With regard to congregations and church-supported schools
it said, "By the same token neither the congregation, nor any
of its auxiliaries, will sponsor a dance," and "the church is not
agreed that dancing should be sponsored as a school activity." [54]

Nothing is said on the attitude toward sex in general, the
restriction of sex activity in marriage, homosexuality, masturbation, and other problems which have beset the church from time
to time. On the matter of sex education, pastors and official
boards of the church body are urged by resolution to see that
proper literature is provided for purposes of education for marriage. Pastors and educators are urged to carry on definite
programs of training for the home and family.[55]

THE UNITED LUTHERAN CHURCH

In its carefully prepared statement of 1956 the United Lutheran Church deals with the problem of sex in our age.

---

[52] Alvin D. Mattson, *Christian Ethics* (Rock Island, Ill.: Augustana
Book Concern, 1938), p. 289.

[53] Alvin D. Mattson, *Polity of the Augustana Lutheran Church* (Rock
Island, Ill.: Augustana Book Concern, 1952), pp. 433—439.

[54] Ibid., pp. 447—454.

[55] Ibid., p. 440. See also *Social Pronouncements of the Augustana Lutheran Church and Its Conferences* (Rock Island, Ill.: Augustana Book
Concern, 1956).

Power of the Sex Drive

The power of the sex drive in human life is recognized by St. Paul in 1 Cor. 6:12; 7:9, 36, 38. The blessings and comforts of sex within marriage should not be withheld except for limited periods, but Christians should shun promiscuity, for they are one body joined to Christ. They are to glorify God in their bodies. While warning against the misuse of sex, Scripture gives to it a rightful place in marriage, where it strengthens the marital bond. Monogamy, therefore, serves as the best channel for the expression of the sex urge. Promiscuity and lust are contrary to divine law and therefore stand under God's judgment and punishment.[56]

Continence Outside Marriage

The whole Christian view of life implies sexual continence before marriage as well as outside of it. The marriage age in America is being lowered, and young people are exposed to more sex stimuli than formerly. Nevertheless the church must insist upon continence before marriage in the interest of the well-being of others, family life in the whole community, and the right of children to be well born. The Christian is called to a life of service, not of pleasure. This is the proper motivation for continence.

Intercourse before marriage, the report says, militates against true oneness in marriage, degenerates to lust and exploitation, frequently robs women of their opportunity for marriage, and involves the possibility of children out of wedlock. While the church should deal sympathetically and constructively with those who err, intercourse demands the permanent and responsible relationship of a marriage.[57]

The Celibate Life

To rate the celibate life higher than the married estate would imply the sinfulness of sex itself. Voluntary celibacy, for good reasons, should not be dismissed as a possibility. But St. Paul

---

[56] *Christian Guidance on Marriage and Family Life,* issued by The Board of Social Missions, The United Lutheran Church in America, 231 Madison Ave., New York 16, N.Y., 1956, p. 13.

[57] Ibid., pp. 14, 15.

makes it quite clear that this is a matter of an individual gift not given to everyone. "But each has his own special gift from God, one of one kind and one of another" (1 Cor. 7:7 RSV). The normal calling is still that of marriage and the family.

The unmarried, says the report, who live continently may play a role which can be holy and healthy. Their need for fellowship finds necessary expression in acts of service to people, church, and community in the same way as that of married persons does. Marriage is not a sine qua non of the successful life. Only a life in God through faith in Christ supplies that fullness and completeness.[58]

Sex Deviations

Homosexuality represents a denial of God's intention in creation (Rom. 1:24-27), expresses selfishness rather than living service and social responsibility, and keeps sex from being a part of a total experience of mutual sharing within the family. When sexual aberrations develop into an uncontrollable compulsion, they become illnesses for which medical and psychiatric attention are necessary. From the standpoint of Christian faith, sex deviates deserve the utmost of understanding and sympathetic help, but their illness can never be accepted as a satisfactory substitute for marriage.[59]

Marjory Louise Bracher, in *Love Is No Luxury*, after tracing the divergent teachings about sex in ecclesiastical history, summarizes a Christian interpretation of sex in marriage as follows: (1) Man and woman complete each other (Gen. 2:18). (2) The sex act itself makes them one flesh, not the outward form of a marriage ceremony (Matt. 19:6; 1 Cor. 6:16). (3) This union or oneness cannot be broken and is not to be violated (Matt. 19: 3-6). (4) It is a function involving the whole body, the entire person (1 Cor. 6:15-20). (5) It is a function given us for the duration of life in this world (Matt. 22:30). (6) Physical union is at once a duty and a right, equally for the man and for the woman (1 Cor. 7:3-5).[60]

---

[58] Ibid., pp. 15, 16.

[59] Ibid., p. 16.

[60] Marjory Louise Bracher, *Love Is No Luxury: A Guide for Christian Family Living* (Philadelphia: Muhlenberg Press, 1951), pp. 100, 101.

About Our Bodies

Mrs. Bracher traces the vague feeling that our bodies are evil or weak, and that they represent the "baser" side of our nature, to a misunderstanding of Matt. 26:41: "The spirit indeed is willing, but the flesh is weak." She writes:

> Perhaps we have thought "flesh" meant the body, that is, the bones, muscles, and organs. But by flesh Jesus meant sinful disobedient "self," the old nature which is against God, as contrasted with the "spirit," the new divine life of faith which is open and responsive to God. In many places in the New Testament the word "flesh" is used in this sense.

> Our bodies and their functions, of which sexual desire is one, are good and perfect creations of God. They are not evil, for God does not make evil. The evil is in our disobedient use of the body and its functions in ways and for purposes not intended by God.[61]

> . . . Sexual desire, as it exists in human beings, is God's provision for binding man and woman to each other for their mutual benefit and for the development of the child. The distinctive characteristic of human sex is not strength of the urge, but its frequency, in both male and female. Sex, in mankind, is more closely related to child rearing than to procreation, though the latter is well provided for.[62]

Significance of Sexual Union

Harold Haas, a contributor to the book *Life in Community,* a United Lutheran Church publication, writes:

> When the sexual union is thought of either as something intrinsically evil or simply as a biological outlet, then marriage can at best serve only as a remedy against sin, a socially sanctioned control of an instinct, or an unwarranted bond interfering with individual freedom.

> Sexual union has, however, a far more profound meaning than either of these alternatives. The creation which God declared to be good contained within it the physical encounter of sex between man and woman. It is true that the sinful condition of man can be expressed through sex in a profound and far-reaching way. This does not alter the basic fact, however, that sex as given by God is good.[63]

Haas shows that the Roman Catholic position on celibacy

---

61 Ibid., pp. 101, 102.

62 Ibid., p. 108.

63 *Life in Community,* Vol. III of *Christian Social Responsibility,* ed. Harold C. Letts (Philadelphia: Muhlenberg Press, 1957), p. 163.

contains "a fundamental suspicion of sex"; that neither the ascetic view of sex, which so long has dominated the church, nor the hedonistic view that sex is mainly for personal satisfaction is Christian and Biblical.[64]

In various pronouncements and articles the United Lutheran Church has counseled the cultivation of sound attitudes toward sex by well-planned sex education at various stages of the boy's or girl's development.[65]

THE AMERICAN LUTHERAN CHURCH

The constituent synods of the American Lutheran Church, as of 1959, comprising the original three synods, the Buffalo Synod, the Ohio Synod, and the Iowa Synod, can be said to a large degree to have followed the trend of writing and practice in the area of sex attitudes which has already been described under The Lutheran Church — Missouri Synod. Like other Lutheran bodies the American Lutheran Church has until recently been silent with regard to printed materials on sex. Parents, it was held, should instruct their children, and "straight talk" on the Sixth Commandment is appropriate in confirmation instruction. Only secondary attention has been given to positive and constructive views of sex and its normal place in human life. The companionship aspect of marriage is now being emphasized more than formerly. Anxieties related to masturbation are frequently mentioned to youth counselors.[66]

In its statement entitled *Marriage, Divorce, and Remarriage,* approved in its 1956 convention, the American Lutheran Church says: "From the beginning man knew that male and female complete and complement one another. . . . As God is love, so male and female, who are created in God's image, seek to make love the characteristic of their marriage. Such love is not the physical passion or erotic satisfaction the world defines as love, although Scripture itself grants sexual satisfaction as one of the joys of marriage." [67]

---

[64] Ibid., III, 163 fn. See also George W. Forell, *Ethics of Decision* (Philadelphia: Muhlenberg Press, 1955), pp. 132—135.

[65] Harold J. Maleske, unpublished research summary, "The Writings of the United Lutheran Church in America on Marriage and Family Life."

[66] Carl F. Reuss, unpublished research summary, "Statement on the American Lutheran Church and Its Teachings on Marriage and Family Living."

[67] *Marriage, Divorce, and Remarriage,* American Lutheran Church Convention, Blue Island, Ill., Oct. 4—11, 1956.

William E. Hulme, professor of pastoral theology and counseling at Wartburg Seminary, Dubuque, Iowa, conveys the
views of the evangelical ministry in the light of and on the
basis of modern counseling in his book *God, Sex, and Youth.*
In his chapter "Sex in Solitude" he disagrees with those who
assert that autoerotic practices are universal and distinguishes
between masturbation as an occasional exploratory venture and
compulsive masturbation. While rejecting the superstitious beliefs not based on facts, he does see in masturbation an escape
from reality and a source of a sense of guilt which is deeply
felt by those addicted to the practice. He writes:

> Some writers on this subject feel that the guilt about mas-
> turbation is the greatest danger in masturbation. They say
> this not only because guilt is painful, but because it may cause
> a person to become even more withdrawn than he already is.
> We have seen that addiction to masturbation may be a
> symptom of difficulty in relating to others. If the symptom is
> followed by a sense of shame and worthlessness, the person
> feels even less qualified to associate with others. As a result
> he withdraws even more into himself, and becomes more
> addicted to his habit. . . . The guilt about masturbation has
> a basis in fact. The real longing has not been met, even though
> the buildup in anticipation seems to indicate that it will be.
> The sexual fantasies appear afterward to be foolish if not
> revolting. We feel let down. A mere physical sensation cannot
> bring the satisfactions of joining with another, any more than
> fantasy can take the place of reality. What follows is a sense
> of being cheated, or even worse, of having cheated oneself.[68]

Hulme shows the relation of masturbation to a sense of self-
worth and to love for others and suggests (1) giving assurances
of God's forgiveness and (2) Christian self-discipline. He writes:

> . . . disciplining sexual desires in line with the best interests
> of all concerned is needed for dating and marriage. Such
> discipline begins in our solitude. If we indulge our imme-
> diate impulses here, we may find it harder to maintain our
> discipline when it concerns others as well as ourselves. From
> my experience I have noticed that people who indulged them-
> selves in masturbation have corresponding trouble with temp-
> tation in dating. Our discipline so far as masturbation is
> concerned should not begin with the physical tensions but
> with the thoughts that encourage the tensions.[69]

68 William E. Hulme, *God, Sex and Youth* (Englewood Cliffs, N. J.:
Prentice-Hall, 1959), pp. 76, 77.
69 Ibid., p. 79.

LUTHERAN SURVEY ON SEX

This review of Lutheran teaching would be incomplete without reference to current attitudes among Lutheran pastors and
their people obtained in a sociological study which is described
more fully in the graphs at the end of this book.

There is always a gap between theory and practice. This is
true also in the realm of sexual expression. While 93 per cent
of the persons questioned agreed that parents should instruct
their children in sex matters, only 33 per cent were giving such
instruction. Fathers, it was learned, give only 6 per cent of the
sex information children receive, while mothers give 18 per
cent, teachers 10 per cent, pastors 3 per cent. While autoerotic
practices were considered wrong by 69 per cent of the clergy
and 75 per cent of the laity, such behavior was reported by
62 per cent of the males and 21 per cent of the females, showing
that this is an area of widespread conflict and confusion. There
was general agreement that sex in marriage is proper even when
procreation is not the purpose in mind; a wide difference in the
opinions exists between various areas of the country.

In comparison with general surveys the Lutheran family has
high moral standards. There is evidence that some of the negative puritan, pietistic, and ascetic views of bygone periods are
still dominant in some Lutheran thinking and that the Biblical
and Christian views more recently enunciated are just beginning
to pass down from the clergy to the laity and to become available in printed form. (See graphs, pp. 239—247)

SUMMARY

1. The Lutheran church bodies of America condemned sharply
   all offenses against the Sixth Commandment in thought, word,
   or deed, but upheld the sanctity of sex relations within marriage and later sharpened their distinctions between the right
   and wrong use of sex.

2. Throughout its history The Lutheran Church — Missouri
   Synod has exalted marriage as God's order for the welfare
   of mankind. There was, however, also a strong tendency
   toward pietistic sex ethics and legalistic procedures toward
   offenders. Masturbation is still condemned as "an unclean

act." Sex education, long frowned upon, is being approved if properly done. Later writings see sex in the light of creation, redemption, and sanctification, not merely as a remedy for "human depravity" but as a part of God's design.

3. Although Lutherans of Norwegian background still have some strong reservations in dealing with sex as a church, they recognize the sex impulse as a gift from God with power for good if properly used. The Augustana Lutheran Church, of Swedish forebears, has given much attention to Christian ethics in its social pronouncements on matters related to sex, warning against all sex deviations. Both groups maintain that Christian homes and Christian standards of purity are the best preventive of sexual liberties.

4. The United Lutheran Church in America has been most explicit in its statements on sex. Recognizing the rightful place of sex in human life, this church has stated that continence before marriage and outside it is a necessary Christian standard; that the Roman Catholic views of sex, and some earlier Protestant ones too, are suspect, for they are out of harmony with the doctrine of creation; and that marriage is more than "a remedy for sin," because sexual desire is God's provision for binding man and woman together in marriage. Both the ascetic view of sex and the hedonistic view so common in current writings are rejected as unscriptural.

5. Although matters related to sex were not treated publicly in the past, congregations of the American Lutheran Church recently in convention adopted a significant statement which embodies a positive, Biblical view of sex. Some important insights into the dangers of masturbation are supplied by a writer of this church.

6. In most Lutheran bodies in America the evil acts associated with sex were sharply condemned, but the positive, God-ordained purpose and use of sex was usually not specifically taught or was neglected. This tradition is being replaced by a clearer, more specific, more complete, and theologically adequate treatment of matters relating to sex.

CHAPTER 10

Contemporary Protestant and Roman Catholic Views

THE PREVIOUS CHAPTERS have revealed the various streams of thought in both Christian and non-Christian cultures regarding a proper view of sex. Because these views and interpretations proceeded from various segments of Christendom which held different basic principles as to what constituted authority in religion, there is much diversity and ofttimes confusion of opinion. The church fathers undoubtedly were influenced by the asceticism of non-Christian cults and Greek philosophies regarding flesh and spirit.

Some theologians constructed their views from the premise of creation, others from the sinfulness of man, still others from Christian freedom. Some developed a new legalism within Christendom, others chose their principles of action from the Gospel of God's forgiving grace.

Christian leaders are called upon to speak out clearly in the face of the "free-for-all morals" which the ethical relativists of our day are advocating. Our pursuits of material satisfactions, our cult of happiness, and the hedonism of our contemporary culture have "developed a strain of influence which favors expediency rather than principle, and which encourages us to be smart, clever, and successful, rather than honest, intelligent, socially useful," [1] and God-pleasing.

In this chapter Protestant and Roman Catholic churchmen

---

[1] Robert E. Fitch, *Preface to Ethical Living* (New York: Association Press, 1947), p. 18.

are called upon to state the basic problems and to set forth Christian principles as they see them. The search for a positive view of sex that can guide Christian people today on the basis of all the facts is not easy. The Scriptures do not specifically answer all questions which arise in this area. Many branches of learning and insights into human behavior are involved. We tend to be creatures of our times, and the temptations are strong to find Biblical sanction for the status quo. Few church bodies have codified their sex ethics, and so we are compelled to find representative views by men at home in this field. It is difficult furthermore because the volume of materials dealing with the Christian and sex produced within comparatively recent years is simply overwhelming. This chapter reviews some of the chief writings that have appeared among Protestants and Roman Catholics, in America and Europe.

AMERICAN PROTESTANTS AND SEX

Several characteristics of Protestant writing on the subject can be distinguished. As more and more churchmen get scientific insights into human personality, sociology and psychology are reflected in all phases of pastoral theology, including the approach to sex. At the same time others are finding in the Scriptural doctrines of creation, redemption, and sanctification the basis for a theology of sex. The unitive function of sex in marriage is being rediscovered. A "sacramental" or symbolic view of sex is now widely held by both conservative and liberal Protestant theologians.

Sex for the Good of Man

Seward Hiltner, representing the historical-critical school, lists six fundamental attitudes toward sex: (1) the *child-of-nature* attitude, which advocates expression rather than restraint as a natural part of living; (2) the *respectability-restraint* attitude — a view which holds that sex is a problem to be feared but still has respectability when kept within its place; (3) the *romantic* view, which consists in finding the proper partner, the emphasis being on real companionship; (4) the *sophisticated no-harm attitude,* holding that anything about sex goes as long as it does not produce harm; (5) the *toleration* attitude, meaning that others need to be understood rather than condemned for

their acts; (6) the *personal-interpersonal* attitude of love and
mutuality, seeking the good of another, finding one's true self
rather than a pseudo self, and not expecting more from the
partner than is possible for a fallible human being. Hiltner points
out that no one of these attitudes is held exclusively or in pure
form.[2]

In a review of Biblical teachings Hiltner makes much of the
fact that Jesus established no new set of laws and codes and that
Paul stressed the freedom of the Christian man, "the spontaneous,
uncoerced, unforced, unimposed character of the whole Christian
life." [3]

He asserts that "a purely reproductive notion of the Christian
view of sex is not possible if one takes seriously the Biblical
views on one-flesh union, on sex as mystery, on sex as the
creation of God, on man's body as fundamental and not peripheral
to his nature and on the freedom of the Christian." [4]

Man's sexual nature is not reprehensible and not accidental.
It is deep and mysterious, but he cannot follow God's will about
this aspect of his being if he ignores sex or flattens it or makes
it his whole being. In itself it is good. It is up to him to use it as
God intended for the fulfillment of his own true being.[5]

Hiltner reports that attitudes toward masturbation differ
sharply among different groups in our society. Modern knowledge holds that frequently it is brief but troublesome and abandoned early. Where it becomes compulsive, it is a symptom of
inner disorder and needs therapy.[6]

Homosexuality in any kind of normative sense is disapproved
by the Christian view. Every possible therapeutic resource should
be made available to homosexuals. A mere condemnation of such
persons would be radically unchristian.[7]

While sex has a positive place in the Christian life, it does
not follow that it is necessary to a full Christian life, because it

---

[2] Seward Hiltner, *Sex and the Christian Life* (New York: Association
Press, 1957), pp. 24—31.

[3] Ibid., p. 46. "The Christian is the freest man of all. If one truly loves
God, he may do as he pleases; because what he freely pleases to do is
to follow the will of God."

[4] Ibid., p. 49.

[5] Ibid., pp. 38, 39.

[6] Ibid., pp. 115, 116.

[7] Ibid., pp. 117, 118.

is not the most important thing in life. The key lies in the inner acceptance of one's sexuality so that even in essentially non-sexual relationships this fosters understanding and love in social and personal relationships.[8]

The Role of Sex in Love

Reuel L. Howe, professor of pastoral theology at the Institute for Advanced Pastoral Studies, Bloomfield Hills, Mich., says we must accept our human sexual nature and the kind of relationship that nature calls for. He believes sex is God's instrument to keep husband and wife united and renewed in their love. With the use of sex go the responsibilities in marriage and the rearing of a family. He calls attention to the basic nature of love in human personality development and distinguishes between romantic love and mature love. Where God in Christ dwells by the Spirit, self-giving love (agape) is added to physical love (eros) and transforms it.[9]

"Each sex has advantages over the other because each possesses that which the other does not have but needs." This need of one for another is back of every true marriage. This relationship can be fulfilled only in true, selfless love. Sex is to be an expression of love in marriage. Marriage needs sex and sex needs marriage. In marriage sex life gets the continuity and stability needed for the fullest realization of the gift of sex. This is more, however, than a physical gift. Lust, on the other hand, is an offense against the right relationship "because it makes flesh serve itself." Prostitution and promiscuity are evil because both persons and society are exploited and injured.[10] From the following it is clear that Howe emphasizes the relational aspect.

> A holy sexual relationship [says Howe] is one in which the interrelatedness and wholeness of the person and his function is preserved and honored in thought and act. In holy love, the lover loves, honors, and cherishes his beloved as a person. It is a wonderful experience to be so revered as a person. And, in gratitude, the beloved gives her lover her functions as a thank-offering, even as he gives her his, so that the receiv-

---

[8] Ibid., pp. 119, 120.

[9] Reuel L. Howe, "A Pastoral Theology of Sex and Marriage" in *Sex and Religion Today*, ed. Simon Doninger (New York: Association Press, 1953), pp. 111, 113.

[10] Ibid., pp. 99, 101, 102, 107.

ing is a result of giving in which there is a minimum of
exploitation. In this sense the sexual act is sacramental, for
the act is an outward and visible sign of mutual union between
two persons in which function serves its real purpose — to be
an instrument for the realization of the fullness of the love
relationship.[11]

Facts of Sex — Not Enough

"The young should have adequate sex education," writes
W. Taliaferro Thompson, Presbyterian (U. S.) clergyman and
professor, "but giving the facts of life is not enough. The all
important thing is a Christian frame of reference." Sex is a strong
urge, pervasive in the girl, more localized in the boy. It is a holy
urge involving the whole personality and to be regarded with
reverence. Religious feelings and background are most important
and make a world of difference. Ideals must be taught so that
boys and girls see the sacredness of personality because of its
relationship to God. Where these two facts, human personality
and the fact of God, are foremost in the mind, it would be difficult
for boys and girls to engage in prolonged petting which majors
in bodily intimacies and measures a date by the physical thrills
experienced. It all starts with the attitude toward sex developed
in earliest childhood. It begins in the attitude of parents before
their children are born.[12] He quotes an experiment of Dr. Richard C. Cabot, who found persons with much biological knowledge (medical students and nurses) not on that account more
chaste than others.[13] He supports the finding of two psychiatrists
who have reached the conclusion that dealing early and frankly
with children when sex questions are asked "denotes to the child
an acceptance of himself, an acceptance of his body and of the
impulses of his body." [14]

---

[11] Reuel L. Howe, *The Creative Years* (Greenwich, Conn.: Seabury
Press, 1959), pp. 101—108. See also Howe, "A Pastoral Theology of Sex
and Marriage," *Sex and Religion Today*, p. 108.

[12] W. Taliaferro Thompson, *An Adventure in Love* (Richmond, Va.:
John Knox Press, 1956), pp. 121—127.

[13] Richard C. Cabot, *Christianity and Sex* (Chicago: Macmillan, 1937),
pp. 7, 8.

[14] O. Spurgeon English and Gerald H. J. Pearson, *Emotional Problems
of Living: Avoiding the Neurotic Pattern* (New York: W. W. Norton & Co.,
1945), p. 76.

"Fundamentalists" and Sex

Writing for some of the "fundamentalist" branches of Protestantism, John R. Rice makes it very clear that, although some
church leaders tend to belittle and despise sex, such an attitude
is not truly Biblical. He asserts that there have been very many
foolish and unscriptural things said about marriage. He refers
to the ravings of some writers who say that married women are
living in "legal prostitution" because they feel obligated to surrender their bodies completely to the will of the husband in the
marriage relationship. "How far fetched, how unscriptural, how
far from the truth are these vain human imaginings!" [15] The
same author says that "sex relations between husband and wife
are normal, beautiful, good, and have not only the permission,
but the blessing of God." But he also writes, "Christians ought
to be temperate in all things, but what is a temperate use of
marriage must be decided by each husband and wife according
to their own happiness and desire, just as each must decide what
is temperate in eating according to the needs and hunger of
his body." [16]

"Fundamentalists" are plain-spoken with regard to the reality
of the sins of sex and are to be respected because of their un-
sophisticated approach to the laxities of our day. They call attention to the frequent warnings in the Scripture against lust of
every kind, to the price that is paid for sexual aberrations, to
the prevalence of sex magazines, and to the deliberately contrived
sexiness of the entertainment world, saturating American life
until people lose their sense of decency and shame. The Christian is to avoid temptations of sex, live a life of Christian self-
control, show Christian modesty in dress, and keep the body
clean and holy not only for the Lord but for the future partner
in life.

In his book *Sex and the Bible* Jack Wyrtzen states that sex
in itself is not sinful; that it belongs to the very fiber of our
being, the warp and woof of our life; that it colors our thoughts
and desires; that sex can be an expression of love and of beauty
in our lives; that every living thing in the universe owes its life

---

[15] John R. Rice, *The Home — Courtship, Marriage, and Children*
(Wheaton, Ill.: Sword of the Lord Publishers, 1946), p. 23.

[16] Ibid., pp. 133—135. See also Frank Lawes, *The Sanctity of Sex* (Chicago: Good News Publishers, 1949).

to the principle of sex; and that God established sex in the marriage relationship before sin ever came into the world. Treating sex according to God's plan will enrich life. Ignoring God's plan degrades life.[17]

The following list of rules for testing a temptation are suggested by one author: (1) Is it of the world? (John 15:19); (2) Is it to the glory of God? (1 Cor. 10:31); (3) Can you invoke the divine blessing upon it? (Prov. 10:22); (4) Is it a stumbling block to others? (Rom. 14:21); (5) Has it the appearance of evil? (1 Thess. 5:22); (6) Is it a "weight"? (Heb. 12:1); (7) Is its atmosphere good? (2 Cor. 6:14).[18]

Sex in Marriage as God's Design

In a chapter on "Sex as Symbol and Sacrament," Presbyterian Dwight Hervey Small, teaching at Wheaton (Ill.) College, sets forth the Christian view of sex over against such false views as sexual experimentation, total denial of any sex expression, mere acceptance of sex as a biological necessity, confining sex to propagation, using romantic love as the only guide, and assigning no moral significance whatsoever to sex.

Sex is a symbolic expression of other values besides sex, intended for the two persons in a mutual commitment of love and trust in marriage. While sex is a biological function, it involves the whole personality and at its highest level is unmistakably spiritual. It is unchristian as soon as it becomes an end in itself and persons are exploited as "things," which is the essence of prostitution. Unless kept in its proper place, that is, in married life, sex becomes a sin against God. Because of sin man needs the forgiving love of God in his sex life as well as in all other areas of living. Sex and marriage need each other. Sex without marriage is devoid of spiritual or personal meaning, while marriage without sex is an incomplete relationship, "a union lacking an indispensable resource for the establishment and maintenance of oneness." [19] Sex is a gift of God and dare not be despised.

---

[17] Jack Wyrtzen, *Sex and the Bible* (Grand Rapids, Mich.: Zondervan Publishing House, 1958), pp. 14, 33, 62. Rolf L. Veenstra, *Christian Marriage* (Hamilton, Ont., Canada: Guardian Publishing Co., Ltd., 1957), pp. 75, 76.

[18] Reginald Wallis, *New Man* (New York: Loizeaux Bros., Inc., 1931), pp. 66, 67.

[19] Dwight Hervey Small, *Design for Christian Marriage* (Westwood, N. J.: Fleming H. Revell Company, 1959), p. 83.

Now if sex is a gift of God, good and holy, it cannot be a regrettable overplus of guilty desire which marriage helps us to dispose of secretly! Nor does it require any justification for its existence apart from its own nature and function. Certainly the fact of propagation cannot itself justify something that otherwise would be not good! Sex is justified for what it is in itself, a medium of expression and unification in marriage. . . . Sexual intercourse in marriage is a means of expressing and communicating the deepest feelings and assurances of love and commitment of the whole life to another, and this in a medium more flexible and profound than speech.[20]

"When sex does not participate in married creativeness, it loses its meaning and becomes instead a degrading thing.[21] Sex in marriage, with mature, self-giving love, is a means of glorifying God in our bodies (1 Cor. 6:19, 20). But outside marriage it becomes a destructive passion, which separates persons and is exploitive and parasitic.

. . . sex is not sinful in itself, but may indeed become sinful because of the way in which it can gather together and bring into abuse so many dimensions of personality, the relationship with God, and the relationship with others of His children. Sex outside of marriage is sinful because it violates God's holy purpose of establishing full and permanent oneness between two persons sealed by the sexual union.[22]

While many couples expect too much of sex in marriage, others expect too little. Small sums up the purposes inherent in normal sexual experience within Christian marriage as follows: (1) Biologically, it releases tensions through ecstatic pleasure and satisfaction. (2) Socially, it is the indispensable part of the full commitment of two whole personalities in a one-flesh relationship. (3) Psychologically, it provides a sense of fulfillment and security and of interdependence as love and understanding are reciprocated. (4) Spiritually, it is the unique symbolical expression of the union of the trusting sinner and the gracious Redeemer.[23]

The Problem of Petting

The case for chastity and against petting is set forth in Small's chapter on "Profile on Petting." Chastity rests on the acknowl-

---

20 Ibid., p. 83.
21 Ibid., p. 84.
22 Ibid., p. 85.
23 Ibid., pp. 88, 89. Small, no doubt, wishes to reflect Eph. 5 here.

edgment of the sanctity of sex. "A chaste person is one whose sexual life in all of its facets is rightly instrumental in the fulfillment of the divine purpose." [24] He is not interested in "margins of safety" but in true, God-given purposes. Small acknowledges that sex appeal is "one of a number of legitimate and necessary elements of attractiveness" in mate selection and that the real question is what form the appeal should take and to what lengths it should go. He also recognizes three typical and common desires for intimacies of a sort between adolescent boys and girls: (1) the curiosity of each to explore further their new awareness of sex differentiation; (2) the excitement and ecstatic pleasure that comes with social contact with the other sex; (3) both the boy's and the girl's basic desire for reassurance of one's desirability and lovableness, of the feeling that one is needed.

Petting is defined as sexually stimulating physical and emotional involvement between two persons of the opposite sex through fondling and kissing — even to the point of bringing about an orgasm (but not including sexual intercourse). What in marriage is love-making "fore play," says Small, in petting is "mutual lust." [25] He rejects as a half-truth that petting is a good thing for maturing young people to prepare them for marriage, because it is a process which belongs within marriage itself. The excuse that it avoids intercourse and preserves the girl's virginity is a moral subterfuge since the integrity of another person is violated. Even for engaged couples it makes a serious moral problem.

Petting cheapens sex. It never stands alone but is a natural prelude to the intimacies of marriage. It often results in nervous tensions, feelings of indignity, resentfulness, hypocrisy. Petting experiences are stored in the subconscious mind to plague and disturb. It is difficult to stop the demands for progressively increasing sex stimulation. Petting becomes a Frankenstein which the creator can no longer manage. "The integrity of persons is inviolable." Selfhood is exploited in heavy petting, and self-respect forfeited. The violation of a person is just as real even though there is no public shame.[26]

---

[24] Ibid., p. 154.
[25] Ibid., p. 155.
[26] Ibid., p. 170.

"Whatever the standard of the non-Christian, the standard for the Christian is clear. His body is a sacred trust from God, its functions meant to be restricted to and preserved for the ends designed by God. Since petting is an unnatural function which substitutes for intercourse when intercourse is not appropriate, it is certainly not within God's will for a child of His." [27] "Petting outside of marriage is sexual immorality (1 Cor. 6: 13; 1 Thess. 4: 4, 5; 1 Peter 2: 11; 2 Tim. 2: 22) ." [28]

"They who preserve love's strength intact [before marriage] will know in God's time a love that will be beautiful, well-adjusted, full and free. They will experience a depth of satisfaction beyond their highest dreams. This is God's sure reward for the self-disciplined Christian!" [29]

Most Spiritual — Most Earthy

Sex, security, and even happiness are not the ends of Christian marriage, according to Episcopalian Thomas V. Barrett, but means and by-products of the greater and more satisfying adventure which comes with the renewing of life through Jesus Christ. Quite realistically he reminds the church that sex was here before the church came into existence, before the Puritans, before the Ten Commandments, and that we are not going to change this characteristic of man's nature nor the wonder of man's way with a maid. To him sexual experience within marriage is a natural but not an ecclesiastical "sacrament" belonging to the order of creation. It is to be enjoyed. If it is not enjoyed, something is wrong with the marriage. He calls sex "the most spiritual experience of marriage as well as the most earthy." The Christian standing before the mystery of sex must uphold the ideal that sexual love is too holy, too wonderful a thing between two lovers to be desecrated and cheapened. "Chastity before marriage is a great good to be desired, for the sexual experience, so intimate, so profound, so complicated in the spiritual and emotional structure of man, involves the giving of the whole person, which cannot be done without love, and which ought not to be

---

27 Ibid., p. 173.

28 Ibid., p. 173. See also Alexander C. DeJong, *The Christian Family and the Home* (Grand Rapids, Mich.: Baker Book House, 1959), p. 37.

29 Small, p. 175.

done outside of the binding loyalty of lifelong marriage, for the
guilt or sorrow, or loneliness it may cause." [30]

Episcopalian theology opposes such notions as "things fleshly
and things external are bad," "that celibacy is in itself higher
than marriage," "that sex and sensual enjoyment are evil in
themselves." [31] Marriage for Christians is not merely legalizing
sexual relations; it is "sacramental" in nature, permanent in
character, reflecting, as the Prayer Book says, the spiritual marriage and unity that exists between the Lord and His church.

Attitudes and System of Values

Many Protestant authors agree with the basic principles derived from what theologians call "the order of creation." Thus
Mary and Harold Walker say:

> If God created our bodies with pleasurable sex response pat-
> terns, He no doubt expected sex to be enjoyed by those
> enjoined in comradeship of marriage. No one needs to be
> shocked by the discovery that married love at its best is
> enjoyable. It was meant to be so. . . . It may be that two
> becoming "one-flesh" is, as Paul said, "a great mystery," but
> it is not a sinful one. . . . Sex is God's gift, and rightly used
> it is a means to mutual self-fulfillment. He and she are "heirs
> together of the grace of life," creating a climate through their
> love in which selfhood can flourish. . . . Healthy growth in
> our children and sane attitudes toward sex are generated not
> by negatives and not by embarrassed silence, but by frankness
> and by the gentle assumption that sex is both important and
> fundamentally good because it is God-given.[32]

Emphasizing the point that sex standards in modern life must
depend for their sanction on devotion rather than dread, Joseph
Fletcher says: "The system of values and philosophy by which
we live, is what determines the particular ways in which we
handle and satisfy the sexual drive. . . . It is not sexual behavior
that determines character; it is character that determines sexual
behavior." [33]

---

[30] Thomas V. Barrett, *The Christian Family* (New York: Morehouse-
Gorham Co., 1958), pp. 62—68, 117.

[31] James A. Pike and W. Norman Pittenger, *The Faith of the Church*
(Greenwich, Conn.: The Seabury Press, 1951), pp. 159, 160, 174.

[32] Mary Alice Walker and Harold Blake Walker, *Venture of Faith:
A Guide to Marriage and the Home* (New York: Harper and Brothers,
1959), pp. 17, 25, 29.

[33] Joseph Fletcher, "A Moral Philosophy of Sex," in *Sex and Religion
Today,* ed. Simon Doninger (New York: Association Press, 1953),

SEX VIEWS OF ENGLISH PROTESTANTS

The Anglican View: A Gift of God

The modern Anglican view regarding sex and marriage is closely in line with that expressed above. Writing on Christian marriage, Derrick Sherwin Bailey says:

> In the first place it must be emphasized that sex is one of God's gifts to man and woman, and as such is good in itself and to be "received with thanksgiving"; there is no place for the unconsciously blasphemous attitude which regards sexual activity as something "nasty" or "impure." On the contrary, the right use of the sexual faculties is one of the most natural ways by which God is glorified in the body. This, however, demands a Godward orientation of the will; in the immediacy of intercourse there can be consciousness of none but the beloved, but the act itself must take place in the context of a common God-centered life and must be offered to Him — in intention beforehand, in thanksgiving afterwards — as husband and wife silently acknowledge the Author of their love. . . . Such intercourse is necessarily pleasurable because of what is expressed, and not merely because it is a means of sensual gratification. There is no doubt that the theological suspicion of sexual pleasure already mentioned has been partly responsible for the fact that this important aspect of intercourse has not been appreciated.[34]

The Lambeth Conference

The Lambeth Conference of 1958 made a special study of marriage and the family. In its carefully considered pronouncements it deals also with human sexuality as a gift of God to be used fully in the marriage union of the two in "one flesh." While procreation is a goal of sexual union, neither the Bible nor human experience makes all other duties and relationships in marriage subordinate to the procreation purpose — a teaching based on the false premise that sex is intrinsically evil. The conference statement considers intercourse as "utterly wrong" when procreation alone is intended. Husbands and wives owe to each other and to the depth and stability of their families the duty to

---

pp. 192, 193. See also Richard A. Fagley, *The Population Explosion and Christian Responsibility* (New York: Oxford University Press, 1960). While this book deals mainly with planned parenthood, it supplies significant insights regarding sex attitudes from various periods of history. The Protestant point of view is set forth in chapter 13, pages 189—209.

[34] Derrick Sherwin Bailey, *The Mystery of Love and Marriage* (New York: Harper & Bros., 1952), pp. 59, 60.

express in sexual intercourse the love which they bear and mean
to bear to each other. In a world that more and more deperson-
alizes life the new freedom of sexuality between man and wife
is a good thing, the report says.

Rejecting the dualism expressed in Puritanism and the theology of St. Augustine, which identified the principle of evil with
the "material" or "the flesh," Lambeth said, "The church holds
as strongly as ever that continence, chastity and self-control are
a positive and creative element in Christian living . . . before
marriage and in it." "If Christian living were to be so influenced by current hedonism as to allow free rein to biological
and sexual urges, it would lose the dimension of holiness and its
power to challenge 'the world.' "

"Premarital intercourse," the report says, "can never be
right; it is selfish and sinful in its irreverence for the sanctity of
both a man's and a woman's life" and prevents "the complete
offering of selfhood unspoiled by any liaison in marriage." [35]

The Unitive Function of Sex in Marriage

David Mace, internationally known authority on marriage
counseling, currently executive director of the American Association of Marriage Counselors, Inc., has written much on
a Christian approach to sex.[36]

Sexual desire, says Mace, is a normal, healthy, God-given
impulse. We are endowed with it with an intensity far greater
than is necessary to propagate the human race. It is an emotional
high explosive, and therefore all communities have had to control it. The best control is through marriage, in which it is not
only "a remedy against sin" but a positive good — not only
a means to generate new life but an instrument of the most tender
spiritual love to refresh, renew, and enrich the whole marriage
relationship. If husband and wife can "rejoice in it as a great
gift from God, then they have achieved a true Christian attitude
to sex." [37]

[35] *The Lambeth Conference 1958: The Encyclical Letter from the
Bishops Together with the Resolutions and Reports* (Greenwich, Conn.:
Seabury Press, 1958), pp. 2.147, 2.150, 2.156.

[36] The editors have chosen to classify Dr. Mace with the English since
he began and did his main work in England.

[37] David R. Mace, *Whom God Hath Joined* (Philadelphia: Westminster
Press, 1953), pp. 22, 23.

Jesus, in Matt. 5:28, "did not mean that a young man seeking a wife should experience no feelings of sexual desire as he contemplated an eligible young woman"; nor did He wish to deny proper admiration of beautiful womanhood or virile manhood. Jesus wanted us to know that "the best way to safeguard ourselves from unfaithfulness is to refuse to let the imagination dwell upon the thought of a sexual relationship which if it actually took place would violate a marriage, our own or another's." The apostle Paul in Eph. 5:25-28 speaks of married people loving each other as they love their own bodies — without shame or false modesty about bodily functions, in full openness and without concealment.[38]

Mace asserts that in the Bible the unitive function of sex in marriage is stressed more than the procreative function. Sex consummates the unity of husband and wife when their marriage begins, and it continuously renews and sustains that unity as they go on through life together. He also calls marriage sacramental, not in the technical sense but in the sense "that what happens on the physical level is not all, and not even the most important part" of the sexual experience. Mace distinguishes love from lust. "The meeting of two bodies cannot make love. It can only express and enrich a love that is already there." "A decline in the fellowship of the marriage will equally disrupt the working of the sexual function, and ultimately destroy it altogether." This is why living in mutual forgiveness is fundamental and why the practice of reasonable self-control is essential to successful sex adjustment in marriage.[39]

Removing Confusion Regarding Sex

William P. Wylie, English churchman and lecturer on marriage, proposes that today's confusion in regard to sex stems not only from modern social freedoms but also from the failure to realize that sex in human beings is fundamentally different in most respects from sex in animals. Animals are in bondage to sex as a fact of nature. In man sex is a gift under the freedom of man's own will. He demonstrates that sex and love are not the same thing, love being the greater and more enduring. While

---

[38] Ibid., pp. 31, 36, 38, 39.
[39] Ibid., pp. 44, 47, 52—54, 69.

love between sexes normally leads to sexual intercourse, only
in marriage are love, romance, and sex fulfilled. "Sex at its
highest and at its best can be the means, the sign and the symbol
of the enduring love in and through which two persons can come
to a fulfillment that neither of them could achieve alone." [40] This
is what God made sex for. In Christian marriage a new dimension is added, agape (Christian love), which has both the warmth
of love and the width of charity. Only in marriage does the one-
flesh union come into reality validly.[41]

He quotes Gilbert Russell on sex outside marriage: "A man's
sexuality belongs to his wife, long before he has met her. If he
never meets her, it belongs to nobody else. Only one human
being has claim on our sexual powers — the one who can claim
the whole of us." [42]

Petting and "love-play" have their place in marriage to cause
necessary tumescence in the male and to prepare the female for
union. They form a chain reaction that leads to coitus. The abuse
of these stimuli merely for a thrill is not only sinful but unwise
and unkind.[43]

As overemphasis of sex is a danger, so, on the other hand, is
underemphasis. Sexual desires and feelings are of themselves
not "impure" or "nasty." Without proper understanding of sex
as a gift of God, Christians are subject to false feelings of guilt
and are ill prepared to fulfill God's purposes in marriage.[44]

Confusion in the church stems chiefly from the fact that three
erroneous "doctrines" have never quite been expelled from popular Christianity: (1) Christian teachers of all ages have talked
as if sex sins were the worst sins of all (sins of the spirit are the
most damaging). (2) The second error is the idea that anything
connected with material things and the human body is essentially
evil (this is the heresy of Manichaeism, perpetuated by Protestants as well as by Romanists). (3) Third is the erroneous
belief that pleasure per se, also the pleasure of sex, is essentially

---

[40] William P. Wylie, *Human Nature and Christian Marriage* (New
York: Association Press, 1959), p. 28.

[41] Ibid., pp. 33, 39.

[42] Ibid., p. 66 (George Lawrence [Gilbert] Russell, *Men and Women*
[Greenwich, Conn.: Seabury Press, 1954], pp. 65, 66).

[43] Wylie, p. 76.

[44] Ibid., pp. 82, 83, 120, 29.

wicked (sexual powers and sex pleasure belong to the order of creation).[45]

Marriage with its God-pleasing exercise of sex is a Christian vocation, but the voluntary renunciation of sex for the sake of service, and the "guarding of sex" by the unmarried (waiting for marriage) are also Christian vocations.

Sexual Morality

In his chapter on "Sexual Morality" the English Christian apologist C. S. Lewis distinguishes between chastity and propriety, or decency, saying:

> While the rule of chastity is the same for all Christians at all times, the rule of propriety changes. A girl in the Pacific Islands wearing hardly any clothes and a Victorian lady completely covered in clothes might both be equally "modest," proper, or decent, according to the standards of their own societies; and both, for all we could tell by their dress, might be equally chaste (or equally unchaste).[46]

He likewise distinguishes between the Christian and the worldly view of sex:

> Modern people are always saying, "Sex is nothing to be ashamed of." They may mean two things. They may mean, "There is nothing to be ashamed of in the fact that the human race reproduces itself in a certain way, nor in the fact that it gives pleasure." If they mean that, they are right. Christianity says the same. It is not the thing, nor the pleasure, that is the trouble. The old Christian teachers said that if man had never fallen, sexual pleasure, insead of being less than it is now, would actually have been greater. I know some muddle-headed Christians have talked as if Christianity thought that sex, or the body, or pleasure, were bad in themselves. But they were wrong. Christianity is almost the only one of the great religions which thoroughly approves of the body — which believes that matter is good, that God Himself once took on a human body, that some kind of body is going to be given to us even in heaven and is going to be an essential part of our happiness, our beauty, and our energy. Christianity has glorified marriage more than any other religion: and nearly all the greatest love poetry in the world has been produced by Christians. If anyone says that sex, in itself, is bad, Christianity contradicts him at once. But, of course,

---

45 Ibid., pp. 116—120.

46 Clive S. Lewis, *Mere Christianity,* 5th ed. (London & Glasgow: Collins Clear-Type Press, 1958), p. 84.

when people say, "Sex is nothing to be ashamed of," they may mean, "The state into which the sexual instinct has now got is nothing to be ashamed of." If they mean that, I think they are wrong.[47]

OPINIONS OF EUROPEAN PROTESTANTS

The One-Flesh Relationship

It is from Europe that the so-called "sacramental" view of marriage and the "mystery of sex" have received their strongest support. Perhaps the best-known advocate of these views is Otto Piper, who has developed them in his book *The Christian Interpretation of Sex*.[48]

Piper centers his whole interpretation of sex in the words "They shall be one flesh." (1) By sexual intercourse a union between the two parties is established such as did not exist before, a union which cannot be understood so long as we regard sexual activity as merely lust or as a desire to propagate. Man and woman thus come to harmony and completion. This is the efficient cause that welds the two persons into a full unity. (2) It is a unity of the flesh or of the body, i. e., of the entire sensuous selfhood of these persons. This union brings the entire natural life of them into a state of mutual dependence, yet without losing their individuality, further seen by the power over their lives which the two persons grant to each other. This union makes a profound change. (3) The union creates a genuine unity and therefore cannot be broken off. It is not temporary or external but genuine and complete. Even a man who has sexual connection with a prostitute is one flesh with her (1 Cor. 6:16). The Bible, Piper asserts, makes the "one flesh" idea central in all its teaching of sex (Lev. 17—20; Matt. 5:32; 19:6 ff.; 1 Cor. 7:4 ff.).[49]

Because this fundamental idea of two-in-one-flesh was allowed to fall into the background and a dualistic metaphysic was accepted instead as a basis, both Roman and Protestant teaching

---

[47] Ibid., pp. 87, 88.

[48] Otto Piper, *The Christian Interpretation of Sex* (New York: Charles Scribner's Sons, 1955). The editors have chosen to classify Piper with the European theologians since the material in his book first appeared in German. He is now a professor at Princeton Theological Seminary.

[49] Ibid., pp. 40, 42, 43.

was distorted, and sex "had to be justified" by various devices.[50] Sex is not primarily connected with the desire to propagate. It occurs in man primarily as a desire for the pleasure one hopes to enjoy in the physical union with another person. Man has a desire both for sexual union and for children. But the mere desire to have children could never stimulate sexual excitement. What binds the two parties together in sexual intercourse is not the intention to have children but the mutual pleasure which they find in each other. To justify sex relations only when procreation is the purpose is to mistake the nature of sex and leads away from the Bible, where sex intercourse per se is regarded as one of the duties of married life (Ex. 21:10; 1 Cor. 7:3 ff.). Neither Paul nor Peter (1 Peter 3:7) limits sex to propogative purposes. The Bible respects fertilization as a mystery and the coming of children as a special blessing.[51]

It is much more than a euphemism when the Bible describes the sex relation as "knowing" a person of the opposite sex. This is not biological knowledge but (1) a strictly personal knowledge; (2) a mutual relationship between the two parties; and (3) an inner secret; it is a mutual self-disclosure, an intuitive knowledge, a knowledge communicable in no other way. It is comprehension of an inner secret. Because of the sanctity of sex this secret is protected in many ways — through privacy, modesty, respect for womanhood. The mystery is this: By sexual contact I learn that by myself I am, and I must always be, a fragment; only my partner enables me to gain my own completeness.[52]

Yet sex is not an end in itself but only a means, nor is the sex relationship the highest goal, for that goal is Christian love (not merely *eros* [physical attraction] or *philia* [friendship], but *agape* [self-giving love]). The two parties find in Christian love that they belong to each other in all the relationships of their life and not merely in those of a sexual character; and the fact that sexual desire finds its true fulfillment in Christian love makes it plain that sex is only one of the many possible genuine relationships between man and woman.[53]

Sex in life is a vital function indispensable for mankind as

50 Ibid., p. 45.
51 Ibid., pp. 47, 49, 51.
52 Ibid., pp. 54, 55, 61.
53 Ibid., p. 77.

a whole only, but not for each individual. While every normal
adult feels sexual desires, these in man are to be under the control of the will.

The Bible bases its valuation of sex on two fundamental ideas:
(1) that the sex function takes the individual out of his isolation
in which he could not fulfill his place in God's creation; (2) that
by virtue of sex the Christian has the possibility of sanctifying
his own body and that of his partner (1 Cor. 7:14; 1 Peter 3:1 f.).
In both ways sex becomes a blessing. The Christian spouse sanctifies even the non-Christian partner by the respectful, reverent
attitude to the other sex, a sort of cleansing effect. Impurity and
lust do not grow in the presence of this sanctity of sex.[54]

"Sex does not represent the animal side of man, nor that of
mere nature as distinct from what is spiritual. Such a deprecia-
tion is in contradiction to the Biblical view of man." "Hence the
real problem of Christian life is not to eradicate sex influence
from the higher realm of life; rather it is to shape and direct sex
through the will of the heart which has been sanctified by God."
It is sex without the knowledge of the inner secret that makes
its destructive and perplexing inroads into our lives.[55]

Jesus left no code of sex ethics but emphasized attitudes in
harmony with life in a one-flesh union. Love, fidelity, accord with
nature, and chastity are the virtues of God-pleasing sex life.
(1) True love is not antithetic to sex love. It is obedience to the
husband, respect for the woman. It regards the partner as a gift
of God, is sacrificial, passionate but not compulsive. (2) Fidelity
depends on respect and can never accept sex relations except
with the marriage partner. (3) Accord with nature means that
the sex relation will be sensuous but not sensual, in agreement
with creation. Both masturbation and homosexuality are contrary
to God's intended heterosexual purposes in creation. (4) Chastity
is the honor paid to the sanctity of the secret of sex. It speaks
reverently of sex and suppresses lustful thoughts. There is
a place for self-discipline, but only the Holy Spirit can give
the Christian awe and respect for sex as God's design.[56]

There is no unconditional right to sexual experience. Sex in-

---

[54] Ibid., pp. 100, 101.
[55] Ibid., pp. 105, 106.
[56] Ibid., p. 148.

tercourse not conjoined with the will for a permanent life in common cannot be justified. Preconjugal sexual intercourse is not outwardly distinguishable from promiscuous intercourse, contributes to the destruction of sex morality, and thus also damages sex life itself.[57]

Sex Life Under Forgiveness

The Danish theologian N. H. Søe holds that the Christian view of sex dare not be founded on the order of creation, since this premise leads easily to natural theology and unbridled naturalism, but rests in the forgiveness of sin by the grace of God in Jesus Christ which covers also the sexual side of life past and present.

For the Christian the will of God is clear and decisive, namely, continence outside marriage (1 Thess. 4: 3-5). The Christian neither rejects sex life as something evil, like the ascetics, nor with Freud accepts sex as the basic human drive, nor with the Gnostics holds that bodily things *(Leiblichkeit)* per se (including sex desire) are evil, but he knows that in the grace of regeneration he receives justification through forgiveness and strives to discover and follow God's will in sexual matters. Not to recognize the place of sex on the one hand is to flatten life. An overemphasis on sex on the other hand actually devalues it. Sex cannot be equated with hunger, since man can live without sexual intercourse but not without food.[58]

Neither License nor Asceticism

A Swedish scholar writing on *Marriage in the New Testament* asserts that primitive Christianity came into contact with two approaches to sex. The one held: "All is lawful for me," and encouraged unbridled license. The New Testament opposed this license. The Christian's entire being, flesh and spirit, lives in Jesus Christ. By fornication he makes his body a member of a harlot.

The other approach was based on the distinction between matter and spirit. Christianity opposed this concept that body is inherently evil and spirit good. Man's flesh as a creation of

---

[57] Ibid., pp. 169, 171.

[58] N. H. Søe, *Christliche Ethik* (München: Chr. Kaiser Verlag, 1949), pp. 288—295.

God is good. Ascetic practices focus a man's attention on himself rather than God. Man may glorify God by living a celibate or a married life.

The essence of marriage is the one-flesh relationship. Man and woman were one in Adam. In marriage that which was one is again reunited. A detailed study of the Hebrew words for flesh and man and woman supports these assertions.[59]

German Churchmen and Sex

Christian Sex Standards

Almost every publisher serving the Evangelical Churches of Germany offers a series of down-to-earth guidebooks on sex and marriage designed for youth and written from a distinctly Christian point of view, upholding Christian standards and calling upon the exercise of enlightened Christian judgment. One such series of books is entitled *Girls, Love, and Young Men*. Warning against identification of love with sexual relations, one of these books says:

> How is it that the same thing, sexual intercourse, is evil, forbidden, and sinful before marriage, while in marriage, all at once, this is allowed, commanded, and "belongs"? This is so because in the second case we are dealing with marriage and the marriage partner. The emphasis is not so much on procedure but on the partner. With whom does one have sexual relations? With a person to whom one is committed and entrusted in marriage for the duration of life. The total life fellowship of marriage requires also a one-flesh relationship (*Leibesgemeinschaft*), the limited relationship before marriage excludes this *Leibesgemeinschaft*.

Careful distinctions are made between things and people, sex exploitation and true regard for persons, true love and lustful desire, mate love and self-love. The emphasis is on respect for the other person, respect for the other sex, respect for the God-instituted marriage relationship. Love, it is said, cannot be forced, made to order, or "organized." What we have experienced accompanies us throughout life consciously or unconsciously. This is true especially of all relations with the other sex.[60]

---

[59] Evald Lövestam, *Aktenskapet i Nya Testamentet* (Lund: C. W. R. Gleerup, 1950), pp. 1, 2, 14—17, 19—33, 34 ff.

[60] G. N. Groeger, *Man hat doch ein Recht auf Liebe*, in the series *Mädchen, Liebe und junge Männer* (Nürnberg: Laetare Verlag, 1953), pp. 21, 22, 30. Other books in this series: *Freundschaft, Verhältnis, Partnerschaft* (1956); *Angst und Freude der Geschlechtsentwicklung* (1954).

The Christian Ethic

Paul Althaus of the theological faculty of the University of Erlangen writes:

> Marriage is the standard for all meeting of the sexes, also for life before marriage. . . . This means a clear "no" to the "affair" or "friendship" which desires no lasting union and still carries through a "one-flesh" relationship. . . . The Christian ethic does not demand of youth principles that destroy life, but, on the contrary, guidelines which lead to a full and wholesome life in love, principles which prove to be always beneficial to those who follow them. God's ordinances in this area do not impoverish life but desire to give full happiness and love to man and woman. God's commandment spares us from immature desire (*Gier*) for each other and from irresponsible love play with each other, by which the precious mystery of sex love is desecrated and loses its dignity and its genuine joy.[61]

Love and Marriage

In his textbook *Grundriss der Ethik* Althaus outlines the relationship between love and marriage in chapter xxxiii, "Liebe und Ehe," which is summarized below.

The norms of relations between the sexes arise out of (1) the equality of man and woman before God, as being heirs together of God's grace, 1 Peter 3:7, and with regard to their relation to God's kingdom, Gal. 3:28; and (2) the duality or diversity of the sexes in creation as intended for living for each other and with each other according to their distinctive gifts (Gen. 2:18).

We recognize the natural love of man and woman for each other as part of God's creation (Gen. 2:24). The purpose and meaning of this love is the full surrender of man and wife in the total surrender of flesh and spirit for full community of life. This full sexual surrender has two purposes: to express the full physical unity and community and to serve the desire for offspring.

The fall into sin has disturbed also God's order for sexual love and adulterated it with lust, self-glorification, and mere sexual gratification, making the man and wife sexually subordinate to each other (*sexuellgehörig*), Gen. 3:16. The original

---

[61] Paul Althaus, *Die Begegnung der Geschlechter* (Erlangen-Bavaria, n. d.).

design for love can be realized *(erfüllt)* only through a constant battle against lust *(Sucht)*.

Thus the Christian cannot accept pure unbridled naturalism on the one hand, nor the asceticism which regards sexual love as sin, contrary to Christian truth, but must hold to God's original design over against and despite misrepresentation.

The sense of shame accompanies the sexual life as peculiar to the human being. It is to be differentiated from shame regarding wrongdoing and shame from a sense of guilt. It goes along with and belongs to the right enjoyment of sexual communion. This sense of shame serves a number of purposes. It veils or covers through silence and concealment the sex organs and act. It tends to preserve privacy and protects the physical aspects of love in which man and wife belong exclusively to each other. It likewise serves to veil the mystery of procreation. It shields coition from constantly threatening desecration. So it assists in the battle for the discipline of the sexual life. Social mores and education should help preserve this useful sense of shame.

Chastity is an attitude which desires to keep physical love wholly within a personal relationship. It is an attitude of the whole person — his thoughts, speech, and behavior in marriage as well as outside marriage. Althaus considers shame an essential characteristic of chastity.[62]

The Basic Nature of Love

Much of the evangelical literature of Germany deals with the basic nature of love in its several aspects. Prof. Karl Seiler of Erlangen speaks of the exclusiveness of mature love. Mature love of the sexes is possible only in relation to one person. Three basic powers belong to this love and harmony in marriage: (1) tenderness *(Zärtlichkeit)*, the capacity and personal need for caresses and fondling, which begins already in earliest childhood and is necessary for marital happiness; (2) idealistic love, known also as *eros,* which seeks an ideal to love and imitate already early in life and looks for this ideal in the beloved during mating; and (3) the sexual attraction *(körperlich-seelisches Hingezogensein)* to the other person with the idea of propaga-

[62] Paul Althaus, *Grundriss der Ethik* (Gütersloh: Bertelsmann, 1953), pp. 113—122.

tion, which awakens at puberty. In order that these three basic powers may mature and marital harmony and companionship be achieved, a fourth power is needed: self-giving, sacrificial love, or *agape*. Marriage will not last or come to its peak of satisfaction without this self-giving love. It is an error to think that this mature love comes without effort. It is rather a development after years of faithfulness. Such love is not impatient or easily discouraged. It is aided greatly by deep religious convictions.

Seiler says: "There is no experience that grows together with religion more intimately than a full and mature love." He compares love and religion to two streams that flow together into the river of full life.[63]

Prudery or Sex Education?

Regarding the necessity of sex education Rudolf Hirzel writes:

> The human being is either man or woman, never just a human being. His sex is determined already in the womb. . . . New human life proceeds only through the union of man and woman. From all of this it is clear that sexual attraction grows in the individual, that it must be strong, and that it begins to assert itself before full maturity, especially mental and emotional maturity, is achieved. It is further clear that we accomplish very little that is intelligent and effective with mere prohibition, scolding, and complaining. He who wants simply to suppress these sexual drives, whether in others or in himself, represses them only to have them break out in an uncontrollable and more dangerous way. (Control is something altogether different than suppression!)[64]

> It is also clear that these powers of sex in themselves are neither good nor bad but simply exist. Whether they exercise good or evil effects is wholly dependent on how they are used. For this reason the traditional prudery of respectable people had only ominous results. This prudery left the discussion of matters of sex to the smutpeddlers (*Schmutzfinken*) . . . and was silent when and where it was a duty to speak. This prudery prevented the discussion of sex questions in the nurture of the child, and a rightful place was

---

[63] Karl Seiler, *Ich bin ja so in dich verliebt,* of the series, *Unser Weg in die Ehe* (München: Claudius Verlag, 1955), pp. 2, 7—13.

[64] Rudolph Hirzel, *Wir Männer und die Frauen,* Heft I in *Schriftenreihe der Protestantischen Eheberatung* (St. Gallen: Vadian Verlag, 1949), p. 7.

denied to it in the training of youth. In doing so prudery made matters of sex something secretive and unwholesome for the child and something unwholesome and lustful (*zu etwas Unheimlich-Reizvollem*) for youth; then, afterwards, it resorted to moralizing! . . . Behind this false position, this incompetence to speak, lies more helplessness and need than folly. The results nevertheless are the same.[65]

German authors treat many phases of the sex drive. Love in marriage as expressed in sexual intercourse is the "continual proving of trust toward the marriage partner." [66] Sex, however, is not primary, as many moderns think. Marriage is not a partial phenomenon of sex, but sex is a partial phenomenon of marriage.[67] Mere sexual union does not really satisfy modern man's mental and emotional needs.[68] It is the spiritual side of sex that distinguishes marriage from prostitution.[69] Nor can love be reduced to glandular or chemical action of the body.[70]

Premarital intercourse, considered by some a safety valve for sex desire, is always a confession of weakness.[71] The unmarried woman can have an abundant life without sex expression, since the woman is by nature sexually passive.[72] Both masturbation and homosexuality frustrate the "sacramental" character of marriage.[73] One author distinguishes between habitual masturbation and "substitute" masturbation.[74]

All of the writers encourage a kind of sex education that is not "too little and too late." There should be no poisoning of the minds by the use of such terms as "lower instincts." [75] Sex edu-

---

[65] Ibid., p. 8.

[66] Ernest Michel, *Ehe, Eine Anthropologie der Geschlechtsgemeinschaft* (Stuttgart: Ernst Klett, 1948), pp. 71—76.

[67] Ibid., pp. 198, 199.

[68] Ibid., pp. 113, 114.

[69] Helmuth Schreiner, *Ethos und Daemonie der Liebe* (Gütersloh: C. Bertelsmann, 1950), pp. 34—36.

[70] Hans von Hattingberg, *Ueber die Liebe* (München-Basel: Ernst Reinhardt, 1949), pp. 24—30. The author mentions the theories of Freud, of Nietzsche (the innocence of the senses), and of Lenin ("glass of water" theory).

[71] Theodor Bovet, *Die Ehe* (Tübingen: Furche Verlag, 1948) pp. 202, 203.

[72] Schreiner, pp. 108, 109.

[73] Ibid., pp. 92—96.

[74] Hattingberg, pp. 55, 56.

[75] Bovet, p. 201.

cation by pastors is strongly urged, and an attitude of acceptance and forgiveness is recommended as absolutely necessary for pastoral counseling on sexual problems.[76]

MODERN ROMAN CATHOLIC VIEWS

Modern Roman Catholic writers speak of the physical relationships in marriage as being natural, normal, and consequently good. They agree with the Code of Canon Law (Canon 1013) that the procreation and education of children is (in the scholastic philosophical sense) the primary, "specifying" purpose of marriage. What they term the secondary but no less real and objective purposes (companionship, relief of tension, satisfaction of desire) are always to be subordinated to the primary purpose; in fact, they exist so that the primary end may be more easily and fully achieved. Marriage, as they view it, places a couple into an "ongoing, procreative status" which embraces all these purposes.

Of sex in human beings Msgr. Fulton J. Sheen writes:

> The equation of man with the animal is a great fallacy. . . .
> In the animal sex is mechanical, a matter of stimulus and response. In man it is linked with mystery and freedom.
> In the animal it is only a release of tension; in man its occurrence is determined by no natural rhythm, but by the will. . . .
> Sex instinct in a pig and love in a person are not the same, precisely because love is found in the will, not in the glands.[77]

A Human Act Full of Grace

Roman Catholic author Thomas Gilbey (T. G. Wayne) points up the more positive, modern approach to sex in marriage:

> It is important to realize that the [sexual] passion is not just tolerated in marriage, condoned as rather unworthy yet all the same necessary. It leads up to and is present in sacramental marriage, and there finds its complete and gracious expression.
>
> Sex intercourse enjoyed rightly and in a human way is an act of the virtue of purity. It is none the colder for that. Purity is not the absence or denial of passion, but is passion justly ordered. In this matter a married couple will help one another. Their bodies are granted, their passions satisfied, not

---

76 Wolfgang Trillhaas, *Der Dienst der Kirche am Menschen* (München: Chr. Kaiser, 1950), pp. 192, 193.

77 Fulton J. Sheen, *Peace of Soul* (London: Blandford Press, 1950), pp. 155, 165.

by indulgence, for that defeats its own end, but by a human act full of grace, that does not diminish but rather increases the ardor, even the passion of love.[78]

In a paper on "Sex Education and Moral Values" Theodore M. Hesburgh, president of the University of Notre Dame, South Bend, Ind., writes: "Both [Puritanism among Protestants and Jansenism among Catholics] regarded sex with great suspicion, in some ways identifying it with concupiscence and sin. Under this scheme of moral values, it was impossible to integrate sex into any healthy philosophy of life. Sex became shameful instead of sacred; it was something divorced from any reasonable consideration of man's personal or social development." [79]

He describes the present situation as one in which sex is divorced from man's destiny and moral values: "The empirical search for 'what is' [the Kinsey Report] replaces the normative study of 'what ought to be.' " [80]

Hesburgh says marriage has a double function, "it is by nature reproductive . . . and it is also a divinely ordained and specially unifying act of love between husband and wife. . . . It seems important for a healthy and wholesome approach to sex education that while the primary and intrinsic function be recognized, the secondary and no less essential function of manifesting mutual love be presented to young people as a purposeful goal for sex." [81] In a summary statement Hesburgh says:

> Nothing is unmentionable about the sexual drive that God designed to bring man and woman together for the propagation of the human race and the personal perfection of each other. Nor need we disguise the pleasure that God designed to ease the burdens and responsibilities of married life, and to highlight the perfect communication of marital love. There is only evil in this scheme when the pleasure of sex is sought for itself, and separated from the responsibilities of sex. . . . Within marriage, seeking only the pleasure of the state with

---

[78] Thomas Gilbey (T. G. Wayne), *Morals and Marriage: The Catholic Background to Sex* (London: Longmans, Green & Co., 1952), pp. 86, 89. See also Marc Oraison, *Union in Marital Love* (New York: Macmillan, 1958), p. 63: "Conjugal chastity shall not then primarily consist in *avoiding sin*, but rather in moving together toward a commonly achieved balance and poise which will be an emancipation from instinctive compulsions."

[79] Theodore M. Hesburgh, "Sex Education and Moral Values," in *Social Hygiene Papers: A Symposium on Sex Education* (New York: American Social Hygiene Association, November 1957), p. 18.

[80] Ibid., p. 19.

[81] Ibid., p. 21.

deliberate and artificial frustration of the procreative purpose-
fulness of the sexual act is another example of divorcing
responsibility from pleasure.[82]

Messenger in his three-volume work first appearing in 1948 [83]
admits that some of the church fathers set forth teachings that
were to all appearances antisex, antimarriage, and even anti-
woman. He cites more than a dozen factors in the popular
teaching and tradition of Roman Catholicism which account for
this antisexual bias. He concedes that this attitude is corroborated by some aspects of Roman Catholic philosophy, doctrine,
and practice. He indicates that much of this opinion still prevails.
However, he maintains that this attitude was never in the main
stream of Christian thought. He cites as an admirable summary
of his own position a statement by Canon Knoch:

> Our aim is to make it clear that the exercise of the marriage
> act (copula maritalis) is an action which is good and holy, and
> not an evil or unclean one (res inhonesta), or something which
> is degrading to man. In point of fact, an inexact and unworthy
> idea of this act is not rare, and it is sometimes supported by
> a certain asceticism: but it is nevertheless erroneous, and in
> opposition to the Christian moral system.

Messenger goes on to say that Romanist theologians and
philosophers frequently confused continence and celibacy with
chastity, which according to Thomas Aquinas is a virtue which
moderates the exercise of the sex function in accordance with
right reason, belonging in the same category with temperance
(not to be confused with complete abstinence). After briefly
reviewing the teachings of the Old and New Testaments and
the findings of natural science and philosophy, he concludes that
"all are bound to observe chastity, but not all are expected to
possess or exercise the virtue of continence." In his conclusion
of Book One Messenger states: "There is, thus, abundant evidence in Scripture, science, and philosophy that sex is a divine
institution, and that its rightful exercise in marriage cannot be
otherwise than good." [84]

---

[82] Ibid., p. 21.

[83] Ernest C. Messenger, *Two in One Flesh*, 2d ed., (Westminster, Md.:
The Newman Press, 1950); Vol. I: *Introduction to Sex and Marriage;*
Vol. II: *The Mystery of Sex and Marriage in Catholic Theology;* Vol. III:
*The Practice of Sex and Marriage with Illustrations from the Catholic
Liturgy.*

[84] Messenger, I, 1—57, especially pages 1—12, 51, 57. On page 12 he cites
A. Knoch, *L'Éducation de la Chasteté* (4th ed., 1921), p. 102. See also Flor-

The Roman Catholic Church, while acknowledging the attend-
ant pleasure in the sex act, rules out intercourse which is divorced from the procreative, primary purpose and pursued for
selfish enjoyment only. One of their writers, in treating of the
moral issues involved, states the point thus:

> Sex pleasure has been added to sex function as an incentive
> for married people to perform the sex function. If the sex
> function is performed normally and naturally, as dictated by
> instinct and reason, it will be in conformity with the design
> of the Creator of man and bring about the result He intended
> by instituting conjugal society and the sexual relations of hus-
> band and wife, namely, the procreation of children and the
> subsequent preservation of the human race.[85]

Referring to the use of sex outside of marriage, another
Roman Catholic writer says: "Any enjoyment of the pleasure
connected with the work of procreation, and deliberate and
voluntary sex enjoyment, apart from the marriage state, is
gravely sinful . . . because it separates the physical act from its
complete purpose, and because it is the enjoyment of an animal
sensation in a manner unfitted for rational creatures destined
for the vision of God."[86] "In her ethics," says Father Schmiedeler,
"the church rejects all gratification of the sex instinct apart from
the responsibility of family life. Any use of the instinct for
purely selfish reasons is ever banned as fundamentally unchristian."[87]

One of the best attempts on the part of modern Roman Catholic theologians to deal with new psychological insights on the
one hand and a more Biblical view on the other hand is made
by the French priest Marc Oraison. He speaks of sex as an
expression of love in marriage, and chastity as sex under control
in marriage.

> Love means the total mutual gift of self; the acceptance of
> the necessity of a corporate asceticism; the joint training
> of the sexual instinct and its orientation toward goals that
> transcend its own quality; the refusal to dissociate sex from

ence Giammarino's article "Married Chastity" in *Marriage,* The Magazine
for Catholic Family Living, XLIII, No. 1 (Jan. 1961), 6—10.

[85] Celestine N. Bittle, *Man and Morals* (Milwaukee: Bruce Publishing
Co., 1949), p. 216.

[86] Wingfield Hope, *Life Together* (New York: Sheed and Ward, 1943),
p. 155.

[87] Edgar Schmiedeler, *Marriage and the Family* (New York: McGraw-
Hill, 1946), p. 216.

its reproductive ends; the curbing in each mate of selfish reflexes even in carnal union. Such are the essential points of the Church's moral and ideal directive teaching on marriage as related to humanity's ultimate destiny: the world of the resurrection.[88]

Thus it would appear that modern Roman Catholic writers are returning to the main stream of Christian thought as regards the exercise of sex within marriage. Many, however, tie it so closely to reproduction and child nurture that one wonders what its function is where barrenness or infertility appears or what its function is after the menopause.

Masturbation

Alexander A. Schneiders, director of the Office of Psychological Services at Fordham University, in the Roman Catholic family magazine *Marriage* writes that masturbation is "a moral problem, objectively sinful" because it is self-gratifying and more or less deliberate. Yet he qualifies this by saying that the circumstances must be taken into account in each instance "before we can say it is immoral or gravely sinful." He states that available evidence indicates that 85 to 95 per cent of young boys masturbate. He warns against the use of false or judgmental labels like "self-abuse" or "onanism," which do much emotional damage and carry unproved implications.

He distinguishes between exploratory sex play and compulsive masturbation. Masturbation has spiritual, social, and psychological aspects. The sex drive is not the only cause. Frustrations, conflicts, deprivations, unsatisfactory personal relations with parents or other persons, and immaturity may be underlying causes. "The more a person is affected by causes he is unaware of the less control he has over his actions." The act itself leads to anxiety, guilt feelings, extreme embarrassment, shame, moral weakness, and a sense of worthlessness. For these reasons people should "be careful not to treat masturbation merely as a moral problem."

Schneiders also warns against moralizing and against using negative approaches and unproved statements regarding the effects of masturbation. Parents can (1) provide adequate sex instruction (which he considers the most effective preventive),

---

[88] Oraison, p. 65.

(2) show that mate love and sex are to be thought of together,
(3) improve their own understanding of sexual development,
(4) help the child develop healthy self-identification regarding
sex through good relations with father (boy) and mother (girl),
(5) use moral and religious means to support the training. Since
neither the parents nor the priest are ordinarily qualified to distinguish one cause from another, there are times when expert
counsel must be sought, especially where deeper personality
problems may be involved.[89]

What Is Impure?

Roman Catholicism has always given a great deal of attention
to moral theology in all of its aspects, basing its teachings on the
principles of Thomas Aquinas. To apply those laws to changing
modern times it has a code of regulations. In the book *Moral
Theology* obscenity is defined as "a quality of words, acts or
objects by which impure thoughts are conveyed, or impure desires
or actions suggested." [90]

> The obscenity of dress is largely dependent on its novelty,
> for things that are usual cease to excite special attention.
> This we can see from the fact that styles that are conservative
> today would have been extreme ten years ago. And so the
> scanty attire of hot countries, the dress of the bathing beach,
> and the moderate decolleté tolerated in private gatherings are
> not obscene in their own proper times and places.[91]

The subject of the dance is treated as follows:

> The fact that some individuals find all dancing a strong stim-
> ulus to impure passion does not prove that every dance is
> obscene. . . . But there are also standard types of dance in
> which many experience not temptation, but innocent pastime,
> and which have also physical, esthetic and social values.[92]

Roman Catholics and Sex Education

Regarding sex education a modern Roman Catholic writer
says: "The church is not in favor of indiscriminate sex education
or exposing youth to the occasions of sin in order to harden them

---

[89] *Marriage,* The Magazine of Catholic Family Living, XLI (Sept.
1959), 38—43.

[90] John A. McHugh and Charles J. Callan, *Moral Theology,* rev. and
enlarged by Edward P. Farrell (New York: Joseph F. Wagner, Inc., 1958),
Sec. 1455, I, 587.

[91] Ibid., Sec. 1457, I, 589.

[92] Ibid., Sec. 1457, I, 590.

against temptation. It insists on the avoidance of the occasion and [on] the positive cultivation of ascetic ideals, reception of the sacraments, etc. . . . It is not forbidden under certain conditions to impart prudently necessary instruction on sex matters, but knowledge alone is not sufficient." [93]

A more encouraging attitude toward sex education is expressed by one Roman Catholic writer when he says: "The knowledge of sex should be given to children gradually in accordance with their needs and natural curiosity, but with sufficient opportunities to forestall the wrong type of knowledge that is very likely to come from undesirable sources. . . . Innocence is not to be identified with ignorance." [94]

The Council of American Catholic Bishops, in a statement of November 1950, "The Child, Citizen of Two Worlds," expressed itself as follows:

> Fathers and mothers have a natural competence to instruct their children concerning sex. False modesty should not deter them from doing their duty in this regard. Sex is one of God's endowments. It should not be ignored or treated as something bad. If sex instruction is properly carried on in the home, a deep reverence will be developed in the child, and he will be spared the shameful references which he often makes when he is left to himself to find out about sex. . . . To be of benefit such instruction must be far broader than the imparting of information. . . . Sex is more than a biological function. It is bound up with the sacredness and the uniqueness of the human personality. It can be fully and properly appreciated only within a religious and moral context. If treated otherwise, the child will see it apart from the controlling purpose of his life, which is service to God.[95]

SUMMARY

1. Protestant theologians in both America and Europe are almost unanimous in developing a view of sex based on the order of creation. Sex is a gift of God, created for the well-being of man, further sanctified by the teachings of Christ and the

---

[93] H. A. Ayrinhac, *Marriage Legislation in the New Code of Canon Law*, revised and enlarged by P. J. Lydon (New York: Benziger Bros., Inc., 1949), p. 295. For a more positive Catholic view on the necessity of sex education see Oraison, pp. 102—105.

[94] A. H. Clemens, *Marriage and Family Relations* (Washington: Catholic University of America Press, 1950), p. 8.

[95] Quoted by Hesburgh, p. 19.

apostles. They trace confusion regarding sex attitudes to three errors, not fully expelled from popular Christianity: that sex sins are the worst sins, that the things of the body are evil, and that pleasure in sex is wrong.

2. They also agree that sexual desire is not in itself a sin, that sexual union for its unitive and pleasurable purposes, rather than for procreative purposes only, is normal, natural, and Biblical. Sex serves man biologically, socially, psychologically, and spiritually.

3. Sex, however, is made for full expression in the marriage relationship and not apart from it. Sexual intercourse is the one-flesh union of man and wife to express a spiritual unity like that between Christ and His church. This union many call symbolical or sacramental. The mystery of sex is finding in conjugal union the completion of self.

4. Sexual intercourse outside the permanent marital union is never right. It exploits other persons, degrades marriage, harms society, and does injury to self and others, disregarding the sanctity of sex and the will of God.

5. Sex is intended for heterosexual use. Masturbation, when continued and compulsive, and homosexuality are contrary to God's purposes and to be treated as personality problems.

6. Self-control and continence have their rightful place in all of life. Chastity is ordering the sex life to conform to God's will for man. Sex in man is under the control of his will. In the Christian this will is to be God-controlled and desires to glorify God also in the body. The human will is, of course, subject to human weakness. Sex attraction and sex appeal within right bounds are part of God's plan, but petting, being part of preparation for coitus, is to be reserved for marriage — outside marriage it is not only sinful but unwise and unkind.

7. Sex can be underemphasized as well as overemphasized. Sex is one of the deepest, most meaningful expressions of mature love between marriage partners. Christian conjugal love will include *eros* (passion), *philia* (companionship), and *agape* (self-giving love).

8. Sex education of the right kind is necessary. It should not be "too little or too late" and should replace prudery, which

is dishonest, unbiblical, and harmful. Accepting a system of Christian values is more important, however, than the mere facts of life. Character determines sexual behavior. Roman Catholic writers are usually fearful of any sex education "outside" their church. It is favored only within a religious and moral context.

9. It is easy to misinterpret the position of Roman Catholicism. The ascetic, almost antisexual tradition in the popular mind is held alongside the writings and teachings which assert that sex in marriage is an ongoing, rightful expression of love and devotion resting upon God's ordinance in creation and is never to be disassociated from its "primary" ends. Some theologians, they say, have misinterpreted chastity by identifying it with continence. Instead they define it as the virtue which moderates the exercise of the sex function in accordance with right reason.

CHAPTER 11

The Views of Social Scientists

THE SCIENTIFIC APPROACH TO SEX

Historical Background

DURING THE LATTER PART of the 19th century the Christian influence was the dominant factor in determining the standards
and patterns of sex behavior. With the passing of the frontier
the pattern of sex attitudes in the United States reached a climax
in the age of Victorianism and the "Gay Nineties." This pattern persisted without serious challenge until World War I.
Restraint in all matters related to sex was regarded as the ideal.[1]

Within the social and ethical milieu of the period, respectability was the reward to women for observing the ideal code;
modesty was the virtue which adorned women and maidens,
although men were allowed more freedom. In this social setting
the natural curiosity of a child about the origins of life was
suppressed; the social penalties visited upon deviations were
quite severe; and the castigations imposed were often illogical,
unfair, and cruel. Yet they were supported because they were
regarded as right and functionally necessary.

When the 20th century began, two significant influences for
change in the prevailing sex mores may be noted. One was the
flood of literature on the subject from London, and the other

---

[1] Sylvanus M. Duvall describes the sex standard of this period in
Men, Women, and Morals (New York: Association Press, 1952), p. 8, as
follows: "This involved, briefly, the elimination of sex from life, at least
outside of marriage, as completely as possible. Really 'pure' Christians
would not only refrain from actual sexual intercourse outside of marriage; they would also avoid minor forms of sex behavior, such as hugging,
kissing, or flirtatious glances and conversation except when marriage was
definitely intended. Even then they practiced chaste restraint."

was Sigmund Freud. Without Englishman Havelock Ellis (1859 to 1939), for example, would there have been an Alfred Kinsey? Without Austria's Freud (1856—1939), would there have come into being the various psychoanalytic interpretations of sex? Ellis popularized frank talk about sex. His seven-volume *Studies in the Psychology of Sex* [2] was kept locked up in most libraries for years but broke the trail for numerous candid paperbacks now commonplace in almost any bookstand. According to William G. Cole, the "house that Freud built" in his writings from 1895 to 1949 (the last published posthumously) "was built upon the foundation of therapy, an intimate and immediate concern for diagnosing and treating patients who were emotionally or mentally disturbed." Freud saw man as a totality, with sex as the most important part of his nature. He was a rationalist who sought to bring the irrational, primitive side of human nature under the disciplined control of reason. Freud believed that when sex plays its proper, ordered role in the total pattern of the personality, it can contribute to growth, development, and physical and emotional health.[3] This latter was the rationale which was adopted by the majority of the social scientists who wrote after 1930.

The 20th century began with a plethora of sexologic writings. The Freudian psychology suited the openness of the age well, championing expression over repression and happily confirming the spirit of revealment as opposed to concealment. Novelists and poets had begun practicing sexual freedom and writing about it in the prewar years and enlarged their output in the years after World War I. Theodoor H. van de Velde's *Ideal Marriage,* a very complete and detailed study of the physiology and technique of sex in marriage, gained him the reputation of "the master sex engineer." [4] Copyrighted in 1926 and translated into English in 1930, the book has had thirty-four printings by Random House since 1941. The "sex engineers"

---

[2] This work was written between 1897 and 1928 and published in this country (1901—28) by F. A. Davis, Philadelphia, in seven volumes, and by Random House, New York, 1936, in four volumes.

[3] William G. Cole, *Sex in Christianity and Psychoanalysis* (New York: Oxford University Press, 1955), pp. 234, 236.

[4] Theodoor H. van de Velde, *Ideal Marriage: The Physiology and Technique of Marriage,* trans. F. W. Stella Browne (New York: Friede Covici, Inc., 1930).

found a ready market, but it is a universally accepted fact among psychologists, psychiatrists, and sociologists (also Van de Velde) that happiness in marriage involves very much more than the ability to employ the proper sex techniques.

As the social science movement began to gather momentum in the United States, more and more effort was directed toward applying the methods of scientific research to courtship, marriage, and family life. This movement has resulted in the publication of a mass of research material, most of it since 1930.

Social scientists have been in the thick of the search for the "greatest good," believing that science offers the essential method for studying phenomena and that the scientific approach can be applied to anything, whether it be rocks, protons, or people. Two main streams of ethical philosophies are distinguishable among the social or behavioral scientists. The one finds the ultimate good on the biopsychological level, that is, in human happiness, however designated or qualified. Adjustment or therapy are the watchwords. The other finds the *summum bonum* in some nonbiological condition or relationship which is often expressed in metaphysical, mystical, or theological terms.

Those who are eclectic in their approach have gathered the largest following and become the most utilitarian.[5] Many sociologists declare that ethical concepts do not belong to their domain, that their task is to describe and explain, not evaluate. These remain on the level of pragmatic humanism. Others, however, taking a different approach, make ethical evaluations and set up norms of human behavior. They base their position on a number of factors: the need for common codes of conduct, the value of true religious and moral convictions for the proper regulation of sex, and personal experience. They assert that biology, sociology, and psychology by themselves cannot settle the problems of human behavior.

It would, however, be misleading to trace the present freedom in sex expression entirely to Havelock Ellis, Sigmund Freud,

---

[5] Cf. Judson T. Landis and Mary G. Landis, *Building a Successful Marriage,* 3d ed. (New York: Prentice-Hall, 1958); Ray E. Baber, *Marriage and the Family* (New York: McGraw-Hill, 1953); Evelyn Duvall and Reuben Hill, *When You Marry* (New York: D. C. Heath & Co., 1953); Paul H. Landis, *Your Marriage and Family Living* (New York: McGraw-Hill, 1946); and Paul H. Landis, *Making the Most of Marriage* (New York: Appleton-Century-Crofts, 1955).

Alfred Kinsey, and the scientific movement they represent. Two world wars have greatly altered our way of life and helped to break down moral barriers. The postwar upgrading of our economy with the increase of material wealth and the resultant softness and ease, the greater amount of leisure, the effect of more leisure on our philosophy of work, the hedonism expressed in so many ways and through so many media, the great increase in the number of women in the labor force, the change of status for women which this has brought about, progress in the realm of transportation and the resultant mobility, household appliances and the greater freedom of women, the change in the functions of the family, the Hollywood type of romance, the movie and television glorification of sex, the exploitation of human sexuality for personal gain, the focus on sex by much of the advertising industry, the sophistication of sex in some magazines and the sadistic treatment in off-color magazines,[6] the sex emphasis in newspaper comics, the popular idea that marriage can be built upon *eros* (romantic love) — all of these and similar influences have made an indelible impression on our society and are among the chief reasons why a total re-education concerning marriage and sex is needed. The changes in our society in a single decade are greater than those which formerly transpired in a century. The social scientist has done much to help the church recognize and evaluate these changes.

The Scientist and Sex Morals

The social scientists, as a whole, do not reject the insights of great philosophies and religious tenets but use them to guide rather than to enslave. To them the final authority will not be a piece of writing or a great person but the actual facts of experience. The social scientist relies on technical research and tries to fit theories to social facts rather than social facts to theories. He is concerned about sex attitudes and sexual behavior because of the problems of health, social relationships,

---

6 It is estimated that pornography in the United States is annually a five-hundred-million-dollar industry. Ralph A. Cannon and Glenn D. Everett, "Sex and Smut on the Newsstands," in *Christianity Today*, II (Feb. 17, 1958), 5—8; Arthur E. Summerfield, "The Challenge of Obscenity — A Major Threat to Our Children," in *American Lutheran*, XLIII (May 1960), 6—8, 30.

and personality adjustment which are involved. Duvall, for example, observes:

> As our sex code becomes more scientific it will also become more precise. . . . A sex code which can draw only one line and call everything on the one side moral and everything on the other side immoral is far too crude. To be usable it must be able to evaluate the relative morality of sex behavior in a large variety of situations. Only a scientific sex code which makes distinctions with some degree of precision can win or even merit general acceptance. . . . A good sex code is the best possible compromise of divergent factors which we can devise.[7]

One may say that at the present moment scientific ideology has transferred the whole field of human emotions and behavior, including sex and reproduction, from the realm and control of magic, metaphysics, and theology to the realm and control of realistic, scientific thinking. Social scientists hold that "freedom" of love today is not simply another outburst of frivolity and licentiousness. Folsom comments on this, saying: "The modern writer is not 'in his cups,' so to speak, when he praises sex, but is very sober. He is advocating not primarily a freedom of love from marriage, but from the supernatural ideology which held it in its chains as an instrument of biological reproduction. Darwin, Pavlov, and Freud, indirectly, have been among the emancipators, and contraception has been the material technique of emancipation."[8]

Hornell Hart, admitting the causal influences of the automobile, birth control, urbanization, and the breakdown of patriarchal ideology, states "that a major factor in recent shifts of attitudes toward sex behavior has been the breakdown of traditional religious control and partially worked out attempts to substitute scientific criteria."[9]

Though many changes have taken place in America since 1900 which have influenced the mores of her people, a careful and

---

[7] Duvall, *Men, Women, and Morals*, pp. 53—55. It is to be noted, however, that his approach from science and reason led to a general confirmation of the Christian code of ethics.

[8] Joseph K. Folsom, *The Family: Its Sociology and Social Psychiatry* (New York: John Wiley & Sons, Inc., 1934), p. 230.

[9] Hornell Hart, *Recent Social Trends in the United States* (New York: McGraw-Hill, 1933), p. 421.

critical appraisal of the present attitudes toward sex reveals
that the ideals which constitute the essence of our inherited sex
code are still with us and that in many respects the approach is
more religious.

Duvall observes:

> Like most moral codes, the sex code will continue to be
> extensively violated in the future as it has been in the past.
> But I can see no basis for expecting that the ideal of restricting
> sexual intercourse to marriage will be significantly changed
> in the predictable future. Some social influences, such as
> the increased social pressures growing out of crisis and the
> greater spirit of "permissiveness," make for more laxity.
> On the other hand, the religious influences which have sup-
> ported the older code have materially increased in influence
> and power, and a much larger proportion of our people are
> now in the middle class which sociologically has been the
> bulwark of the code. In short, the predominant weight of the
> agencies of "respectability" are still solidly behind premarital
> chastity and postmarital fidelity.[10]

Though there may be laxity of morals today, the cause may
not be traced alone to the scientific view of life. Social scientists
view sexual activity as a psychophysiological function having to
do with those instincts which are at the root of social affections.
They also maintain that unrestricted license is psychologically,
no less than socially, incompatible with those instincts which
constitute the psychical bond of the relation between men and
women. These bonds, say the social scientists, cannot be preserved without subjecting sexual activity to the limitations dic-
tated by mutual devotion and common interests.[11]

The social scientists have gathered much factual data which
has been incorporated into their psychological-sociological-ethical
systems. One cannot say that the sexual behavior of the modern
human being has not come under careful scrutiny. Let us turn
now to what the social scientists have to say about sex attitudes.

---

[10] Duvall, *Men, Women, and Morals*, p. 27. See also Henry A. Bowman,
A Christian Interpretation of Marriage (Philadelphia: Westminster Press,
1959), pp. 29—48.

[11] See Robert Briffault's discussion under "Chastity" in *Encyclopedia
of the Social Sciences*, ed. Edwin R. A. Seligman (New York: Macmillan,
1937), III, 358.

THE PLACE OF SEX IN MARRIAGE

Modern secular literature maintains that sex is not the whole of marriage [12] and that there is no sound reason for assuming that the purpose of sexual union in human beings is only or primarily for reproduction.[13] At the same time it also affirms that in most societies sexual gratification is not the primary purpose of marriage, but rather the legitimacy of the offspring and their care and training through the early years.[14] Yet sexual expression in marriage is useful because it serves as a release of physical tensions, satisfies in a purely physical sense, and expresses fulfillment for the entire marriage relationship.[15] This is confirmed by sound medical opinion.[16]

Social scientists agree that the attainment of sexual togetherness is an important factor in achieving cohesiveness in marriage. Optimum sexual satisfaction comes, however, only to those couples who have found a high degree of happiness in other areas of their lives.[17] Sexual union is but one of a complicated set of relationships and activities which make up the whole interactional pattern of a marriage.[18] The sex attraction can serve to enhance and color all husband-wife associations. Studies among happily married couples all agree that a mutually satisfying sex relationship is one of the important factors that contribute to happiness in marriage.[19] Kinsey's study con-

---

[12] Henry A. Bowman, *Marriage for Moderns,* 3d ed. (New York: McGraw-Hill, 1948), p. 339.

[13] Ibid., p. 340.

[14] Kimball Young, *Sociology* (New York: American Book Co., 1942), p. 402.

[15] Duvall and Hill, *When You Marry,* p. 277.

[16] "Most people would answer the question 'Why sexual desire' by saying, 'Obviously so the race can continue.' True, without sex the human species would not survive. But sex is also the basis of married love, the means of deep spiritual communion between partners. . . . Regular sexual activity contributes to physical and mental health." Bernard Greenblatt, *A Doctor's Marital Guide for Patients* (Chicago: The Budlong Press, 1957), p. 27.

[17] James A. Peterson, *Education for Marriage* (New York: Chas. Scribner's Sons, 1956), p. 296.

[18] Landis and Landis, *Building a Successful Marriage,* p. 377.

[19] Ibid., p. 377. See also the findings of judges in domestic courts. For instance, Louis H. Burke, *With This Ring* (New York: McGraw-Hill, 1958).

cludes that when sexual adjustments are poor, marriages are maintained with difficulty.[20]

The Burgess-Wallin research revealed that a successful marriage in our society needs more than sex to keep it alive.[21] Terman found that sex is indeed a basic factor in marital adjustment but only one of four or five basic factors. He concluded that the "sexologists" had overestimated the role of sex in marriage.[22] In a study of 666 couples who had been married from three to five years, those factors which are essential to happiness in the initial years of marriage were found to be (1) love and affection, (2) satisfactory sexual relations, (3) emotional interdependence, and (4) temperamental interaction. Burgess and Wallin remark that for "practically all couples" sex is secondary to companionship and other aspects of marriage.

Duvall and Hill affirm that happiness in marriage demands more than mutual sex fulfillment.[23] Clinical evidence has richly indicated that happiness lies within the personality adjustment of each of the married partners and in their larger relationships as two whole persons rather than in any physical tricks or techniques.[24] Social scientists concur that true married living revolves around such interchange as is found in planning for the children, spending the family money, making plans for vacations and holidays, rejoicing over personal advances, and comforting each other in times of illness or disappointment. It is these day-by-day experiences in common that set the stage for the fullness of sexual response which for most couples symbolizes their unity and is far more satisfying than the purely physical release involved. Sex satisfaction or dissatisfaction reflects the whole husband-wife relationship. Almost all writers agree with the comment of Groves: "We have come to appreciate that sex offers relaxation and creative vitality that give it a value aside from its relation to reproduction." [25]

---

20 Alfred J. Kinsey et al., *Sexual Behavior in the Human Male* (Philadelphia: W. B. Saunders Company, 1948), p. 563.

21 Ernest W. Burgess and Paul Wallin, *Engagement and Marriage* (Philadelphia: J. B. Lippincott Co., 1953), pp. 679, 680.

22 Lewis M. Terman et al., *Psychological Factors in Marital Happiness* (New York: McGraw-Hill, 1938), Appendix I.

23 Duvall and Hill, *When You Marry*, p. 125.

24 Ibid., p. 125.

25 Ernest R. Groves and Gladys Groves, *The Contemporary American Family* (Philadelphia: J. B. Lippincott Co., 1947), p. 40.

That sex needs are psychological as well as physical and organic is held among others by Paul H. Landis, who says: "The romantic marriage of our day, in fact, integrates the psychological and physical aspects of sex and makes them inseparable." [26] "High on the list of personal needs which marriage now seeks to satisfy are those of intimacy, companionship, and love. These needs, as has been observed, derive their fulfillment in large part from the sexual relations of man and wife. This elevates sex to a position of new importance in marriage." [27]

Sex in Marriage a Positive Value

That a satisfying sex relationship is one of the positive elements contributing to the well-being of the individual and of the married pair is unanimously affirmed.[28] The opportunity which marriage affords for constant and complete companionship with the person most loved, with the full sanction of society, is its greatest single attraction.[29] Sexual expression means more than the gratification of erotic urges or bringing the next generation into being.[30] Neill observes: "It [sex expression] is not the reason for true love between husband and wife; it is the product of true love. It is not the objective of marriage, it is, rather, the most perfect expression of the mutual interest and the kindly devotions that bind the lives of the happily married husband and wife." [31]

---

[26] Landis, *Making the Most of Marriage*, p. 26. Landis also says: "Once the sex relationship is entered into by married couples it becomes the regular habitual way of meeting the physical need for sex expression, bringing relief, pleasure, psychological relaxation, comfort, and closeness of the marriage relationship." (P. 27)

[27] Ibid., p. 512.

[28] Landis and Landis, *Building a Successful Marriage*, p. 379. "Its value consists not only in the function of reproducing the race but it is a constructive force for the happiness of the individuals. It can be the most complete form of love expression, contributing to the mental, emotional, and physical balance which is necessary if two people are to have a happy and successful marriage." (P. 399)

[29] Baber, p. 163. "In our present culture, sex attraction, in the broad interpretation of the term, is the dominating reason for marriage. Sex, in both its physical and psychological aspects, is without question the basic attraction between men and women."

[30] For the philosophical approach read Peter A. Bertocci, "The Place of Intercourse in Human Experience," *The Human Venture in Sex, Love, and Marriage*, 5th print. (New York: Association Press, 1958).

[31] Alexander S. Neill, *The Problem Family: An Investigation of Human Relations* (New York: Hermitage House, 1949), pp. 173, 174.

Sex Has Been Overrated

Though the sexual relationship is a vital part of marriage, social scientists are quick to affirm that the nonsexual interests and activities in which the husband and wife engage together far outweigh, in both interest and time consumed, their strictly sexual behavior.[32] No sane person, they say, would deny the power and importance of sex, but neither will the thoughtful be misled by the present-day emphasis on it. Terman admits that certain sex factors do contribute materially to marital happiness or unhappiness, but he is careful to conclude that sex has been overrated. "The data in fact indicate," he says, "that all of the sex factors combined are far from being the one major determinant of success in marriage that many writers have sought to make them." [33]

THE CASE FOR PREMARITAL CHASTITY

There are at least four identifiable schools of thought among social scientists on the subject of sexual intercourse before marriage. The one suggests that it is better in the long run to abide by the accepted social standards because it makes more sense and is healthier. (Writers with this view do not always state their own position. They write with tongue in cheek as if to say, "Society has made the rules. Whether they are right or wrong, I will not say.") The second argues on the basis of morality and integrity. (These take a philosophical view rather than a religious one.) The third suggests that the ideals of premarital chastity and postmarital fidelity may be questioned on reasonable grounds. A fourth group operates with a Christian, or theological, frame of reference and within the Christian tradition.

---

[32] Baber, p. 237.

[33] Terman, p. 373. Terman also says: "We have no ambition to add anything to the professional sexologist's glorification of sex as a psychological experience. The lily has already been sufficiently gilded. One even becomes a bit weary of the constantly reiterated emphasis upon sex as the primary basis of marital happiness, at once the soil in which it roots and the choicest product of its flowering. The sexologist is not wholly wrong, but it is pretty certain that his emphasis has been overdone. There is more to the marriage than the sexual embrace" (p. 247). "Our data do not confirm the view so often heard that the key to happiness in marriage is nearly always to be found in sexual compatibility. They indicate instead that the influence of the sexual factors is at most no greater than that of the combined personality and background factors, and that it is probably less." (P. 376)

Most sociologists would agree that premarital sex relations do not rest on sound judgment [34] and that social and religious disapproval are sufficient reasons for abstinence. They admit, however, that for the present, at least, the most effective deterrent is fear of disease, pregnancy, ostracism, disgrace, and loss of self-respect. Magoun says flatly: "The only intelligent reason for restraint is that the long-run results are not worth the effort." [35]

Baber states that "it is difficult to make a strong case for premarital sex relations, for most of the arguments seem to stem from the rationalization of one's desire to satisfy his sex urge whenever he wishes without regard to the social experience of previous generations. It is based upon the assumption that a physical urge must be satisfied at once because self-control either is impossible or will frequently result in psychoneurosis. But the facts do not fit such assumptions." [36] He discusses at some length eight objective reasons against premarital coitus. The weight of the arguments against outweigh those in favor, and the consensus of opinion is that it creates more problems than it solves.[37]

One high school study lists *Ten Scientific Reasons for Chastity:* (1) The physical relationship has no meaning of value outside of a loving marriage. (2) The physical relationship for complete satisfaction demands the security of marriage. (3) Adjustment to the physical relationship takes time. This rules out experimentation. (4) Controls in all societies have been placed on the physical relationship to protect children. (5) The welfare of society, of civilization, of democracy demands the preservation of the family unit. (6) Man understands best what he himself experiences; to experience the physical relationship at its best, promiscuity is ruled out. (7) Habit is a strong force; promiscuity before marriage is likely to continue after marriage. (8) Chastity

---

[34] Bowman, for example, says that sex is not something to be tested or played with but is to be built within the context of love and family (p. 239). He also says that premarital sex experiences are often followed by a deep sense of guilt which may produce regrets, marital conflicts, worry and strain (p. 234). See also Bowman, *A Christian Interpretation of Marriage*, pp. 29—40.

[35] F. Alexander Magoun, *Love and Marriage* (New York: Harper & Bros., 1948), p. 96.

[36] Baber, p. 596.

[37] Ibid., pp. 596—599.

is not harmful to either young men or women. (9) The possibility of an unwanted child cannot be ruled out. (10) There is always the risk of venereal disease.[38]

Burgess and Wallin conclude from their data "that husbands and wives with no experience of premarital intercourse have the greater probability of marital success." [39] Duvall and Hill build a chapter around the question "Does Morality Make Sense?" and conclude that freedom for the individual comes through conformity to the traffic rules of life's highway and that morality does make sense.[40]

The Liberal View: Freedom of Sex Expression

A few counselors are taking a position in favor of premarital sexual experience. Walter Stokes, M. D., for example, is strong in the belief that the best sexual development is possible through premarital sex experience under emotionally favorable conditions.[41] Dr. Albert Ellis, clinical psychologist and counselor in New York City, likewise takes the position that virginity and chastity represent cultural lags in our thinking about marriage preparation. He believes that extreme sexual difficulties in his clients are directly attributable to taboos against premarital sexual relations, masturbation, and so forth.[42] Robert A. Harper,

---

38 *Course of Study for Family Life Education*, Senior Schools — San Antonio (San Antonio, Tex: Independent School District, n. d.). See also the significant article by Margaret Culkin Banning, "The Case for Chastity," in *Reader's Digest*, XXXI, No. 184 (Aug. 1937), 1—10.

39 Burgess and Wallin, p. 370. Others question this and cite cases but usually fail to indicate previous religious convictions, precise feelings, or the basis of present happiness.

40 Duvall and Hill, Ch. vii. This is a pragmatic-moralistic approach to the problem based on "responsive integrity."

41 See the extended discussion on the Stokes position as reported in *Marriage and Family Living*, XV (Aug. 1953), pp. 234—249. Published by the National Council of Family Relations, 1219 University Ave., S. E., Minneapolis.

42 Albert Ellis, in *Marriage and Family Living*, XV (Aug. 1953), pp. 249—254. Ellis also states his position in a recent book (*Sex Without Guilt* [New York: Lyle Stuart, 1958]): "Every human being . . . should have the right to as much (or as little), as varied (or as monotonous), as intense (or as mild), as enduring (or as brief) sex enjoyments as he prefers — as long as . . . he does not needlessly, forcefully, or unfairly interfere with the sexual (or non-sexual) rights and satisfactions of others." Ellis belongs to the same school as his greater namesake, Havelock Ellis, and all those students who have attacked what he calls the cant, hypocrisy, ignorance, supernaturalistic sentimentality, and primitive-mindedness which still characterize 90 per cent of those who talk, think,

in *Marriage,* copyright 1949, held, in the main, to an objective utilitarian view. In the February 1959 issue of *Marriage and Family Living,* however, he says: "All the realistic evidence points to the desirability not only of fully educating children about sex, but of making contraceptive and prophylactic information and equipment completely available to all persons who reach the age of possible fertility." He catalogs the long list of social ills and personal sufferings which follow the alternative and concludes: "It is only because we keep rigidly reciting to ourselves the moral ditty about the catastrophic nature of premarital coitus that we cannot even clearly see, let alone do anything constructive about, our completely unnecessary, utterly idiotic premarital sexual morality." [43]

The General View: Society Demands Restrictions

Paul H. Landis, who has written an evaluative chapter on this whole conflict, disagrees. He says: "Social systems have always operated on the assumption that maximum physical satisfaction is rarely or never possible in human relationships — that only through restraint on biological appetite, by restricting it to customary channels of expression, can human society as such exist. The sex impulse is, therefore, always regulated in relation to the goals and objectives of the family itself." [44] He further observes that "only in marriage does sex become a responsible act." [45]

Most counselors are firmly convinced that conventions must be given a place in appraising premarital sex behavior and feel just as certain that premarital chastity is not only justified but

---

act, pontificate, and "legalize" about sex matters. These instances are cited here to give a realistic view of what the libertines of our day are advocating.

[43] *Marriage and Family Living,* XXI (Feb. 1959), 1. In defense of the free-love advocates Robert Briffault states: "The testimony of cultural history tends to show that not only are great evil and suffering produced by the coercive enforcement of stringent sexual codes, but that the effect of such coercion on loose conduct and unwholesome sexual manifestations is not proportionately appreciable. The freedom which modern criticism of coercive marriage has in view is not the promotion of individual happiness by license, but the abatement of needless suffering and evil resulting from groundless and unwarranted coercion based upon authoritarian and dogmatic traditional grounds insofar as these are productive of suffering which is not adequately justified or necessitated by social requirements." Cf. "Free Love" in *Encyclopedia of the Social Sciences,* VI, 433—436.

[44] Landis, *Making the Most of Marriage,* p. 250.

[45] *Ibid.,* p. 27.

desirable. Among counselors and authors who are strong in their support of the mores are David Mace, Harold T. Christensen, Abraham Stone, and Emily H. Mudd. Evidence available to date suggests that marriages of the chaste are most successful under the culture pattern of the United States and that premarital sex relationships frequently result in feelings of self-betrayal and inner conflict.[46]

The generally accepted view is that without firm rules favoring premarital chastity we would have social chaos.

THE RELATIONSHIP OF LOVE AND SEX

Social scientists are rather reluctant to commit themselves definitely as to what love really is and how it relates to sex. Some, however, do attempt some explanation or description. Henry A. Bowman says: "Romantic love, the love which prefaces and carries over into marriage, is distinguished from other types of love— filial, parental, brotherly — by the fact that it grows out of an awareness of and response to sex differences." [47]

People in many cultures have considered romantic love a sign of weakness and have ridiculed the person who yields to it, but our culture has glorified it in music, poetry, fiction, screen, and in adolescent experience. Throughout the Eastern world, for example, love is not considered a significant part of relationships between men and women. Sensuous desire is known and looked upon as a kind of human madness.[48] In most of the world's societies marriage is, in fact, primarily a status of relationship which does not require love before or after marriage.[49]

Social scientists are agreed that at least in Western society there comes a time when the young person begins to show an increase in interest in age mates of the opposite sex. Actually

---

[46] Where there is an intent to marry, one writer claims, "we have no conclusive scientific evidence that one or the other — the continent or the permissive — will achieve the better marriage." Lawrence S. Bee, *Marriage and Family Relationships* (New York: Harper & Bros., 1959), pp. 213, 214.

[47] Henry A. Bowman, "The Diagnosis of Love," in *Modern Marriage and Family Living,* ed. Morris Fishbein and Ruby J. R. Kennedy (New York: Oxford University Press, 1957), p. 133.

[48] Oswald Schwarz in *Women: The Variety and Meaning of Their Sexual Experience,* ed. A. M. Krich (New York: Dell Publishing Co., Inc., 1954), p. 290.

[49] Burgess and Wallin, p. 395.

there is no way of knowing how much of the awakening is due
to physical maturation and how much is a consequence of social
customs. That both operate, most students of the subject agree.
Just what the state or emotion of love is is difficult to explain.
Is it a mixture of many things, or is it essentially sexual? The
schools of opinion say either that it is too profound to define
or that it is simply the sex drive in motion. They agree that the
normal love (excluding the possibilities of parental fixation,
narcissism, and the predatory or exploitive attitude, etc.) which
wells up emotionally is focused in a person of opposite sex who
is considered an outlet for sexual urges (not necessarily overtly
expressed), a stimulator of sexual responses (likewise not necessarily overtly expressed), and an object of marital aspirations.
Also there is general agreement that the love which an individual
has for the opposite sex may be said to contain three basic elements: (1) attraction, (2) satisfaction of need, and (3) sexual
interest. To deny that sex is important to love between the sexes
is to argue uselessly against an obvious fact.[50]

Sexologist Havelock Ellis states baldly: "Love is a synthesis
of sex and friendship." [51] Sociologist Willard Waller, a follower
and interpreter of Freud, maintains that love involves idealization.[52] Walter R. Stokes, M. D., has said: "The only sound motive
for a happy marriage is being overwhelmingly in love on
a frankly sexual basis, centering about sexual desire." However,
he qualifies his statement in the same article by adding: "There
is much more to a good marriage." [53]

Harper is bold to say that romantic love, whatever its other
components, is preponderantly the sex impulse in action. "Although various high-sounding rationalizations may be offered,
it takes little insight to realize that sex is the sine qua non of
romantic love." [54]

---

[50] Landis, *Making the Most of Marrriage*, p. 103. Landis has two chapters which treat this subject: "The Genesis of Love" and "Romantic Love:
Can One Count on It?" — chs. vi and vii.

[51] Quoted by Paul H. Landis, *Making the Most of Marriage*, p. 98.

[52] Cited by Landis, ibid., p. 98.

[53] Quoted by Landis, ibid., p. 98.

[54] Robert A. Harper, *Marriage* (New York: Appleton-Century-Crofts,
1949), p. 48. Harper also states: "In present-day society, most young people
who enter marriage are seeking two primary goals: sex satisfaction and
security of intimate companionship" (p. 123). "It is this combination of
friendship and sexual satisfaction that is the essence of the modern conception of marital love." (P. 12)

Leslie Weatherhead does not shadowbox with the question. He says: "The most glorious fact of sex is that it makes falling in love possible." [55] He goes on to say: "Falling in love ought to be a very religious matter. . . . Any man who does not feel drawn nearer to God on falling in love may well ask whether he has fallen into lust instead of love." [56]

A more conservative position is taken by others. Love is an emotional response to others who meet our basic personality needs.[57] Love is of all natures and kinds and is made up of many wishes and needs.[58]

James A. Peterson holds that "in all love-making which is on a high level of adjustment, there is much complementary interaction. . . . In the mature sexual relation this effort to please the other brings profound psychological closeness between the two. The sexual act is thus both an expression of and an undergirding of companionship love." [59]

Paul H. Landis says: "Sex alone is hunger — raw animal hunger. Love is a combination of sexual desire with all the other impulses that go into the highest type of association between the sexes. . . . Love is sexual desire idealized, controlled, and made to conform to social living." [60]

Sex on the one hand kindles love and on the other hand serves as a medium through which love is expressed. Love and sex are not held to be the same thing.[61]

In any event, love seems to be here to stay in spite of the fact that science, although it observes it and describes it, does not attempt to define it. In one instance the authors quietly walk

---

[55] Leslie D. Weatherhead, *The Mastery of Sex Through Psychology and Religion,* 17th ed. (London: SCM Press, Ltd., 1954), p. 47.

[56] Ibid., p. 47. He also notes: "It is dangerously easy in the teen-age to confuse real love with physical attraction." (P. 50)

[57] Robert F. Winch, *The Modern Family* (New York: Henry Holt & Co., 1952). See chs. xiv and xv for a full discussion of romantic love and complementary needs.

[58] Joseph K. Folsom discusses the nature of love in *The Family: Its Sociology and Social Psychiatry* (New York: John Wiley & Sons, Inc., 1934), pp. 58—77, and in *The Family and Democratic Society,* rev. ed. (New York: John Wiley & Sons, Inc., 1943), ch. xi.

[59] James A. Peterson, *Education for Marriage* (New York: Chas. Scribner's Sons, 1956), p. 313.

[60] Landis, *Making the Most of Marriage,* pp. 104, 105.

[61] Lawrence S. Bee, *Marriage and Family Relationships* (New York: Harper & Bros., 1959), pp. 138, 139.

around the whole matter by saying: "One of the outstanding characteristics of modern American marriage is the fact that couples are expected to marry only if they are in love, and marriage for any other reason is judged questionable behavior." [62]

PROPER AND IMPROPER USE OF SEX

Lust and Promiscuity

Social scientists admit that it is not at all uncommon for the terms love and lust to be confused, that what may be disguised as the activity of love is promiscuity in fact. Ligon defines lust as any sort of unbridled, selfish desire. He adds that whenever any urge becomes strong enough to dominate one's entire personality, even temporarily, it may be described as lust.[63] Admittedly, the sex urge has great power and can seduce a person into regarding other persons, especially members of the opposite sex, as mere instruments for his own satisfaction. This makes sex an end in itself and exploits the other person for selfish purposes. On the other hand, sex can be an increasing source of personal enrichment when it is dedicated to objectives other than self-satisfaction. Bertocci notes: "The fact of human experience seems to be that persons enjoy deeper, more lasting and more profound satisfaction when the normal experience of sex lust is not primarily an end in itself but a symbolic expression of other values." [64]

Bovet calls lust "impersonal sexuality" and notes that in marriage, sex pleasure sought for its own sake disturbs the harmony of the marriage. He says specifically: "The greatest enemy of love is lust, which wants to get something for itself and employs the other as a means of satisfying this want." [65]

The destructive force of lust is described in this fashion: He who "lusts after" a woman makes her into an impersonal object and therefore falls away from love.[66]

---

[62] Burgess and Wallin, p. 393. See also Herbert Spencer's description of love above, p. 65.

[63] Ernest M. Ligon, *The Psychology of Christian Personality* (New York: Macmillan, 1953), p. 125.

[64] Peter A. Bertocci, *The Human Venture in Sex, Love, and Marriage*, 5th print. (New York: Association Press, 1958), p. 48.

[65] Theodor Bovet, *Love, Skill and Mystery* (Garden City, N. Y.: Doubleday & Co., 1958), p. 59.

[66] Ibid., p. 85.

Promiscuity takes many forms when a person wishes to get all he can out of sex as sex, and all of these forms are emotionally unhealthy in their origins and in their effects. Polatin and Philtine say that "as a rule, pronounced promiscuity of any kind masks a neurosis which will interfere with the mature sexual adjustment required of marriage. It indicates that somehow the act of sexuality has become dissociated from feelings of love." [67]

Medical people conclude that promiscuity is a psychiatric problem. "Our psychiatric study indicated that much of the sexual behavior of promiscuous men and women represents an effort to substitute sexual activity for more appropriate responses as a solution to emotional problems not related to sex needs or sex expression." [68]

Cole agrees. He says: "Psychoanalysis recognizes that promiscuous sexual behavior springs from a disturbed personality. Maturity demands sexual behavior that is motivated by respect for persons. Sex at its best, that is, when it fulfills its inner essence and purpose, is the union not simply of two bodies but of two persons." [69]

Although the specific terms lust and promiscuity are not often used, the social scientists take a dim view of sex on the mere biological level. They agree that it is a strong appetite and that its expression has always been a problem to civilized man. Mere expression is and cannot be the way. Marriage is not always the solution to the sex problem nor a certain guarantee of healthy adjustment. However, authorities agree that the experience of sex may enrich or endanger love, that it may bless or be a constant source of friction in marriage, and that it may be a solid foundation for co-operative family life or a source of frustrating disharmony. All of this indicates that a high level of regard for the other person and ability to seek the good of that person is requisite for the proper use of sex in marriage.

Recent writings show concern about the meaning of love in marriage as contrasted to exploitation of the other person. Two

---

[67] Phillip Polatin and Ellen C. Philtine, *Marriage in the Modern World* (Philadelphia & New York: J. B. Lippincott Co., 1956), p. 54.

[68] Richard A. Kock, "Penicillin Is Not Enough," in *Readings in Marriage and the Family*, eds. Judson T. Landis and Mary G. Landis (New York: Prentice-Hall, 1952), p. 429.

[69] Cole, p. 297.

views of love may be noted. Some say: "People have the ability
to love, and it is good. It is touched off by the natural love
of a child for its mother and father, grows into love for playmates
and friends, comes to a deep intensity in romantic love, and
develops in marriage in a deep regard and concern for the other's
welfare. This is mature love." Others say: "One must be realistic
and regard people as egocentric in their motives. These emotional drives in people, stripped to their most elemental terms,
are anything but loving, tender, solicitous. A person loves another for his own selfish ends. However, the mature person
is able to do this in a socially acceptable way. He covers up the
crass egotism of his self-centered love by humanizing it. Although he is actually exploiting the other person for his own
ends, he is subtle and indirect about it, even respecting the other
person and serving his needs." [70]

Sexual Activity in Marriage

In answer to the question, What is normal sexual gratification? Polatin and Philtine, the former a practicing psychoanalyst
and chief of female services at New York Psychiatric Institute,
say: "If there is conflict over any practices and if they prove
distasteful to either husband or wife, then they are not healthy
for that couple, although they may be perfectly acceptable to
another." [71]

William Graham Cole observes: "There is nothing either perverse or wicked about any behavior which precedes that union
and its climax, providing only that it is directed by mutual
respect and mature love. . . . An activity does not become a perversion until it is used compulsively as a substitute for the
standard coital pattern." [72]

Duvall and Hill say simply: "Caressing, fondling, and assurance of endearing love are as much a part of the sex act as the
more highly dramatic climax that is to follow. . . . Any activity
or position in coitus is normal and acceptable if it brings satisfaction to the couple." [73]

Paul H. Landis sets up a guiding principle. He stresses the

---

[70] Bee, pp. 113—155.
[71] Polatin and Philtine, p. 70.
[72] Cole, p. 303.
[73] Duvall and Hill, *When You Marry,* pp. 120, 121.

fact that "young people who hope to make a healthy sexual adjustment in marriage must learn to distinguish between behavior that is not normal and behavior that is merely not typical." [74] He emphasizes that sexual attitudes and practices which spell abnormality need professional care. The limits within which variations should be practiced are few and simple, he claims. He notes that they should bring neither physical nor emotional harm to either mate and that they should be indulged in by mutual inclination.[75]

One to three sexual contacts a week seems to be the average practice of the people interviewed by the various investigators. However, any individual couple might well go over or under that average and still be regarded as perfectly healthy and normal.

A study made by psychiatrists E. Gustave Newman and Claude R. Nichols, Duke University, of 149 elderly married couples ranging in age from 60 to 93 showed that 54 per cent of them were still sexually active. The average age of persons in this study was 70. One person 91 years old reported regular sexual activity. The report said: "Given the conditions of reasonably good personal health and marital partners who are also physically healthy, elderly persons continue to be sexually active into their seventh, eighth, and ninth decades." The frequency showed a wide range, from four or five times a year to three times a week, depending largely on health.[76]

Peterson maintains: "The main criterion for love play is that it expresses the mutual desire of the couple and that it be spontaneous, creative, and tender." [77]

No fixed rules of "courtship" in marriage are laid down. Lewin and Gilmore in their widely used book, *Sex Without Fear*,

---

[74] Landis, *Making the Most of Marriage*, p. 320.

[75] Ibid., p. 321. A further note from the medical point of view is expressed by Greenblatt: "Probably the most neglected part of successful intercourse is the complicated process of getting ready for it. This involves the attitudes with which young people come to marriage, and their ability to open up and share themselves freely and gladly with their life partners. Frankness is essential in reaching an understanding of the other partner's needs, desires, pace, and preferences. The marriage bed is the last place in the world for reticence. Too much is at stake — perhaps the very success of the marriage itself." (P. 36)

[76] See newspaper report, Orlando (Fla.) *Sentinel* (Nov. 15, 1959); also *Time*, LXXIV (Nov. 23, 1959), pp. 52, 55.

[77] Peterson, p. 305.

maintain that it is neither possible nor desirable to prescribe any routine forms of behavior or any set rules to be followed. Mutual understanding and adaptation is the guide.[78]

In summary, the opinion is expressed that sexual activities in marriage must be expressive of conjugal love and be aesthetically and physically enjoyable.

Masturbation

Masturbation is usually defined as "any self-excitation of the genital organs through manipulation or friction, for the pleasure involved and for the release of tension." [79]

Since the beginning of the study of the sex life of man, no other subject has been more frequently discussed, no other practice more roundly condemned and more universally practiced than masturbation.[80]

Two trends are manifest in the thinking in the recent literature and on the subject. The first is a tendency to consider masturbation in any form, under any circumstances, and with any frequency completely harmless. The writers holding this view are convinced that the morbid conditions and results which were attributed to the practice by many preceeding generations were groundless. The second trend wells up out of the studies and observations made by students of psychiatry and psychoanalysis. They see dangers in the practice, such as fixations, repressions, psychoneuroses, maladjustments to the sexual phase of marriage, and other mental effects. This latter school is reluctant to release all restrictions lest complete abandonment be encouraged which may lead to possible if not definable negative results.

According to Kinsey, masturbation and other sexual expressions are nearly universal for the young male. The teen-age female, however, may often have little or no localized sex desire and is less likely to masturbate.[81] If the histories of men and women who had reached the age of 25 were taken from all studies to date, they would show (1) that masturbation has

---

[78] Samuel A. Lewin and John Gilmore, *Sex Without Fear* (New York: Medical Research Press, 1950), p. 42.

[79] Lester W. Dearborn, "Masturbation," in *Modern Marriage and Family Living*, p. 484.

[80] Ibid., p. 484.

[81] Alfred C. Kinsey et al., *Sexual Behavior in the Human Female* (Philadelphia: W. B. Saunders Co., 1952), p. 126.

played a part in the lives of more than 90 per cent of all males and about 70 per cent of all females, with the frequency running from once or twice a month up to several times a week; and (2) that no evidence exists to prove that the greater frequency was any more productive of harm than the lesser.[82]

Those who discount any subsequent harmful effects of masturbation speak in this wise: The outlet of masturbation, resorted to by many who are sexually deprived, is not harmful. It will not cause loss of manhood, mental debility, nervous troubles, inability to have children, or any of the horrible consequences imagined by those who have been taught to fear and deny their genital sensations.[83] Others say the same but qualify by adding: "We know of no harmful effects of masturbation other than the mental conflict engendered." [84]

William G. Cole regards masturbation as no more serious than thumb sucking or nail biting and suggests that it should be regarded as a stage through which all children pass (particularly during the so-called "phallic period," three to six years, when masturbation is a rather universal phenomenon). He says that it is scarcely necessary any more to point out that masturbation can do no physical or psychological harm. He adds this qualification, however: "The sole danger of masturbation lies in the feelings of guilt attached to it. The Christian acceptance of the body has an important place in the training of the young. Children should be taught to value and appreciate their bodies, that sensual pleasure is one of God's gifts to His creatures, not a snare set to trap them." [85]

There are others who weigh the balance more carefully. Some say that the desirability or undesirability of masturbation apparently depends entirely on the attitude of the individual, that no scientific evidence has been produced to establish any absolutely good or bad effects. They assert that as a tension release for many adolescents, masturbation undoubtedly does no harm. For the introverted person, on the other hand, it may

---

82 Dearborn in Fishbein and Kennedy, p. 489.

83 Polatin and Philtine, p. 52.

84 O. Spurgeon English and Gerald Pearson, *Emotional Problems of Living: Avoiding the Neurotic Pattern* (New York: W. W. Norton & Co., 1945), p. 83.

85 Cole, p. 319.

symbolize the escape from the necessity of making adjustments with the other sex.[86]

The important question for others is why a person indulges in the practice. Is it a retreat from life, a comfort-finding device used to compensate for a life that has little joy and constant defeats? When masturbation becomes compulsive, it is a result, not a cause, of neurotic conditions associated with the lack of love in the home. Without the assurance of love from the outside, the only pleasure a person can find is in his own body.[87]

Peterson is one who believes that the practice will disappear if a child masturbates only for sensual pleasure. However, if the behavior is compulsive, it is symptomatic of deeper problems.[88]

A conservative view is taken by Bertocci. "Masturbation may produce as many problems as it solves, both in the present life of the individual and, probably, for the future." [89]

Bovet takes an interesting stand. He says: "Most of the so-called repressions — masturbation, sex curiosity, exhibitionism, fetishism, sadism, etc. — are simply fixations of the struggle against sex, isolated and more or less repressed, and they can only be overcome by accepting sex and combining it with *eros*. Most young men stop masturbating as soon as they fall in love with a real girl, and an erotically happy relationship is hardly ever disturbed by perversion." [90]

Modern writers generally agree that masturbation, according to the best medical authorities, causes no physical or mental injury. Any harm resulting from it is caused entirely by worry or by a sense of guilt due to misinformation. Emotional damage may result if the child is severely censured and made to feel guilty and fearful about the habit. If the behavior is continued and habitual it is most likely compulsive. Such behavior indicates an inner disturbance, the need for therapy. Patient attempts to discover the source of the problem, not scolding and punishment, and to deal with the problem instead of its symptoms will prove the only adequate approach.

[86] Harper, p. 81.

[87] English and Pearson, pp. 80, 221, 222. See also the analysis of Wm. E. Hulme, *God, Sex and Youth* (Englewood Cliffs, N. J.: Prentice-Hall, 1959), above, p. 143.

[88] Peterson, p. 58.

[89] Bertocci, p. 34.

[90] Bovet, p. 24.

We cannot close this section of the chapter on proper and improper use of sex without a further reference to the studies of Alfred C. Kinsey and his associates. These studies were variously evaluated as invalid and exaggerated or as revealingly real, presenting the status quo. They gave some new insights and further opened up the whole area of sexual behavior. Even conservative scholars feel that these studies cannot be ignored. Christian writers agree that they expose the extent of human weakness.[91]

SEX EDUCATION

Sex education is now commonly understood to include all educational measures which in any way prepare human beings, especially during childhood and adolescence, to deal with life situations and social relationships directly or indirectly arising out of the sex instinct. [92]

The movement for organized sex education had its origin in the worldwide medical attack on venereal diseases. The extent to which ignorance was a factor in the spread of venereal diseases led to a recognition of the necessity of sex education for both children and adults. The first societies were formed in Europe and America between 1900 and 1905 as the result of national and international medical conferences. Later these societies were reorganized as social hygiene associations. Their program has shifted from direct emphasis on disease to proper sex education.[93]

---

[91] For responsible sociological evaluations see *Sexual Behavior in American Society: An Appraisal of the First Two Kinsey Reports*, ed. Jerome Himelhoch and Sylvia F. Fava (New York: W. W. Norton & Co., Inc., 1955), 446 pp. Russell L. Dicks, head of the department of pastoral care, Duke University, writing in *The Pulpit* (March 1955) says the following: "The best reply to the Kinsey reports is not to question their accuracy. It will not help to dismiss the sex behavior or misbehavior of his subjects as unimportant because his figures are believed to be inaccurate. Surely no one of fair mind can read our newspapers or study the records of our clinics and courts without knowing that all of the undesirable sex behaviors described by Dr. Kinsey do occur in definitely unwanted amounts. Some ministers have been so busy moralizing over Kinsey's figures that they fail to see the need for a better understanding of sex. . . . We should turn our attention and energy to the ways in which we neglect, or sexually miseducate, our children and recognize our failure to prepare young people for marriage. . . . Ministers need to seek opportunities for training to help them achieve objective standards in sex education for the children and youth in their church schools and provide adequate premarital and marital counseling for their adult members."

[92] Maurice A. Bigelow, "Sex Education and Sex Ethics," in *Encyclopedia of the Social Sciences*, XIV, 10.

[93] Ibid., XIV, 10.

The following may be considered to be a summary statement of the philosophy of the social scientists: The widespread acceptance of the idea that young human beings need sex instruction is connected with the biological fact that in the human species there is a strong hereditary drive toward sexual functioning but no instinctive mechanism for control or regulation of sexual impulses. If the latter were limited strictly for reproduction and instinctively managed toward that biological end, as is true of animals, with the possible exception of some of the high primates, sex education would be unnecessary. The development of sexual gratification as an end in itself has led to many of the complicated problems of sex and has made it necessary for society to devise some means of controlling the sexual impulse. Since control must be based on intelligent choice, young persons can be expected to manage their inherited sex impulses within the limits of health and social requirements only when they have been instructed by parents and teachers.

Sex education in America for many years stressed the common evil results of mismanaged sex instincts, such as personal ill health, illegitimacy, promiscuity, and venereal disease. This attack on the negative side has been considerably modified. With more effective drugs now available to combat venereal diseases, the emphasis has shifted from the remedial approach to the preventive approach. Sex education is now based on an understanding of sex in its relation to the individual and the family and directed toward successful marriage and parenthood. Extensive knowledge of sex pathology — physical, mental, or social — has no place in modern programs of sex education.[94]

Responsibility for Sex Education

Opinion as to the primary responsibility for sex education is divided. Some posit that the chief opportunity and responsibility for sex instruction of children before high school age rests on the home. To this end they advocate adequate training for parents. Others say flatly that the home is not prepared to give proper sex instruction and that the schools must take over. Still others take a position in the middle and agree with Charles E. Manwiller, director of research and curricular planning, Pitts-

---

[94] For fuller treatment see whole article, ibid., XIV, 8—12.

burgh Board of Education, who says: "If one aim of sex education is to preserve the family, there is little doubt that it should
be introduced at the nursery-school or kindergarten level and
be continued throughout the high school as an integral part of
a positive planned approach. Even though wholesome sex training should start in the home, the school should supplement home
training, when given, and follow it through the maturation levels
of the child by correlating it with subject matter and the activities
in the curriculum." [95]

Landis discusses the problem in this fashion: "Assuming that
sex education is in itself desirable, one still may question the
desirability of putting it into the hands of the school. The fact
that this is being done represents realism, rather than any ideal
arrangement. Ideally, most agree, the intimate, unrestricted atmosphere of the home is the proper place for sex education.
Realistically, however, most concede that too few parents are
willing or able to accept the responsibilities of this task." [96]

The need for giving children information concerning sex,
right attitudes toward it, and truthful answers to their questions,
usually born of natural and normal curiosity, is now generally
recognized. There is a strong conviction that ignorance leaves
one vulnerable and that knowledge and understanding make
chastity easier. The fear that sex instruction will lead to immorality and promiscuity is challenged by most authorities and an
opposite opinion expressed.[97]

The Child Study Association expresses the belief that children who are given information about sex are less likely to
experiment than those who are not.[98]

Studies of marital adjustment point to the fact that the chil-

---

[95] Charles E. Manwiller, "Sex Education and the Child," ch. 6 in Morris
Fishbein and Ernest W. Burgess, eds., *Successful Marriage: A Modern Guide
to Love, Sex, and Family Life*, rev. edn. (Garden City, N. Y.: Doubleday & Co., 1955), p. 370.

[96] Landis, *Making the Most of Marriage*, p. 513.

[97] English and Pearson, writing from a psychiatric and psychoanalytical
background, respectively, comment: "Case histories indicate that information that is given to children about sexual matters and that is given early
will not cause them to misuse the information or become sexually delinquent
during grade school years or during adolescence. Children do not misbehave
by utilizing what they know nearly so often as they misbehave because of
what they do not know. It is the unsatisfied curiosity . . . that causes so
much of the sexual experimentation." (P. 76)

[98] See Landis and Landis, *Building a Successful Marriage*, p. 472.

dren who have had sex facts presented to them in an open and
frank manner by their parents were sexually more adequate
in marriage later on.[99]

Landis and Landis in their study conclude that sex education
gives better chance for happiness in marriage.[100]

In a study of 3,000 college students, 1952—1955, the factor
of chastity was related to childhood sources of sex information.
A larger percentage of those who had maintained socially acceptable standards of behavior had gained their sex education
from parents or from school classes. Those who reported having
had premarital sexual experiences learned sex facts from brothers or sisters or from other children. The research supports the
belief that parents who give their children rather complete sex
information also influence their children toward developing attitudes and standards with which they can live comfortably in
our society.[101]

It is generally recognized that parents hesitate to give sex
information because of inadequate information and inadequate
vocabulary. That questions on the facts of life should be answered continually from early childhood until marriage is also
generally recognized. This is essentially the job for parents.[102]
Beginning in early childhood, before there is emotional involvement, is emphasized.

The Scope of Sex Education

Manwiller, in his chapter on "Sex Education and the Child,"
shows that awareness of sex has its beginnings in the wholesome
family life environment, is learned from the love and respect of
parents for each other, progresses as the child develops, continues at the elementary, high school, and college level. He cites
examples of integrating it into the curriculum, setting up special
courses, and brings the consensus of the educators to bear on
the problem that children have a right to get their knowledge
of sex from adults having normal and healthy attitudes without
fears and anxieties.[103]

----

[99] Folsom, p. 436.
[100] Landis and Landis, p. 464.
[101] Ibid., pp. 628, 629.
[102] Robert G. Foster, *Marriage and Family Relationships* (New York:
Macmillan, 1950), p. 71.
[103] Fishbein and Burgess, pp. 362—380.

The evidence from research studies on the sexual experiences of youth indicates that (1) an early beginning in sex education is needed, preferably before age seven; (2) emphasis on broad social implications of sex with regard to long-range, individual adjustment is important; (3) social responsibility associated with sexual behavior needs to be emphasized; and (4) opportunities for youth to get together in wholesome, happy situations under guidance should be provided by the school. Two extremes are to be avoided in sex education, it is agreed: (1) teaching sex as something evil and (2) teaching sex in an openly brazen and crude manner. The first makes for prudery, the latter for immorality.[104]

From painstaking research Jerome Himelhoch, sociologist at Brandeis University, hypothesizes three major value conflicts affecting sexuality in our highly heterogeneous and rapidly changing American culture: tenderness vs. toughness, present-orientation vs. future-orientation, and hedonism vs. asceticism. In his paper "Sex Education in Sociological Perspective" he adapts evidence primarily from the Kinsey reports to outline the major patterns of American sexual behavior and interprets these prevailing patterns, including evasions and violations of publicly affirmed norms, in terms of his value-conflict theory as attempts to realize often radically contradictory sexual values according to sex, age, religion, educational level, occupation, and the cultural or class categories indicated by the two latter factors. Through informal sex education it is likely that basic conflicts in attitudes, values, and patterns of response will continue, for though modified and refined by selective learning in adolescence and early adulthood, the sexual conduct of the American adult, particularly that of the male, is largely an outgrowth from decisive social orientations of early childhood. During the age span from 16 through 20 years, when young people are most likely to receive formal sex education, the basic attitudes and major patterns of sexual behavior are already apparent, though the incidence of deviations from the "official code" does not peak till a more advanced age. Himelhoch, who is concerned primarily

---

104 For a list of basic principles in sex education consult Maurice A. Bigelow, "The Established Points in Social Hygiene Education," quoted by Manuel C. Elmer in *Sociology of the Family* (Boston: Ginn & Co., 1945), pp. 131—137.

with the social effectiveness of formal sex education, deduces from his discussion

> . . . that basic patterns of sexual attitude and conduct are formed in the preschool and grade school years; that they are learned as interdependent parts of a subcultural value-orientation; that indirect, characterological learning is more effective than direct indoctrination; and that such learning comes from groups and persons who constitute primary points of reference for the individual; and, finally, that the teacher and school must compete as reference groups with family and peers. If we wish to alter basic sexual patterns, the argument might be that we must start much earlier than high school and must change the child's reference groups.[105]

Public educators commonly agree that youth should be trained for more knowledgeable sex roles as adults, but there is much less agreement on the proper function of the schools and the scope of such instruction. At least two states have passed specific laws authorizing professionally supervised sex education in public elementary and high school curricula and exempting from such courses pupils whose parents object on constitutional or religious grounds. About half of the nation's high schools, especially in larger cities, offer courses, many still on an elective basis, which include at least some aspects of sex education. Integrating information on anatomy, the function of the sexual parts of the human body, and social hygiene into units on family life education and personal living in social studies, home economics, and biology courses with more organized and comprehensive instruction during the junior and senior high school years seems to be favored.

In her paper "Some Objectives of Sex Education" Catherine T. Dennis says sex is related to the total development of the individual. Sex "is the motivation behind most of our actions throughout life — our personal self-respect or esteem, our affection and love for other people, our sense of social values for all peoples, our moral code in dealing with others, our biological

---

[105] *Social Hygiene Papers: A Symposium on Sex Education* (New York: American Social Hygiene Association [now the American Social Health Association], November 1957), pp. 10, 11. In accord with Himelhoch's analysis many sociologists emphasize social and cultural influences and the prevailing sex ideologies and mores as major determinants of sex attitudes and conduct. See, e. g., Seward Hiltner, "Sexual Patterns and the American Class Structure," ch. xvi in *Sexual Behavior in American Society*, pp. 175 to 190. See above, n. 91.

desire for the continuation of the race, and our inter-personal relations with the opposite sex." [106] Because sex education is a part of total education involving not only physical growth but contributing also to the child's emotional, spiritual, and social development, "it should be included in all learning experiences from elementary through high school grades under conditions that foster wholesome and desirable growth patterns." [107]

This chapter cannot go into the needs of children for specific sex education at various developmental stages. Those interested will find much helpful information by social scientists and educators in *Social Hygiene Papers,* now referred to as *Social Health Papers,* and other publications of the American Social Health Association [108] and in other resources suggested in the footnotes of this chapter.

The Place of the Church in Sex Education

The question as to who should be responsible for sex education is a very difficult one to answer. It is agreed that the family must play a strategic role, but many parents are themselves confused and are giving little reliable help. This is borne out also in the Lutheran survey, which shows that the father's contribution is very negligible (see graphs). To what extent must the school help? Are teachers prepared to give such instruction? In what general frame of reference will they carry on this work, and with what motivation? The church should play a significant role. But is the church so concerned with instruction in ritual and doctrine that there is neither understanding for the basic Christian attitudes and principles in this area nor actual teaching of them? [109]

The social scientists assert that what is needed most is the setting of moral standards and a code of spiritual values by the youth of this generation under the guidance of adults. These standards, they assert, must not be built on the "fear theory"

---

106 *Social Hygiene Papers: A Symposium on Sex Education,* p. 24.

107 Ibid., p. 26.

108 A listing is available on request from the association, 1790 Broadway, New York 19, N. Y. Also consult the social hygiene (or health) center in your city or state.

109 Adah Peirce, "The Family in the Anxieties of the Fifties," in *Social Hygiene Papers,* pp. 27—31.

so prominent in past teaching but on the sociological, spiritual, and psychological facts involved in the relations between the sexes. They insist that facts alone are never adequate, that proper attitudes and appreciation are necessary, and that the church is the source of these values. There is more than theology involved, they contend, and what is needed is a far more realistic approach by the church on the basis of sound study which, in close co-operation with the social scientists, takes into account all of the related factors. Will the churches rise to meet this challenge — this combination of forces that make sex education so important and necessary?

The social scientists, on the other hand, have something to receive as well as give. A Christian interpretation of sex is coming into clearer light and is being developed on the basis of a sounder re-examination of the whole Christian Scriptures and as growing out of the doctrines of creation, redemption, and sanctification. This clearer light it is hoped will remove some of the confusion caused by disparate religious teaching in the past. The social sciences have some new things to learn from the church; and the church has some new things to learn from the social sciences with regard to sex education.

Home, church, and school — all have a role to play. Here an interdisciplinary approach seems necessary. But before it can be a reality, there must be communication between theology and sociology. Hardly a beginning has been made on this important task on the level of the local community.

Because the biological, sociological, and psychological sciences are involved in dealing with human sexuality alongside theology (both systematic and pastoral), the church, in order to minister understandingly and constructively to this age, needs not only a clearer theology of sex but also the insights and approaches which the social sciences give in the area of sex. Every pastor can profit from the basic studies in marriage and family living and from sound marriage-counseling guides.[110]

The social sciences are getting at the psychological sources of emotionally unhealthy sex behavior, such as (1) the quest for satisfaction at the expense of another person; (2) the desire to bolster the ego by a demonstration of sex capacity; (3) the

---

[110] For instance: *Marriage Counselor's Manual*, developed by Gelolo McHugh (Durham, N. C.: Family Life Publications, Inc.).

exploitive conquest of another person; (4) the rebellious desire to get even with parents or a spouse.

The social sciences are also pointing to the healthy or proper use of sex when they speak of (1) becoming partners with God in responsibly creating new life; (2) finding completeness in the "better half," the marriage partner; (3) using sex as an expression of genuine love, the love that is already there; (4) finding the normal and moral pleasure of the sex relationship in marriage a pleasure that is both lasting and growing.[111]

SUMMARY

1. The research activities of the social scientist provide valuable data regarding the sex habits and attitudes of the people of the twentieth century. Social scientists are quite pragmatic in their conclusions and for the most part align their value judgments with regard to tested experience and the standards of approved social behavior.

   Two schools of thought are evident among them. One group studies man on the biopsychological level and advocates behavior which makes him happy and well adjusted in his environment. A second group sees a deeper dimension in human relationships and develops ethical principles as norms of human behavior.

   The findings of the social scientists and their subsequent postulations are useful to discriminating students of sexual behavior who understand and believe that the problem of man is theological, that what a person is depends on his relationship to God in Christ. In all human relationships the dimensions of faith in God and concern for the other person are vital.

2. That sex plays a very important and constructive role in marriage is unanimously affirmed. Some are quick to affirm that sex is not the mainspring of life and marriage but that other factors and relationships play a large role. Nevertheless, the scientists agree on the unitive value of sex in marriage.

3. Premarital unchastity is frowned on by most social scientists because of the dangers involved. Social pressures and fixed

---

111 Howard Whitman, "Science Takes a New Look at Sex in America," in *This Week* Magazine, Oct. 25, 1959 (United Newspaper Magazine Corp., 485 Lexington Ave., New York 17, N. Y.).

standards are usually named as the only valid deterrents. Sex restricted to marriage is generally accepted as the better course of action because of the configuration of advantageous factors surrounding it.

4. Social scientists are not quite sure what love between the sexes actually is. While love is not to be identified with sex, the relationship between love and sex is very real. Sex on the one hand kindles love and on the other hand is the medium through which love is expressed. There is a complementary interaction between the two. The sex drive has been compared to hunger by both theologians and social scientists. Love is wider and broader than sex, being an emotional response to others who meet our basic personality needs. Sex alone can be very self-centered and exploitive; coupled with love, however, it can be very creative and constructive.

5. Sex for the sake of sex and disregard for the other person (exploitation) are characteristic of promiscuity and prostitution. Free love and libertinism advocated by a few extremists find little acceptance on the part of responsible social workers and scientists. Love, not lust; marriage, not promiscuity, are regarded as normal. Sex abnormalities indicate emotional problems and demand special care.

6. Clinical studies show that masturbation is common, does no harm physically, may do harm psychologically, usually arouses guilt feelings, and is overcome by a healthy, socially approved sexual outlet and emotional satisfaction. Where masturbation is compulsive, special therapy is needed.

7. Caressing, fondling, and love-making are a normal part of the sex act. Such activities in marriage must be expressive of conjugal love, be aesthetically and physically enjoyable, be mutually acceptable, and lead to normal coitus. None of the authorities consulted speak for restrictions.

8. Sex education is both necessary and desirable. All voices speak in unison for the values of giving the proper sex information at the right time, and the data support the assertion. The home and the school are to do the job from early years on, giving not merely sex knowledge but also training in personal and social responsibilities. Since moral and spiritual values are decisive in proper sex education, the church has a duty here.

CHAPTER 12

A Christian Interpretation of Sex

THE NEED for this investigation and the purposes of this study have been set forth. We have reviewed the thinking, writing, and teaching of the church from pre-Christian times to the present day. It has not been easy to find these teachings and the attitudes behind them. Frequently no specific sex ethics had been formulated. Only in comparatively recent times have some church bodies prepared statements on sex. Various streams of thought, some chiefly cultural, some philosophical, some religious, have either flowed together or flowed apart. We are now ready to answer the ten questions which were set forth in Chapter One. In this final chapter we draw together the mass of material and set forth a Christian interpretation of sex.

1. What Is the Place of Sex in God's Design?

Sex is God's idea, not man's. Sex is a gift of God, and like all other things God made, it has the design of the Creator in it. Sex was not an accident. As science delves deeper into natural phenomena, it discovers purpose in the universe, sees the infinite wisdom behind it, and finds reason for wonder. This is true also of sex, which is a vital part of all animal and most vegetable life. It varies in different species of animals. In plants the fertilization of the female by the male takes place in several ways. Sex is part of the structure of all animate life. Sex in its highest and most complex form is found in man.

Sex in animals is regulated by nature and in the female follows definite cycles. It may be regarded as automatic and guided by mysterious instinct. "Animals (with the exception of some primates) have no sex life apart from procreation, which

is seasonal and entirely outside their conscious control."¹ In
man sex is not cyclical. The sex drive is continuous after
puberty and left to the control of the individual. For this
reason sex in animals and sex in human beings dare not be care-
lessly equated.²

God's design of sex in the creation of Adam and Eve is not
only purposeful but wise and good. All creation is called "good"
in Scripture; the creation of male and female is called "good."
Adam's loneliness and separateness (not having a sexual counterpart as the other creatures) God called "not good." Heterosexual human beings are God's design. The female was made
to complement the male. Without woman man could never
fulfill God's creative design. What is more, each sex needs the
other socially, psychologically, physically, and spiritually. This
built-in longing and desire of the one for the other penetrates
into all phases of living. There is no domain where this inter-
relationship does not come to some expression. We are not
born merely human; we are born either male or female, and
masculinity or femininity begins to assert itself at once.

Although sex is basically biological and physiological, its
expression among human beings involves more than mere dif-

---

¹ Marjory Louise Bracher, *Love Is No Luxury* (Philadelphia: Muhlenberg Press, 1951), p. 95; William P. Wylie, *Human Nature and Christian
Marriage* (London: SCM Press, 1958), p. 15.

² In view of the careless equation of sex in animals with sex in the
human being, of which preachers are often guilty, we give the following
quotations from recognized scientific works supplied by Harold J. Maleske
and John W. Klotz of Concordia Senior College, Fort Wayne, Ind.

"In most lower forms [of animals] receptivity of the female to the
sexual advances is determined by hormone balance and by other accompanying physiological changes occurring during the period of heat, or
estrus. With some exceptions, the female animal is receptive only when
she is in heat. This is, of course, not true of the human female, who may
actively desire or entirely reject sexual relations at any time during
the menstrual cycle."

Authors Lindesmith and Strauss after examining the scientific literature in the field write: "This literature clearly shows that human sex
behavior is not controlled in the same way or to the same degree by
physiological processes and mechanisms as is that of lower animals. In the
sex practices of human beings mental processes play a preponderant role.
... Moreover, it is a logical fallacy to try to account for the unique features
of human sex behavior in terms of the biological conditions which man has
in common with other animals." (Alfred R. Lindesmith and Anselm L.
Strauss, *Social Psychology*, rev. ed. [New York: Dryden Press, 1957],
pp. 316, 317; see also Clifford Kirkpatrick, *The Family as Process and
Institution* [New York: Ronald Press, 1955], pp. 28, 29.)

ferences in sex organs with complementary functions. There
are many differences (innate or conditioned) in temperament,
in feelings, in ways of response. This is acknowledged by all who
participate in human relations, especially in marriage. Many of
these differences are part of God's design and belong to the complementary nature of the two sexes. In sexual intercourse two
persons are "merged" into one flesh. This union is not only physical in nature, it is also emotional, spiritual, and psychological.

Discriminating theologians say the sexual drive as such is
to be accepted as part of the original and ongoing order of
creation and not as a result of the fall into sin.

Sex is of God. This is the first basic fact that must be completely recognized. Much of the confusion in and outside the
church regarding sex is directly traceable to the fact that sex
as God's design is not fully accepted. Sex was often considered
more or less evil in the civilizations and religions of the East.[3]
The concept that sex is evil has also been taught for hundreds
of years within the Christian church. This is the chief error
behind most asceticism and teachings that exalt virginity and
celibacy above marriage. While voluntary asceticism is within
the rights of free man, much religious asceticism and sex denial
is a full or partial rejection of the creation doctrine that heterosexual human beings were designed for each other. In theology
the order of creation is basic to the order of redemption and
the order of sanctification, and it precedes them. We are redeemed as bodies as well as souls, and sanctified wholly, also
in body and soul.

What God in His wisdom has made for the honor of His
name and the welfare of mankind, what He Himself has called
"good," is to be accepted by the creature as a sacred, honored
thing. It is to be received with thanksgiving and respected as
a gift (1 Tim. 4:3, 4) which in many respects is more mysterious
and wondrous than other gifts because it includes the gift of
life itself. And it is neither to be ignored nor despised nor
maligned — but properly used in accordance with the divine
will of the Creator.

---

[3] David Mace and Vera Mace, *Marriage: East and West* (Garden City,
N. Y.: Doubleday, 1960), pp. 90—97.

2. What Is the Proper Place of Sex in Marriage?

For centuries the dogma has been taught that sex has only one purpose, that of procreation. To this day this characterizes most Roman Catholic teaching, and it has at one time or another crept into the teaching on sex of many Protestant denominations. Other purposes of sex in marriage have been proposed from time to time, such as "to avoid fornication," "a remedy for sin," "to serve a unitive function." Dogmaticians usually list three purposes of marriage: companionship, sex relations, procreation. Procreation is frequently given first rank.

Gen. 1 associates sex with procreation but has nothing to say of marriage as such. Gen. 2 adds the significant feature that sexual union is a blessing in itself; that the one-flesh relationship is an end in itself; that husband and wife are to cling to each other in love and lifelong companionship. In the New Testament our Lord endorses the Genesis account and emphasizes the one-flesh relationship in marriage (Matt. 19:4, 5). The apostles do the same. In the most extended statement by the apostle Paul (1 Cor. 7) there is no reference to children, but a strong emphasis on conjugal relations. His statement, "It is good for a man not to touch a woman," has been much discussed and distorted. Protestant theologians, following the total context of the chapter, find Paul advising against prolonged periods of sexual abstinence between married partners (1 Cor. 7:3-5). Paul considers the exercise of the sex privilege a debt each spouse owes the other. This is the emphasis throughout the New Testament.

In both the Old and the New Testament sexual intercourse is presented as an experience to be anticipated with pleasure and to be prepared for with affection and love, without necessarily having procreation as the conscious purpose. It pleased God to arrange for procreation through the sexual act. However, God does not make procreation the sole purpose of the sexual act; and nowhere does He restrict cohabitation to the generation of offspring.

On the other hand it is neither Biblical nor realistic to think of sexual relations divorced from the conception and training of children. The two belong together. Children are a joy and a blessing (Psalm 127 and 128). They are also a responsibility

(Deut. 6:6-9). Unfortunately many popular books on sex almost ignore this aspect of sexual relations. The conception, birth, and care of children belong to the burden of marriage, which should not be evaded. Procreation is tied by the Creator to the unitive function of sex. The use of contraceptives does not change this fact; on the contrary, contraceptives are a recognition of this fact. This is a burden of marriage, on both man and woman, but the woman lives with it more closely. (Gen. 3:16, 20; Is. 21:3; John 16:21)

Frequent sexual activity in marriage is the general intention or implication of Scripture (1 Cor. 7:5; 1 Thess. 4:4, 5; Heb. 13:4). Yet this judgment of Scripture is not always accepted. Because all sex activity was erroneously classified as "sin" or "evil" and even the begetting and conceiving of children was considered a means of communicating original sin, the theologians sought ways of "excusing" or "sanctioning" ordinary intercourse in marriage. Roman Catholicism did this by making marriage a sacrament; some Reformers covered it by saying "it is a remedy for fornication"; others held that because marriage is an institution of God, what goes on in marriage cannot be sin. There seems always to be some hesitancy or scruple. This is not necessary. For sexual intercourse is God's ordinance for marriage.

Sex in itself is good, being a work of creation. It is, however, used by people who are evil (since the fall). But this does not make sex evil. Similarly covetousness is attached to trade and gainful occupation, gluttony to eating, and an inordinate craving for intoxicants to drinking. But these do not make drinking, eating, or working for wages per se sinful or evil.

Indeed, the fall into sin has affected all of life, including the emotions and the will. Since the fall nothing man does is absolutely perfect. "The imagination of man's heart is evil from his youth" (Gen. 8:21). The apostle Paul confesses: "For I know that nothing good dwells within me. . . . for I do not do the good I want, but the evil I do not want is what I do" (Rom. 7:18, 19 RSV). But this fact does not make the sex act as such any more sinful than any other act.

When people express themselves in any area of living, respecting any of God's Ten Commandments, in thought, word, or deed contrary to God's will, that is sin, and the sinner needs forgiveness. This forgiveness has been earned by Christ with

His redemptive sacrifice on the cross. In conversion the Holy
Spirit applies this forgiveness to the believer for all imperfect
or sinful acts and claims both the body and the soul as His
dwelling place (1 Cor. 6: 19, 20). In this sense also the Christian's sexual activity in marriage is always covered by the
redemption.

Marriage is God's ordinance for the good of man, and sex
is a part of marriage. A proper desire for marriage is hardly
possible without sex drive. Normal marriage would be incomplete without sexual cohabitation. (Gen. 24: 67)

God made marriage for sex and sex for marriage. God
made sex one of the means for continuously uniting a man and
his wife in the deepest and most realistic way, a unique way
in which they are "known" to each other as they could not
otherwise know each other, in the fullest expression of mutual
love unlike any other demonstration. The "one flesh" concept
is basic and dominant in the Bible's teaching on marriage.
(Gen. 2: 24; Ex. 21: 10; Lev. 18; Deut. 24: 5; Matt. 19: 5, 6; Mark
10: 6-8; 1 Cor. 7: 2-6; Eph. 5: 31)

Sex in marriage has in addition to the procreative function
a unitive function. This Biblical truth (Gen. 2: 24; 1 Cor. 7: 2-6)
has been strongly corroborated by psychology, psychiatry, social
studies, the clinical experience of marriage counselors, phy-
sicians, judges, and Christian ministers.

Conjugal intercourse before and after the birth of children,
before and after the menopause, continuing throughout married
life is normal and so intended by the Creator. Biologically it
releases tensions through ecstatic pleasure and satisfaction. Socially it is the indispensable part of the full commitment of two
whole personalities in an intimate relationship. Psychologically
it provides a sense of fulfillment and security and of interdependence as love and understanding are reciprocated. Love in
Christian marriage (including sex) is used by Paul as a symbol
of the union of Christ and His church. (Eph. 5: 30-32)

While it is to be doubted if normal marriage exists where
there are no sex relations, Christian love and commitment forbid
a disruption of marriage because illness or some misfortune
has suspended sexual relations. Companionship and care, total
commitment and Christian love continue. (Heb. 13: 1; 1 Cor. 13)

3. What Is the Proper Place of Sex Outside Marriage?

Sex in the wider sense of sexuality concerns married and unmarried. We are either men or women. We carry our sexual characteristics and feelings with us wherever we go. Some by creation or cultivation carry with them what is popularly called special sex appeal. This raises the question: How should a person outside marriage act toward persons of the opposite sex?

Sexual attraction is a part of God's design. It need not and should not be denied or ignored. But sex expression in its fullest sense is reserved for marriage only. Gilbert Russell puts it succinctly: "A man's sexuality belongs to his wife, long before he has met her. If he never meets her, it belongs to nobody else. Only one human being has claim on our sexual powers — the one who can claim the whole of us." (See page 160.)

The Christian regards sex as sacred, a thing of God's design, restricted for use in keeping with God's will, a wonderful, mysterious gift. He also believes in the dignity and worth of the individual person and refuses to exploit another person for his own selfish purposes or to do bodily, social, mental, or spiritual damage to another person. This sanctity of sex combined with respect for the other person — no matter who it may be — comes from respect for God, a Christian sense of values, and orientation of life to God's will.

This does not mean we cannot appreciate beauty, grace, and the sexual characteristics of others. The person of the opposite sex is to be regarded as "a creature of God," in whose life God is to be honored in all things. The Christian's feeling toward his neighbor will be disciplined and directed by the spirit as well as the letter of the divine law. The Christian's regard for the person of the other sex is based on moral integrity and on the believer's commitment to Christ and his neighbor.

When God sets up a single moral standard for men and women and demands that sex relations are to be reserved for marriage, He is not unjust or unmindful of human weakness or giving principles that destroy life, but He is guiding man into a way of life which has proved to be beneficial. Following God's will leads to the full happiness of marriage and a wholesome life of love. "The talent of waiting is the most priceless gift

youth can have," said a family service director. Overstepping
God's law means a disservice to self, to the other person, and
to society.

Modern freedoms in dating and courtship, the widespread
availability and use of contraceptives, theories of testing companionability through sexual experimentation, the depletion of
men in war, the deep sex hunger in the human being fanned
to a flame by sex-saturated advertising and entertainment do
increase sexual temptations and make premarital chastity difficult. But none of these conditions alter the divine principle,
given in love, "Keep thyself pure." None of these factors and
circumstances can justify extramarital sex affairs. What is more,
Christian principles are supported by experience. The human
conscience is sensitive to sins of sex which are not easily forgotten or ignored.

Christ in His mercy forgives all who come to Him in repentance and faith. The church must not make sexual sins "unforgivable" by judgmental attitudes and legalistic actions and so mis-
represent the abounding grace of God in Christ. It should not
castigate sexual sins while excusing the sins of pride, hate, greed,
and hypocrisy. Sexual aberrations are not unforgivable, nor
are they to be identified with the sin against the Holy Spirit.
Jesus forgave the woman taken in adultery (John 8). When the
church is known for its "laws" and not for its "Gospel," it is
misrepresenting Christ. This, of course, does not deny that even
the Christian daily has need of the restrictions of the Law for his
guidance, nor that a church dare ignore God's Law in its ministry.

Sex relations are proper only when there is willingness to
enter upon a permanent husband-wife relationship and assume
all the responsibilities that go with intercourse. "Sex outside of
marriage is sinful because it violates God's holy purpose of
establishing full and permanent oneness between two persons
sealed by the sexual union." (Small, above, p. 153)

Intercourse before marriage is irresponsible, undermines true
oneness in marriage, exploits the other person, frequently robs
women of their opportunity for marriage, and may involve children born out of wedlock and deprive them of the love of a normal family.

It should be noted that studies of extramarital sex relations by
social scientists on the basis of the empirical approach have gen-

erally agreed that the single standard of morality for both men and women is basic for the welfare of society and ordinarily most conducive to personal happiness.

In most societies there are both men and women who have never had or taken the opportunity for marriage or who by force of special circumstances have remained unmarried. Not only is their sexual nature denied fulfillment but also their longing for a child. Is their sex drive to be completely submerged?

Sexuality plays some type of role in every person's life. It belongs to personality and is a part of all interpersonal relations. It is, however, only one of man's endowments. Nor is it the highest of all human powers. It has been given by God as a means and not as an end in itself. Sex does not exist for itself. There are many other ways of expressing affection and human consideration of one person for another.

Sexuality is always to be regulated by chastity. Only this is responsible living. While it is true that the normal calling for the average person is that of marriage and the family, God in His wisdom has not made the full use of sexual powers necessary to happy, useful existence. In this respect the sex drive differs from hunger for food. The sex drive is to be under control. Where this is difficult, Scripture recommends marriage. Continence is not every person's gift. (1 Cor. 7:7)

Both feminine gifts and masculine gifts are needed in all spheres of action; in practically all professions and vocations; in the fields of education, science, business, industry, government services, and social welfare. Some of the very great achievements in practically every sphere of human activity are attributed to men as well as women who never married and yet kept the sex impulse under control. The longing for a child is usually satisfied by working with children and being with families. Because here also the burden falls more heavily on women than on men, the church can help provide more opportunities for unmarried persons to meet socially, to be with families, to work with children.

The unmarried who live continently may and do play a role that can be healthy, holy, and richly blessed, not only in a chosen profession but in the higher calling of service to people in the church and in the community. Marriage is not a requisite for a successful life. The new life in Christ is both full and complete. It is life's highest good. Marriage is an honorable and worthy vocation. Serving God outside marriage is equally honorable and worthy.

4. When Is Sexual Desire Sinful (Lust)?

Sexual desire is not in itself sin. Man and woman are made to attract one another and eventually to leave father and mother and cling to each other as husband and wife. In marriage wife and husband are to desire each other, also sexually. When then is sexual desire sinful?

Some would have all desires of the body considered sin. This would make hunger sinful. Both Greek philosophy and Manichaeism taught that the body is evil and only the soul is good. Some of this unbiblical thinking crept into the church. This accounts for such statements as: "Because sex belongs to the body, it is sinful." Bodily desires and indeed all natural desires are not in themselves sinful. Neither is the body to be despised and hated; it is rather to be loved, cared for, and protected (Eph. 5:29). The body is to be used, not abused; to be enjoyed, not punished.

Nor is every interest in the other sex forbidden. Jesus' words about the lustful look (Matt. 5:28) spoken in connection with a discussion on adultery are not to be interpreted to mean that the young man seeking a wife is to have no sexual feelings at all, but, as the context indicates, Jesus wanted to say that the Christian must discipline his desires so that they do not include thoughts of sexual relations with another man's wife (2 Sam. 11:2) or outside marriage. Any other interpretation of this passage violates the order of creation.

The God-created sexual desire as such is not sin. To this desire may be attached sinful lust, sometimes called concupiscence. It is this that is wrong. Sex as such is not sinful; man is. Man sins, sex doesn't. It is only when sexual desire becomes perverted by lust that it becomes "unchaste" and sinful. Rightful sexual desire is directed to the marriage partner and is accompanied by considerations of love. Wrongful or lustful sexual desire overrides the limits which God has set, ignores the welfare of other persons, is directed to the wrong person, and may also be excessive and inconsiderate. (1 Peter 3:7)

Since the fall man's heart is evil. Out of the evil heart proceed immoral thoughts which are exploitive, egotistical, and selfish, which do not regard the wellbeing of the partner but seek sex relations where God has forbidden them. This is sin, just as covetousness is sin. Desire that is directed toward forbidden ends is always sinful.

The theologians have rightly called concupiscence, or sexual lust, sin, sometimes, however, without carefully distinguishing it from the sex drive itself (Augustine). In Gal. 5:16-24 Paul speaks of the conflict between flesh and spirit, saying: "Do not gratify the desires of the flesh. For the desires of the flesh are against the spirit, and the desires of the spirit are against the flesh; for these are opposed to each other, to prevent you from doing what you would" (vv. 16, 17 RSV). He does not here refer to the gratification of proper sexual desires in marriage but to fifteen sins (against six commandments), only three of which refer directly to sins of sex: immorality, impurity, licentiousness (19 to 21; see also the contexts of 1 Cor. 6:13; 1 Thess. 4:4, 5; 1 Peter 2:11; 2 Tim. 2:22). The New Testament uses the term "flesh" not of the physical body but of the sinful, disobedient "self," of the old nature which is against God, as contrasted with the spirit, the new life of faith which is open and responsive to God.

This still leaves the question: What is moral and immoral in the realm of sex? The New Testament knows no double moral standard, one for men, another for women. It broadens the meaning of "adultery" in the Decalog. In the wider Christian interpretation all immorality inside and outside wedlock, all homosexuality, all filthy talk, all impure, lustful desires are sinful. The essence of the moral law here is that God made sex for use within the marriage bond where the true two-in-one-flesh relationship is God's design. By and large the experience and practice of the whole human race confirms this meaning.

To youth's question: Why is it that sexual intercourse is sinful before marriage but allowed and commanded after marriage? there is only one answer. God has arranged it so for the welfare of man. God ordained marriage, not harlotry. God desires that sex be used responsibly, within wedlock, with fidelity toward the spouse, and with provisions for the care of children.

5. What Is the Relation of Love to Sex?

Although in some societies marriage for love is incidental or
not the usual practice, in Western civilization romantic love plays
an important role. Even in societies where marriages are arranged by parents, love and devotion are not altogether absent,
and they develop and grow within marriage.[4]

In the New Testament, love for the spouse is the ideal, and
Christ's great love for the church is made the pattern (Eph. 5).
This love *(agape)* is sacrificial, self-giving, fully committed, undying, like Christ's love for us. This love helps to make marriage faithful and enduring. This kind of love is responsible to
God and to man. It is to be differentiated from companionship
(philia), which is expressed in mutual helpfulness, friendship,
common interests. These also are important. Sacrificial love is
furthermore to be distinguished from physical attraction, or
sex love and desire *(eros)*. Actually none of these three should
be absent in marriage. Without physical attraction, or *eros*, there
would be no sexual union; without companionship, *philia,* there
could be no life in common, or union of two whole personalities;
and both of these are lifted to a new level by the bond of a common faith and by self-giving devotion to each other *(agape)* out
of commitment to Christ.

The relation of love to sex has been set forth in Chapters Ten
and Eleven. Love and sex are not the same thing. There can
be sexual activity without love. There can also be love without
sexual relations. In marriage, sexual activity should be an expression of mutual affection. Where this is the case, love matures
to weld husband and wife ever more closely together. Thus sex
serves as a medium through which love is expressed. The meeting of two bodies cannot of itself make love. It can only express
a love that already exists. "A decline in the fellowship of the
marriage will equally disrupt the working of the sexual function,
and ultimately destroy it altogether" (David Mace, above, p. 158).
This is why the practice of mutual forgiveness and reasonable
self-control is essential to successful sex adjustment in marriage.

This conjugal love builds family harmony and happiness and
has salutary influence on children, relatives, and friends. Con-

---

[4] Mace and Mace, pp. 197—220.

jugal love is not identical with parental love or with the love between brothers and sisters or with the love for relatives and friends.

Petting and love play have their place in marriage because they prepare male and female for union. They form a chain reaction that leads to coitus. The Christian brought up in a tradition in which sex is frowned on is often disturbed over pleasure sensations in sexual activity. The Bible everywhere implies that such conjugal enjoyment is normal and not displeasing to God. God made man and woman with pleasurable sex-response patterns. That God meant sex to be enjoyable in the marriage comradeship is clear from Gen. 24:67; Prov. 5:18; Eccl. 9:9.

As sex and love are not identical, neither are love and lust. Lust is selfish, exploitive, seeks personal gratification; it desecrates sex because it violates personality. Lust is the greatest enemy of love. To lust is to fall away from love. It makes people promiscuous, irresponsible, criminal (rape). It wrecks marriages because it offends against a basic principle of true sexual union.

The Christian will reject also the popular notion that "falling in or out of love" determines whether or not sex relations are permissible. Mere infatuation with an unmarried person or a person already married gives no marital privileges. Married men belong to their wives and to no one else. The Christian will not even permit such an affair to get started. (Gen. 39:9)

6. What Shall the Church Teach Regarding Aberrations in Sex Practice?

Evidence reveals that sex crimes and perversions are on the increase. Social studies indicate that masturbation and homosexuality are far more prevalent than was formerly supposed; at least, expanding social case work and better record keeping now bring them to the surface more frequently.

Masturbation in childhood and early adolescence is common (Kinsey reports an incidence of 90 per cent among males and 70 per cent among females; note also the high incidence in the Lutheran survey). See graphs. Formerly masturbation was considered physically harmful. Clinical studies do not prove this to be the case. It is usually a passing phase. Where it does become compulsive, it almost always arouses guilt feelings and is an escape from reality. Neither New Testament nor Old Testament seems to speak specifically about masturbation.

Homosexuality is considered a more serious practice that frequently shows emotional imbalance and need for professional treatment. The Scriptures speak of homosexuality as "leaving the natural use" of the sex organs and perverting God's creation.

The use of sex contrary to God's design is condemned in Scripture. It militates against heterosexual creation, arouses serious guilt feelings, and is frequently a deterrent to marriage and good marital adjustment.

Those who deal with these problems, though not condoning the behavior, advise against condemning the person, since this makes recovery more difficult; they rather suggest an approach of forgiveness, understanding, sympathy, and, where necessary, professional help. It is the duty of the church to give the assurance of full forgiveness in Christ, provide sound counseling, and educate parents.

Promiscuity, prostitution, and harlotry are severly condemned in the New Testament as contrary to God's will, as an offense to the community, and as excluding from the kingdom of Christ him who impenitently persists in these sins. Some medieval churchmen tolerated brothels as an unavoidable social evil because of the widespread corruptness of public morals. The enforcement of celibacy in the Roman Church and false teachings regarding virginity only worsened the situation. Some of the reformers, convinced of the need for marriage as an antidote for sin, allowed exceptions to monogamy, but the church has always condemned polygamy, the establishment or operation of brothels, clandestine love affairs, and whatever desecrated marriage and promoted unchastity.

The church today needs to be conscious of the state of public morals, of the high incidence of extramarital sex relations, and of such deviant behavior as homosexuality. It should be acquainted with rehabilitation processes and should utilize, where indicated, the services of the psychiatrist. It must, however, first of all realize that in the Gospel of redemption it possesses the only power that can re-create all of life (2 Cor. 5: 14-21) and give men and women a new start by means of Christ's forgiveness.

The church, with its moral and spiritual teachings, more than any other institution is the chief support of public morals. It should reappraise, in the light of the changes in present society, the adequacy and effectiveness — both as regards content and methodology — of its instructional program and of the guidance it actually is offering to children, young people, and adults, particularly parents. Mere warning and denunciation are not enough. What the church offers may be too little and too late. Also in such matters let the church be the church, not merely as an upholder of moral standards but above all as a teacher of the Gospel. Christian sex attitudes and practices are products of "being in Christ." (2 Cor. 5:17)

7. What Is the Place of Chastity, Modesty, and Shame in Matters of Sex?

The New Testament says lewdness, impurity, lasciviousness, licentiousness, and unchastity are not for Christians and that those who delight in such things have no place in the kingdom of Christ, because they are yet living in the lusts of the devil, the world, and the flesh. (Eph. 5:3-12)

Chastity is a badge of the Christian, part of his witness to the new life in Christ, and a mark of his concern for the neighbor. Christians are called unto holiness, not uncleanness (1 Thess. 4:3-8); their bodies are members of Christ and temples of the Holy Spirit (1 Cor. 6:15-20), not instruments of unrighteousness (Rom. 6:11-23); they have been taught by Christ to put off the lasciviousness of the unconverted (Eph. 4:17-24) and to regard filthy communication as something unbecoming a child of God (Col. 3:1-8). These passages of Holy Writ are the Christian's code of purity.

The terms *modest* and *decent* are especially applied to behavior and dress as outward manifestations of inward chastity or purity. What is decent in one age or climate or setting may be considered immodest in other times, places, and circumstances. The Christian is concerned that his dress is in good taste and that it does not encourage lustful desires or cause a weaker person to fall. His chief criterion will be: Does my behavior and dress help me to be a good witness to the Christian way of life (1 Tim. 2:9, 10)? In the desire to avoid prudery there is a danger of cultivating laxity and indifference. How to be in the world

and not of the world will always require keen Christian judgment.

While modesty in dress may be considered somewhat relative,
chastity is universal and constant. God has established the rule:
continence before marriage and outside marriage. Chastity is
a purity of mind and heart that regards sex sacred, marriage
honorable, and the other person one whose sexuality is not to
be exploited. Chastity extends to thoughts, speech, and behavior.
Even the respect of spouses for each other can reveal chastity
or unchastity (1 Peter 3:2), for God looks at the heart, and Jesus
judges the motives.

Premarital chastity is a conquering and constructive force
that views the giving of oneself through sexual union as a most
precious gift. It is an expression of personal integrity that looks
forward to the ultimate choice of another person with whom one
is to achieve fulfillment and completion in marriage.

Postmarital chastity is fidelity to one's spouse, using the gift
of sex responsibly as God intended it, in mutual love and respect
and fulfillment.

The new freedom evident today especially in dating practices
includes petting and sexual experimentation. Although interest
and affection may and should be expressed on an increasing scale
as courtship ripens into love and nears engagement, yet the modern heavy petting practice starts an emotional and physical involvement that frequently "goes all the way." This is not only
sinful, but it is also unkind and unwise for one person thus to
exploit basely the sex of another. Heavy petting, or fondling,
tends to cheapen sex, to build up tensions, and to result in feelings of resentment and hypocrisy, thus doing deep damage.

Sex is sacred and has in it an element of mystery. It is hedged
about with privacy, modesty, and respect for womanhood.
A wholesome sense of shame (not of guilt) shields coition from
desecration and assists in the battle for the discipline of the
sexual life. Luther says it nicely: ". . . that we may lead a chaste
and decent life in word and deed, and each love and honor his
spouse."

The Biblical concepts of modesty (1 Tim. 2:9) and chastity
(Titus 2:5; 1 Peter 3:2) will never be outmoded. They are part
of God's order for the welfare of mankind.

This study has not examined the cult of nudism. Christian

opinion generally has not found this view of life reconcilable with Biblical concepts of the avoidance of those things which may occasion another person to fall into sin.

Only if the church — in its witness, in the attitudes of its people, in the lives of the Christians in the community — holds to standards of chastity and each family firmly maintains a Christian sense of values — only then can the next generation learn to live in common decency. The old fear approaches were legalistic instead of evangelical; they forbade but only infrequently offered positive guidance; they did nothing to create a new inner spirit and attitude (Psalm 51:10). Both motivation and guidance should be given to help Christian adults and youths set up and maintain Christian standards with an emphasis on the positive, Christian ideal of sex as part of God's order of creation.

The cultivation of Christian chastity puts a heavy responsibility especially on today's parents.

8. What Is a Christian Attitude Toward the Modern Emphasis on Sex?

Churchmen, philosophers, statesmen, educators, public health authorities, and social workers have testified that in their opinion, based on careful observation, America is experiencing a moral breakdown which is doing deep damage to its children. Much of their evidence has already been cited earlier in this book. School authorities are rightfully alarmed over the sharp rise in pregnancies and illegitimate births among high school girls. The incidence of petting to climax, of premarital coitus, and of homosexual orgasm is disturbingly high among young men during the age span from 16 through 20, as the Kinsey studies report. (See Table C, p. 248)

A number of secondary causes for these conditions have been cited by various observers, for instance: the special strains and tensions in our modern culture; the prolonged period of education which postpones marriage far beyond that of older civilizations; the humanistic philosophy of our times; the sex-saturated entertainment, literature, and advertising; the availability of contraceptives, which to a considerable degree have removed the fears of conception, infection, and detection; juvenile delinquency and the lack of proper home guidance; the coarsening influence of two world wars; the postwar materialism and prosperity; the present imbalance between science and religion; and the use of new scientific discoveries to destructive ends.

But these are only symptoms of a much deeper malady, the secularization of life for many people who formerly lived under social and religious sanctions and who seem to have lost their sense of moral direction and of responsibility for their acts. As respect for God has decreased, sensitivity to sin seems to have been erased from many consciences.

Modern man needs desperately to regain the real meaning and purpose of sex in its religious and moral context as related to the divine institution of marriage. More than that, he needs to rediscover the meaning of life itself under God. This discovery cannot be fully made until God's Law breaks down indifference and irresponsibility, and the Holy Spirit through the Gospel gives repentance and faith and creates a new spiritual life. Christian character can be found only at the foot of the cross.

To this transformation by the Gospel the Christian is to give constant witness by his testimony and way of life. In his dress, speech, and social ideals the Christian bears witness to a Christian standard of morality. He upholds the sanctity of sex in belief and practice. He stands up against immorality. The Christian family, in which parents surround their children with Christian influences and guide youth step by step toward Christian manhood and womanhood with the Gospel and a Christian interpretation of sex and marriage, is one of the most powerful forces for combating false sex attitudes and false standards of behavior.

Here the Christian church can do much more than it has in the past to inculcate positive understanding of sexuality consistent with the Christian faith. It can correct erroneous opinions with a program of constructive teaching and action. Especially can the church help parents become equipped for their role — since homes that stand firm, maintain a Christian sense of values, and are evangelical rather than legalistic in their teaching and training are the strongest dike against immorality of every kind.

To curb the unwholesome emphasis on sex, a Christian can do the following: (1) accept the fact of sex with reverence, as God-given, not as a joking matter; (2) speak respectfully of marriage as an ordinance of God for the blessing and happiness of man; (3) affirm, by word and by example, sensible, realistic, and healthful attitudes toward boy-girl relationships, marriage, and family life; (4) safeguard the sanctity of sex by modest and chaste interpersonal relationships but not in ways that deny sex as a gift of God; (5) hold to Christian standards of morality (Sixth Commandment) and give to children a Christian sense of responsibility toward others as persons whom they are to love for the sake of Christ; (6) endeavor to express sex with propriety as a means, under God, which promotes human happiness and welfare in the family — not as an end in itself for selfish indulgence.

Moral order and the suppression of immorality is also the duty of the state (Rom. 13). Lawmakers, law-enforcement officers, and social scientists are properly concerned with human behavior. Psychology tries to discover why human beings behave as they do. Psychiatry penetrates into the deeper subconscious reasons for antisocial behavior. Social scientists contribute new insight and understanding based on human experience and suggest tools that have been helpful in treatment. The Gospel alone is the real transforming, life-changing power, but the clergyman and the Christian educator can apply Law and Gospel more understandingly and effectively if they have good insights into human behavior, gained from scientific studies. This knowledge is needed particularly for good marriage education and counseling.

There are times when the church needs to join forces with social and law-enforcement agencies to clean up a situation which is threatening the moral welfare of a whole community. Because the peer group wields such a strong influence on youth, many problems must be attacked by parents on a neighborhood or community basis. Although the church is a "transforming" agency rather than a "reform" agency, it is also called to be a witness for righteousness like the prophets of the Old Testament. No less than the prophets and apostles the Christian church should speak out and recognize its God-given task. It can and should cooperate in well-conceived programs of community action together with statesmen, teachers, and editors in molding public opinion that we and our children "may lead a quiet and peaceable life, godly and respectful in every way." (1 Tim. 2:2 RSV)

9. What Is the Church's Responsibility and Role in Sex Education?

The long debate in the church on the propriety of sex education seems tragic in the light of all the facts. Not to give the right kind of sex instruction seems inexcusable now. While knowledge of sex facts doesn't make people chaste if the heart is wrong, ignorance and silence have done more harm than sex education. Prudery has failed miserably. It made matters of sex secretive and unwholesome for the child, lustful for youth, and then often resorted to face-saving moralisms. A proper acceptance of self and a wholesome self-image require that the child know and accept the impulses of his body. Even with its silence and quiescence the church was as a matter of fact doing some sex educating. It was saying sex is beneath the dignity of Christian teaching and must be "picked up" elsewhere. This hardly makes sense, especially since most social scientists realize that biological and social facts are ineffective without a spiritual sense of values and Christian attitudes. The secular press is saying, "Sex education is a job for the clergy!"

There are nevertheless some questions: By whom? When? and How? Church educators agree that the home must play a vital role in sex education, but they find most parents uninterested or unequipped or embarrassed. (The Lutheran survey showed 90 per cent in favor of parent-child sex discussions but only 20 per cent having such discussions.) Other persons cannot really take the place of father and mother in this matter and do not have the teaching opportunities parents have. In the nature of the case parents *do* play a role, negative or positive, and should be equipped by the church and others to do their part well. School and church can only supplement the home. This is a big, new task for the church.

The schools (public *and* parochial or private) also have a task. Here the questions increase: How much? With what religious orientation? Is the average teacher adequately equipped? The social contacts of our youth are not restricted to church people. For the protection of our children other boys and girls of the community need proper sex education. A problem as widespread as the sex revolution needs to be attacked on a broad front, not merely by a few isolated columns of soldiers. Here the church school is in a better position than any other school because it has a religious approach and can deal with the whole person in the whole curriculum.

Authorities also agree that sex education begins at birth and is to be integrated with daily living. It is not to be given in isolated little doses but when the child asks questions, progressing to greater details as need dictates until adequate understanding is attained. Sex is to be interpreted spiritually. Educators say it must begin before the child is involved emotionally in early adolescence.

It is hoped that books like this one will help the church select both context and content of sex education. The social and educational sciences can supply the necessary techniques for good teaching and learning.

The church has an important role in sex education. (1) It can give parents the content, materials, methods, and above all, the attitudes which will equip them to do the basic task. (2) It can supplement the work of parents in the teaching program of the church. (3) It can train its teachers and youth leaders to do their part with understanding and in close co-operation with parents. (4) It can show interest in and help develop adequate public education, which supplements the work of the church and is not in conflict with Christian ideals.

Whatever the process, the attitude of the teacher is fundamental: Sex is both important and fundamentally good because it is God-given. It is not sexual behavior that determines character; it is character that determines sexual behavior.

10. What Is a Christian Interpretation of Sex?

The right view of sex begins with a person's right view of life. If his view is Christian, he will trust God, who created sex, and in faith accept the limits of its use which God has set. By faith the Christian embraces his sexual life as a divinely given part of creation. He identifies himself with God's plan for human life and well-being, viewing his own life of sex in its light. This means that all things are looked upon spiritually and accepted gratefully in faith. "Everything created by God is good, and nothing is to be rejected if it is received with thanksgiving; for then it is consecrated by the Word of God and prayer." (1 Tim. 4:4 RSV)

God made man a sexual being. Sex has many useful functions. It is part of the warp and woof of life and belongs to the
fiber of our being. Most living things in the world owe their
existence to the principle of sex. Sexuality gives a new dimension
to life; without it life would not only be flat, it could not even
exist. God puts beauty, happiness, children, and countless other
blessings into our world through sex. Sex existed before sin came
into the world. God made it and pronounced it good. God instituted marriage as a holy state and as a God-pleasing vocation.
Through sex we become partners in God's ongoing creation.
Through sex, marriage is consummated. The one-flesh union continually re-creates and renews the marriage. Sex is reserved for
full use only in marriage, where it strengthens man and wife
physically, socially, spiritually, and psychologically.

Sex is not divorced from religion for the Christian. He accepts it as a gift of God (Gen. 1:31) and uses it according to
God's will (Matt. 19:4, 5), to His glory (1 Cor. 10:31), and for
His purposes (Gen. 1:28; 2:24). The proper use of sex is part
of the Christian's grateful response to God, who made sex in
creation (Gen. 1:27), redeemed sex as part of the total person
(1 Cor. 6:19, 20), and sanctifies the proper use of sex through
the Holy Spirit (1 Thess. 5:23). Sex is included in the Christian's
total dedication to God according to Rom. 12:1: "Present your
bodies as a living sacrifice, holy and acceptable to God, which is
your spiritual worship." (RSV)

Although sex is a good gift of God, like other gifts of God
it can be and is misused by reason of sin, which dwells in all
people since the fall. Satan has adulterated every aspect of sex
(Rom. 1). He exploits the dynamic power of sex for demonic
ends. Sinful people have taken a good thing and through misuse
made it perplexing, destructive, and explosive. The fall brought
lust in beside love, and wrong desire beside right desire. Also
the Christian still has the effects of the fall in his bosom, and
like every other sinful human being must do combat against lust
and exercise self-control. In this struggle the Christian has the
Holy Spirit as a powerful aid at his side.

Though justified by God's grace and fully forgiven, the Christian nevertheless lives in the sinful flesh. Thus he is at the same
time, as Luther put it, a saint and a sinner *(simul justus et pec-
cator)*. The Christian's words, thoughts, and deeds, also those

in the area of sex, are imperfect while he is in this world. Daily the Christian, following the covenant of his baptism, repents of and confesses his sins, receives assurance of full forgiveness, and in the Spirit's strength mortifies his "sinful self." He daily prays for a clean heart and a right spirit.

Because sex is not a thing to be despised or treated with apologies, because it is created by God and is not sinful, because there is no special merit or virtue in the unmarried, or celibate, state, and because marriage is an institution of integrity and honor, there will be no room for a false asceticism in the Christian view of sex. Sex is not "evil" or "dirty" or "a regrettable overplus of guilty desire which marriage helps us to dispose of secretly."

The Christian views sex as being part of his total personality and part of the total context of life. This view is in contrast to the strictly scientific view that it is purely a biological phenomenon or a biochemical function in man. Nor does he accept a purely naturalistic or humanistic view which divorces sex from moral law and rejects man's accountability to a higher being for his use of sex. This view is practically atheistic in its orientation. Nor does the Christian view sex as merely a phenomenon in human life with sociological aspects, as if sex were to be evaluated only as it affects society. Each of these views lacks the full dimension of the concept of man as a moral creature responsible to Almighty God.

The Christian and Biblical view of sex rejects the many half-truths and errors that have crept into the thinking of the church down through the centuries and have never been entirely expelled from popular Christianity: (1) that sex per se is sin; (2) that sex sins are unforgivable or the worst sins in God's sight; (3) that the body is evil and bodily functions are "nasty"; (4) that only the things of the spirit or soul can be good; (5) that anything connected with the material things of the world is of itself evil and displeasing to God; (6) that all pleasure, particularly all pleasure connected with sex, is sin; (7) that the commandment against adultery is only negative, a prohibition without a positive side; (8) that in sinful man there can be no right sexual desire; (9) that virginity is the only pure state; (10) that the celibate life is holier than married life; (11) that such ascetic acts as continence in marriage help to earn the favor of God;

(12) that the first sin was a sexual act (the eating of the fruit being a metaphor for it); (13) that Christianity is a matter of regulations: Do not handle, Do not taste, Do not touch (Col. 2:21); (14) that marriage merely legalizes sexual relations; (15) that sex activity is animallike and unworthy of man; (16) that sex desire belongs to our "lower instincts." These and similar half-truths or errors have brought not only confusion, uneasiness, and wrong attitudes, but they have also unnecessarily burdened consciences and spoiled many a marriage. Where the traditional view that "sex is essentially sinful" has been taught, it is very difficult to grasp the truth that sex can be good.

Conclusion

This study has revealed how central and fundamental the order of creation is for a proper understanding of the place of sex in life. The order of creation includes the sanctity of sex, the worth of man, and the significance of the one-flesh relationship in marriage to create life and to renew marriage. Equally important is the doctrine of redemption. The body as well as the soul is redeemed. Sinful, fallen man now reconciled to God can use sex to God's glory because sex, too, has been redeemed. The doctrine of sanctification is also involved. In Christian marriage sex is sanctified as husband and wife live with God, with self, and with each other in daily contrition, repentance, and faith, drawing forgiveness out of the fountain of God's grace in Christ.

The Christian life is not mere separation from evil but separation for good, for intimate personal fellowship with the living God. It is to be lived within the entire framework of the Christian ethos, which is predicated on the doctrine of atonement based on the morality of the regenerate man, having Jesus as its ideal, the New Testament as its general frame of reference, the Holy Spirit as its dynamic power, a Christian conscience as its monitor, a life to the glory of God as its goal, and gratitude for God's grace in Christ as its motive.[5]

---

[5] Carl F. H. Henry, *Christian Personal Ethics* (Grand Rapids: Wm. B. Eerdmans Publishing Co., 1957), pp. 427—435.

Graphs, Tables, Bibliography, Indexes

The Sociological Survey

In the sociological study of 3,400 couples, 750 unmarried young people, and 1,000 pastors in three Lutheran synods (The Lutheran Church — Missouri Synod [Mo.], The Evangelical Lutheran Church [ELC], The Augustana Lutheran Church [Aug.]) residing in all parts of the United States and chosen by an approved, objective method (random sampling), the following questions on sex attitudes were asked. The most significant answers tabulated by machine are summarized in the following graphs.

Questions asked of all (married persons, single persons, pastors):

SEX ATTITUDES

	YOUR BELIEFS			YOUR ACTIONS	
	RIGHT	NOT SURE	WRONG	HAVE	HAVE NOT
1. Do you believe that it is right for young people to receive a thorough sex education before marriage? (Circle one answer in each column)	RT	?	WR	H	HN
2. Do you believe it is right to have a frank and sober discussion of sex —					
a. Between parents and children? (Circle one answer in each column)	RT	?	WR	H	HN
b. Between friends of the same sex? (Circle one answer in each column)	RT	?	WR	H	HN
c. Between couples in serious courtship? (Circle one answer in each column)	RT	?	WR	H	HN
3. Do you believe that frank sex education (correctly given) will lead to immorality? (Circle in first column only)	RT	?	WR		
4. Do you believe that there are any circumstances under which masturbation (handling of one's own sex organs for pleasure) could be right? (Circle one answer in each column)	RT	?	WR	H	HN

Two additional questions were asked of married couples and pastors:

	YOUR BELIEFS			YOUR ACTIONS	
5. Do you believe that it is right to have sex relations for the enjoyment of husband and wife without the intention of conceiving children? (Circle one answer in each column)	RT	?	WR	H	HN
6. Do you believe that in marriage it is right to engage in any type of sex activity agreeable to both husband and wife? (Circle one answer in each column)	RT	?	WR	H	HN

The questionnaire to those not yet married asked also for the sources from which the best sex education was received:

Please number in the order of their importance the sources from which you received your best sex education.

1. Father _____   6. Teachers _____
2. Mother _____   7. Pastor _____
3. Both parents _____   8. Brothers and sisters _____
4. Books _____   9. Friends and playmates _____
5. Physician _____   10. Other (state which) _____

The only difference in the questions was that those directed to the pastors asked not for "beliefs" and "actions" (practice) but "do you teach (or advise)" and gave the choice between "yes," "no," and "never mention," as per sample of question 1:

	YES	NO	NEVER MENTION
1. Do you teach (or advise) that it is right for young people to receive a thorough sex education before marriage? (Circle one)	YES	NO	NM

Graph 1

SEX EDUCATION BEFORE MARRIAGE

APPROVE SEX EDUCATION

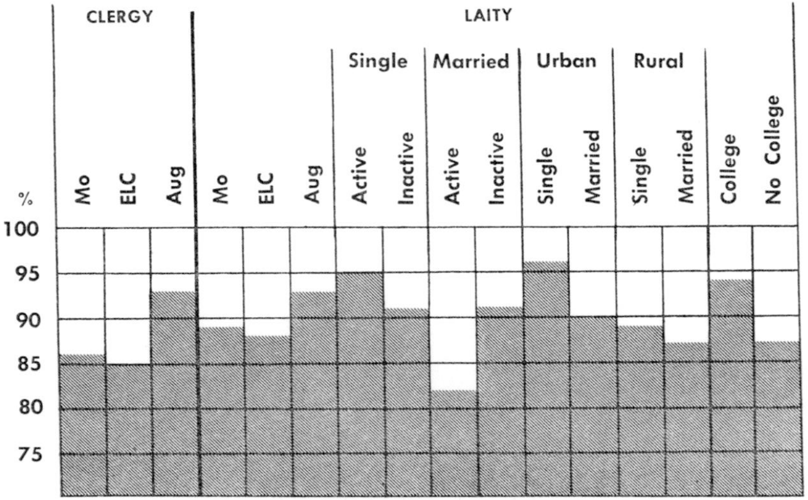

RECEIVED SEX EDUCATION

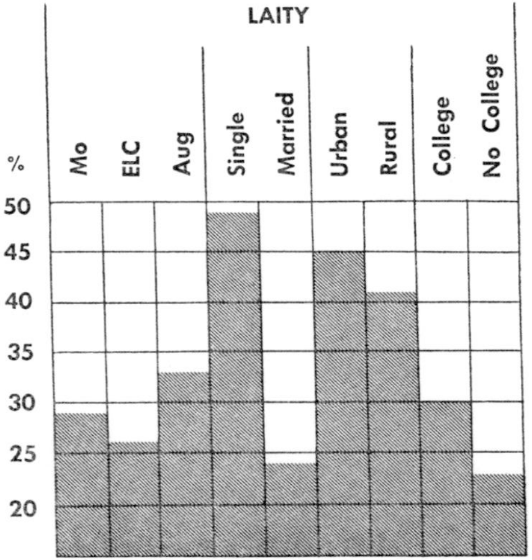

There is general agreement favoring sex education by as high as 93 per cent of the clergy and laity. As the graph shows, there was only a slight variation between the respective synods. This approval varies only slightly between single and married, urban and rural, college-educated and such as have no college training, active and inactive Lutheran church members.

The most striking discovery is in the low number of persons who have received sex education, as low as 29 per cent of all persons included in the survey. This reveals the inadequacy of the sex-education program in home, school, and church. The low figures for the married (24 per cent) and for those who did not get college education (23 per cent) may reflect age of the respondents and may indicate that more sex education is being offered now.

SOURCES OF SEX EDUCATION

Graph 2

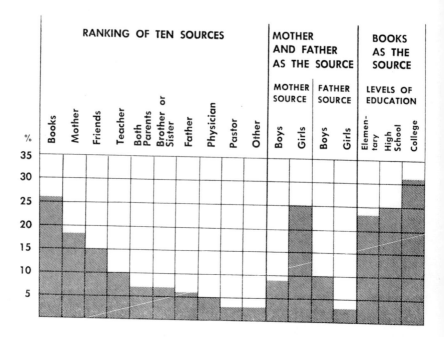

500 persons not yet married were asked to indicate the source of their sex information and education. The respondents checked ten items in the order of their importance as sources from which they received the best sex education. Three votes were given for first place, 2 for second, and 1 for third. No votes were given for placing lower than third. The percentages were then established on the basis of total votes.

This part of the survey reveals the very small role in sex education played by father, physician, and pastor. Books are the chief source. This may indicate the general feeling of incompetence on the part of so many parents. The mother rates three times more as a source than the father and six times more than the pastor. The church's role seems to be quite negligible, very likely because of false views of sex and traditional taboos. The mother is as influential as the father with boys and eight times more influential regarding sex education with girls.

Books become a greater source as the person moves from elementary school through high school and college.

SEX DISCUSSION APPROVED AND PRACTICED

Graph 3

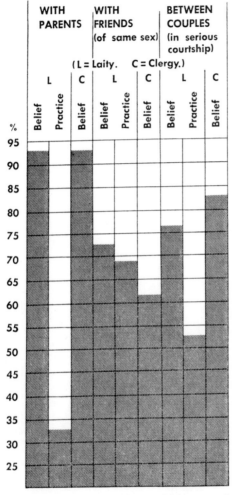

There is complete agreement between laity (married persons [parents included], single persons) and pastors that frank and sober discussion of sex should take place between parents and their children. Yet only in one third of the cases is this belief or opinion put into practice. This shows how great is the need for supplementing home instruction with proper sex orientation in church and school.

Children apparently talk more freely about sex to their friends (of the same sex) than to their parents. Only in a little more than half of the cases did respondents report that frank sex discussion took place during their courtship.

[For Question 3, dealing with the opinion as to whether frank sex education (correctly given) will lead to immorality, no graph was constructed. 71 per cent of the laity replied that it would not, 15 per cent that it would, and 14 per cent were not sure. 90 per cent of the clergy did not believe that such education would lead to immorality.]

MASTURBATION

Graph 4

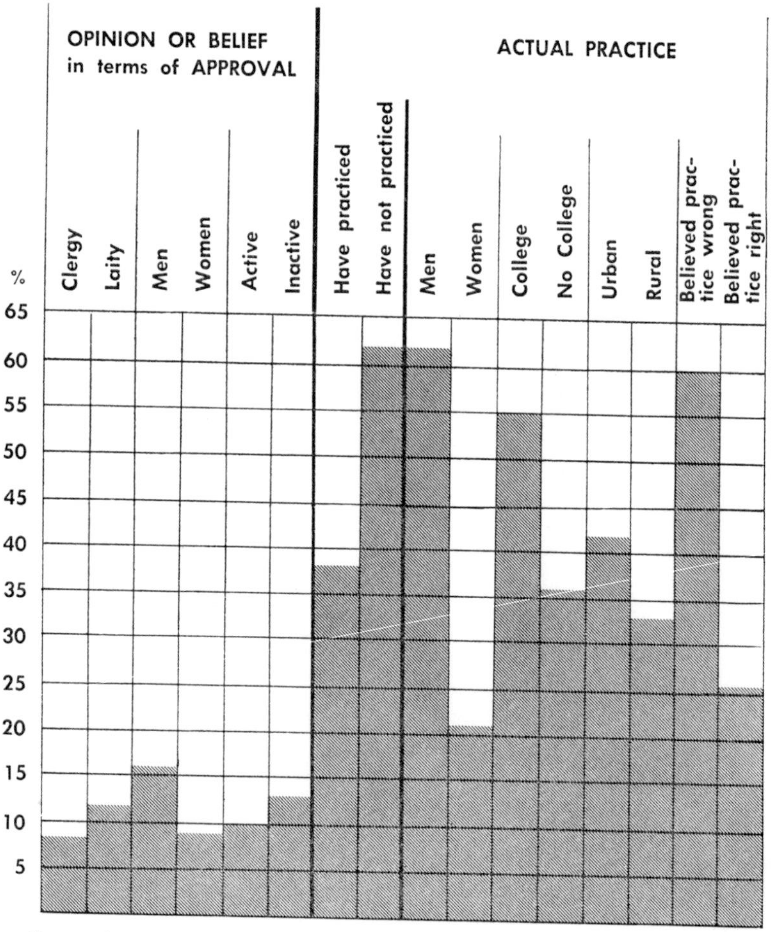

The number of lay respondents to Question 4 was 3,868. 12 per cent approved masturbation, 13 per cent were not sure, 75 per cent considered masturbation wrong. Only 8 per cent of the clergy approved, 23 per cent were not sure, 69 per cent believed masturbation to be wrong. About half as many women as men approved the practice. There was only a small difference when the approvals by active church members were compared with approvals by inactive members.

2,703 married and single people answered the question regarding their own practices, and of these, 38 per cent had practiced masturbation, and 62 per cent had not. These percentages are broken down as regards men and women, college-trained and non-college persons, urban and rural residents.

The inconsistency between belief and practice is shown in the last two bars of the graph, where 60 per cent of those who believed masturbation wrong (2,290 cases responding) practiced it just the same, while only 35 per cent of those who believed masturbation right admitted to having practiced it.

SEX ENJOYMENT IN MARRIAGE
APART FROM PROCREATION

Graph 5

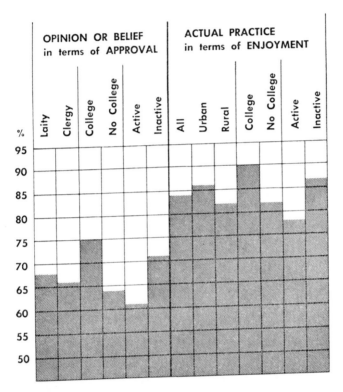

68 per cent of the married laity approved the enjoyment of conjugal sex relations (apart from procreation), 10 per cent were not sure, 22 per cent believed such enjoyment to be wrong. 66 per cent of the clergy approved such enjoyment, 19 per cent were doubtful about it, and 15 per cent considered it wrong. These figures reflect somewhat the general uncertainty growing out of variant teachings in the church through the centuries. Note also that those without college training and active church members express less approval.

The total number of the laity responding to this question was 3,232. Only 2,440 filled in the column on practice ("Your Actions"). 84 per cent of these reported enjoyment of the conjugal act, or 16 per cent more than considered enjoyment "right." The variations between urban and rural persons, college trained and others, active and inactive church members are not too significant. It should be noted that the question included the phrase "without the intention of conceiving children."

[With regard to Question 6 the replies were considered invalid and no graph was constructed, because the question itself seemed to be variously interpreted by the respondents.]

TABLES A and B

Tables A and B are from "Opinions of a Group of Lutheran High School Students Regarding the Sources of Influence of Their Attitudes in the Areas of Morals, Marriage, Sex, and Family," a Master's thesis by Mardelle Meyer, submitted to the College of Education, Michigan State University, in 1959. Using the opinionnaire "Survey of Attitudes and Beliefs, Form AH" (Chicago: Science Research Associates, 1955) by Leslie W. Nelson, professor of education, Los Angeles State College, Miss Meyer chose 25 items for her study, four of which dealt with sex:

Item   14   A girl has to neck to have a second date with a boy.

Item   87   Heavy necking and petting are not so bad unless they lead to extremes.

Item 105   If young people want information about sex problems, they should ask their parents or teachers.

Item 135   Intimacy with the opposite sex (from Section III, ". . . things that some people believe are wrong").

Participating in the survey were 88 senior students of Detroit Lutheran High School West. The "N" in the tables represents the number of cases or students in the group.

This limited survey shows that mother influence is strongest where sex information is correct and weakest where sex information is incorrect. It gives pastors a high rating but the organized teaching functions of youth group and Bible class re sex education a low rating. Compare with Graph 2 for similarities and dissimilarities.

TABLE A
Sources of Influence Listed Most Often by Students
*Answering **Incorrectly** Items in the Area of Sex*

Sources of Influence	Items:				
	14 N = 6	87 N = 21	105 N = 10	135 N = 56	Total
Friends, Community	2	3	1	3	9
Movies, Nonreligious		3		4	7
Friends, School		3		3	6
Books, Religious				5	5
Friends, Church	3				3
Father				3	3
Mother				3	3

TABLE B

Sources of Influence Listed Most Often by Students
*Answering **Correctly** Items in the Area of Sex*

Sources of Influence	Items:				
	14 N = 82	87 N = 67	105 N = 78	135 N = 32	Total
Mother	18	24	24	15	81
Pastor	9	28	13	12	62
Books, religious	13	26		16	55
High school, teachers	12	15	20	7	54
Father		19	20	8	47
Friends, school	29	8			37
High school, classes		9	13		22
Church, Walther League	9	7			16
Friends, church	10				10
Church, Bible class		9			9

TABLE C

To permit the reader to make a comparison between sexual behavior in the Lutheran survey and the findings of the Kinsey reports Table C below is included. It was prepared by Jerome Himelhoch and appeared in *Social Hygiene Papers: A Symposium on Sex Education,* published by the American Social Hygiene Association, 1790 Broadway, New York 19, N.Y., November 1957. Mr. Himelhoch with S. F. Fava is coeditor of *Sexual Behavior in American Society* (New York: Norton, 1955), an evaluation of the Kinsey studies by representative scholars in the field. You will note that the age span includes the last two high school years, during which young people are most likely to be exposed to courses in sex education. We attach also Mr. Himelhoch's footnote to the table. In this note "I" is used as an abbreviation for A. C. Kinsey, W. B. Pomeroy, and C. E. Martin, *Sexual Behavior in the Human Male* (Philadelphia: Saunders, 1948), and "II" refers to A. C. Kinsey, W. B. Pomeroy, C. E. Martin, and P. H. Gebhard, *Sexual Behavior in the Human Female* (Philadelphia: Saunders, 1953).

Himelhoch's footnote: "Source of Data: I: 240, 244, 248, 258; II: 178, 267, 271, 334, 491. For the females, Kinsey gives statistics based upon his own sample only. In his end-of-chapter summaries in the volume on the female he compares his female sample incidence percentages with the male sample incidence percentages *corrected in terms of the United States Census population of 1940.* Even though it might be argued that it would be more logical to compare uncorrected male statistics with uncorrected female statistics, I have followed Kinsey's usage in the above table. For no apparent reason, however, Kinsey departs from his own procedure on II: 478 by comparing uncorrected single male active incidence of homosexual orgasm, age 16—20 (22%) with the uncorrected female percentage. In the interest of consistency I have given above the *corrected* percentage for male homosexual incidence, as given on I: 258. In the case of the male median frequencies, I have followed Kinsey's practice of basing these upon the uncorrected male sample."

TABLE C

*Active Incidence and Frequency of Sexual Activities
During Age Span 16 Through 20 Years*

ACTIVITY	SINGLE MALES		SINGLE FEMALES	
	Incid. %	Median Freq. per yr.	Incid. %	Median Freq. per yr.
Masturbation to Orgasm	88	57	28	21
Petting *	80—90	—	80—90	—
Petting to Climax	32	5	23	5
Premarital Coitus	71	31	20	10
Homosexual Orgasm	31	6	3	10

* Kinsey's definition of petting includes necking.

Bibliography

Althaus, Paul. Essay, *Die Begegnung der Geschlechter*. Erlangen-Bavaria, n. d.

——. *Grundriss der Ethik*. Gütersloh: Bertelsmann, 1953.

Aquinas, Thomas. *Summa Theologica*. London: Burns, Oates, and Washbourne Ltd., 1932.

Arndt, William F., and F. Wilbur Gingrich. *A Greek-English Lexicon of the New Testament*. London: Cambridge University Press, 1957.

Augusti, Johann C. W. "Von der Ehe," *Handbuch der christlichen Archaeologie*, III. Leipzig: Dyk'schen Buchhandlung, 1836.

Ayrinhac, H. A. *Marriage Legislation in the New Code of Canon Law*, rev. and enl. by P. J. Lydon. New York: Benziger Bros., Inc., 1949.

Baber, Ray E. *Marriage and the Family*. New York: McGraw-Hill, 1953.

Bacon, Leonard. *Thirteen Historical Discourses*. New Haven: Durrie and Peck; New York: Gould, Newman and Saxton, 1839.

Bacon, Leonard Woolsey. *History of American Christianity*. New York: Christian Literature Company, 1897.

Badger Lutheran. Publ. by Milwaukee, Wis., Federation of Lutheran Churches. Jan. 22, 1959.

Baier, John Wm. *Compendium theologiae positivae*, ed. C. F. W. Walther. St. Louis: Concordia Publishing House, 1879.

Bailey, Derrick Sherwin. *The Mystery of Love and Marriage*. New York: Harper & Bros., 1952.

——. *Sexual Relation in Christian Thought*. New York: Harper & Bros., 1959.

Bainton, Roland H. "Christianity and Sex," *Sex and Religion Today*, ed. Simon Doniger. New York: Association Press, 1953.

——. "Marriage and Love in Christian History," *Religion in Life*, XVII (Summer 1948), 399, 400.

——. *What Christianity Says About Sex, Love and Marriage*. New York: Association Press, 1957.

Balduin, Friedrich. *Commentaries in omnes epistolas beati apostoli Pauli*. Francofurti: A. D. Moenum, 1691.

Banning, Margaret Culkin. "The Case for Chastity," *Reader's Digest*, XXXI, No. 184 (Aug. 1937), 1—10.

Barrett, Thomas V. *The Christian Family*. New York: Morehouse-Gorham Co., 1958.

Bee, Lawrence S. *Marriage and Family Relationships*. New York: Harper & Bros., 1959.

Behlmer, Reuben D. *From Teens to Marriage.* St. Louis: Concordia Publishing House, 1959.

Bente, G. Friedrich. *American Lutheranism.* St. Louis: Concordia Publishing House, 1909.

Bertocci, Peter A. *The Human Venture in Sex, Love, and Marriage,* 5th prtg. New York: Association Press, 1958.

Bittle, Celestine N. *Man and Morals.* Milwaukee: Bruce Publishing Co., 1949.

Bouma, Clarence. "Calvinism in American Theology Today," *Calvinism in Times of Crisis* (papers read at the 1947 American Calvinistic Conference). Grand Rapids: Baker Book House, 1947.

Bovet, Theodor. *Die Ehe.* Tübingen: Furche Verlag, 1948.

———. *Love, Skill and Mystery.* Garden City, N. Y.: Doubleday & Co., 1958.

Bowman, Henry A. *A Christian Interpretation of Marriage.* Philadelphia: Westminster Press, 1959.

———. *Marriage for Moderns,* 3d ed. New York: McGraw-Hill, 1948.

Bracher, Marjory Louise. *Love Is No Luxury: A Guide for Christian Family Living.* Philadelphia: Muhlenberg Press, 1951.

Brav, Stanley. *Marriage and Jewish Tradition.* New York: Philosophical Library, 1951.

Brayshaw, Alfred Neave. *The Quakers: Their Story and Message,* 2d ed. London: The Swarthmore Press Ltd.; New York: The Macmillan Co., 1927.

Bruce, Gustav M. "The Evangelical Lutheran Church and Family Life" (unpublished research summary, 1953).

———. *Marriage and Divorce.* Minneapolis: Augsburg Publishing House, 1930.

Buddeus, John Francis. *Institutiones theologiae moralis.* Leipzig: Fritsch, 1715.

Burgess, Ernest W., and Paul Wallin. *Engagement and Marriage.* Philadelphia: J. B. Lippincott Co., 1953.

Burke, Louis H. *With This Ring.* New York: McGraw-Hill, 1958.

Cabot, Richard C. *Christianity and Sex.* Chicago: Macmillan, 1937.

Cadoux, Cecil John. *The Early Church and the World.* Edinburgh: T. & T. Clark, 1925.

Calverton, Victor F., and Samuel D. Schmalhausen, eds. *Sex in Civilization,* 7th prtg. New York: The Macaulay Co., 1929.

Calvin, John *Commentary on Corinthians,* I, trans. John Pringle. Grand Rapids: Wm. B. Eerdmans Publishing Co., 1948.

———. *In Defense of the Reformed Faith.* Vol. III in *Tracts and Treatises Relating to the Reformation.* Grand Rapids: Wm. B. Eerdmans Publishing Co., 1959.

———. *Institutes of the Christian Religion,* trans. John Allen. Grand Rapids: Wm. B. Eerdmans Publishing Co., 1949.

Cannon, Ralph A., and Glenn D. Everett. "Sex and Smut on the Newsstands," *Christianity Today,* II (Feb. 17, 1958), 5—8.

Catholic Encyclopedia, The. New York: Robert Appleton Co., 1908.

Central Illinois District Lutheran, October 1937, p. 22.

Chemnitz, Martin. *Loci theologici,* ed. Polycarp Leyser. Frankfurt-Wittenberg: Christian H. Schumacher; type by B. C. Wust, 1690.

Chemnitz, Martin, Polycarp Leyser, Johann Gerhard. *Harmonia Evangelistarum,* I, II. Geneva: Chouet, 1645.

Christian Guidance on Marriage and Family Life, issued by The Board of Social Missions, The United Lutheran Church in America, 231 Madison Ave., New York 16, N. Y., 1956.

Clemens, A. H. *Marriage and Family Relations.* Washington: Catholic University of America Press, 1950.

Coiner, Harry G. *The Christian View of Sex.* St. Louis: Concordia Tract Mission, 1960.

Cole, William Graham. *Sex in Christianity and Psychoanalysis.* New York: Oxford University Press, 1955.

Concordia Pulpit 1950. St. Louis: Concordia Publishing House, 1949.

Concordia Theological Monthly, III (Nov. 1932).

Course of Study for Family Life Education, Senior Schools. The San Antonio, Texas, Board of Education, n. d.

Cross, Frank Moore, Jr. *The Ancient Library of Qumran and Modern Biblical Studies.* New York: Doubleday, 1958.

Crump, Charles G. and Ernest F. Jacob. *Legacy of the Middle Ages.* New York: Oxford University Press, 1926.

Crusius, Christian August. *Kurzer Begriff der Moral Theologie,* II. Leipzig: Saalbach, 1773.

Dakin, Arthur. *Calvinism.* Philadelphia: Westminster Press, 1940.

Dannhauer, John C. *Theologia casualis.* Greifswald: John W. Fickweiler, 1706.

De Rougemont, Denis. *Love in the Western World,* trans. Montgomery Belgion. New York: Harcourt, Brace and Co., 1940.

Dedekennus, George. *Thesaurus consiliorum et decisionum,* III, ed. John Ernst Gerhard. Jena: Hertel, 1671.

Deems, Mervin Monroe. "The Sources of Christian Asceticism," *Environmental Factors in Christian History,* ed. John Thomas McNeill, Matthew Spinka, Harold R. Willoughby. Chicago: University of Chicago Press, 1939.

DeJong, Alexander C. *The Christian Family and Home.* Grand Rapids, Mich.: Baker Book House, 1959.

Denomy, Alexander J. "An Inquiry into the Origins of Courtly Love," *Medieval Studies,* VI (1944), 175—260.

Dierks, Hartwig. *Social Teachings of the Old Testament.* St. Louis: Concordia, 1940.

Doninger, Simon, ed. *Sex and Religion Today.* New York: Association Press, 1953.

Dunte, Louis. *Decisiones mille et sex casuum conscientiae,* 3d ed. Lübeck: Wetstein, 1664.

Duvall, Evelyn, and Reuben Hill. *When You Marry.* New York: D. C. Heath & Co., 1953.

Duvall, Sylvanus M. *Men, Women, and Morals.* New York: Association Press, 1952.

Eckhardt, Ernst. *Homiletisches Reallexikon,* II. St. Louis: Success Printing Co., 1908.

Eichrodt, Walter. *Theologie des Alten Testaments,* 3d ed. Berlin: Evangelische Verlagsanstalt, 1950.

Ellis, Albert. *Sex Without Guilt.* New York: Lyle Stuart, 1958.

Ellis, Havelock. *Studies in the Psychology of Sex.* In seven vols., 1897 to 1928. Now four vols., New York: Random House, 1936.

Elmer, Manuel C. *Sociology of the Family.* Boston: Ginn & Co., 1945.

252   *Sex and the Church*

Encyclopaedia Britannica, XVIII. Chicago: Encyclopaedia Britannica, Inc., 1951.

Encyclopedia Americana, The. XXII. New York: Americana Corporation, 1955.

English, O. Spurgeon, and Gerald H. J. Pearson. *Emotional Problems of Living: Avoiding the Neurotic Pattern.* New York: W. W. Norton & Co., 1945.

Evangelisch-Lutherisches Schulblatt, II (May 1867); III (Oct. 1867); XVI (March-April 1881); XXIV (Aug. 1899).

Fagley, Richard A. *The Population Explosion and Christian Responsibility.* New York: Oxford University Press, 1960.

Fishbein, Morris, and Ernest W. Burgess, eds. *Successful Marriage: A Modern Guide to Love, Sex, and Family Life,* rev. ed. Garden City, N.Y.: Doubleday, 1955.

Fishbein, Morris, and Ruby J. R. Kennedy, eds. *Modern Marriage and Family Living.* New York: Oxford University Press, 1957.

Fitch, Robert E. *Preface to Ethical Living.* New York: Association Press, 1947.

Folsom, Joseph K. *The Family and Democratic Society.* New York: John Wiley & Sons, Inc., 1943.

————. *The Family: Its Sociology and Social Psychiatry.* New York: John Wiley & Sons, Inc., 1934.

Forell, George W. *Ethics of Decision.* Philadelphia: Muhlenberg Press, 1955.

Foster, Robert G. *Marriage and Family Relationships.* New York: Macmillan, 1950.

Fritz, John H. C. *Pastoral Theology.* St. Louis: Concordia Publishing House, 1932; 2d ed., 1945.

Fuerbringer, Ludwig, Theodore Engelder, Paul E. Kretzmann, eds. *The Concordia Cyclopedia.* St. Louis: Concordia Publishing House, 1927.

Geiseman, Otto A. *Make Yours a Happy Marriage.* St. Louis: Concordia Publishing House, 1946.

Gerhard, John. *Loci theologici,* ed. Ed. Preuss. Berolini: Sumptibus Gust. Schlawitz, 1869.

Good, James I. *History of the Reformed Church in America.* Reading, Pa.: Daniel Miller, 1894.

Graebner, August L. *Doctrinal Theology.* St. Louis: Concordia Publishing House, 1910.

Graebner, Theodore. *The Borderland of Right and Wrong.* St. Louis: Concordia Publishing House, 1932; 8th ed., 1951.

————. *Pastor and People.* St. Louis: Concordia Publishing House, 1932.

Greenblatt, Bernard. *A Doctor's Marital Guide for Patients.* Chicago: The Budlong Press, 1957.

Groeger, G. N. *Man hat doch ein Recht auf Liebe,* in the series *Mädchen, Liebe und junge Männer.* Nürnberg: Laetare Verlag, 1953.

Groves, Ernest R. and Gladys. *The Contemporary American Family.* Philadelphia: J. B. Lippincott Co., 1947.

Guenther, Martin. *Populäre Symbolik,* 3d ed. St. Louis: Concordia Publishing House, 1898.

Haller, William. *The Rise of Puritanism.* New York: Columbia University Press, 1938.

Harless, G. Chr. Adolph von. *Christliche Ethik.* Gütersloh: C. Bertelsmann, 1875.

Harman, Carl H., and Edward W. Marquardt. *Vital Facts of Life*. St. Louis: Concordia Publishing House, 1949.

Harper, Robert A. *Marriage*. New York: Appleton-Century-Crofts, 1949.

Harper's Latin Dictionary, ed. E. A. Andrews. New York: American Book Co., 1907.

Hart, Hornell. *Recent Social Trends in the United States*. New York: McGraw-Hill, 1933.

Hattingberg, Hans von. *Ueber die Liebe*. München-Basel: Ernst Reinhardt, 1949.

Heiler, Friedrich. *Der Katholizismus: Seine Idee und seine Erscheinung*. München, Germany: Verlag Ernst Reinhardt, 1923.

Heinecken, Martin J. "A Theology of Marriage" (unpublished paper, delivered at Seminar on Christian Education and the Family, St. Olaf College, Northfield, Minn.), 1957.

Heinisch, Paul, and William Heidt. *Theology of the Old Testament*. Collegeville, Minn.: The Liturgical Press, St. John's Abbey, 1950.

Henry, Carl F. H. *Christian Personal Ethics*. Grand Rapids: Wm. B. Eerdmans Publishing Co., 1957.

Henslow, George. *Present-Day Rationalism Examined*. London: Hodder and Stoughton, 1904.

Hiltner, Seward. *Sex and the Christian Life*. New York: Association Press, 1957.

———. *Sex Ethics and the Kinsey Reports*. New York: Association Press, 1952.

Himelhoch, Jerome, and Sylvia F. Fava, eds. *Sexual Behavior in American Society: An Appraisal of the First Two Kinsey Reports*. New York: W. W. Norton & Co., 1955.

Hirzel, Rudolph. *Wir Männer und die Frauen*, Schriftenreihe der Protestantischen Eheberatung, Heft I. St. Gallen, Switzerland: Vadian Verlag, 1949.

———. *Zur heutigen Ehenot*. St. Gallen, Switzerland: Vadian Verlag, 1949.

Hollaz, David. *Examen theologicum acroamaticum*. Leipzig: Godfrey Kiesewetter, 1741.

Hope, Wingfield. *Life Together*. New York: Sheed and Ward, 1943.

Hosemann, Abraham. *Verus amor conjugalis, Das ist: Eheliche Liebe Zweyer Ehegatten usw.* Brunswick: Zilligern, 1682.

Howe, Reuel L. *The Creative Years*. Greenwich, Conn.: Seabury Press, 1959.

Huizinga, Johan. *Herfstty der Middeleeuwen*. Haarlem: H. D. Tjeenk Willink en Zoon, 1928.

Hulme, William E. *God, Sex and Youth*. New York: Prentice-Hall, 1959.

Husted, Alice. *Strictly Confidential*. Minneapolis: Augsburg Publishing House, 1944.

Jackson, Samuel M. and George M. Gilmore, eds. *The New Schaff-Herzog Encyclopedia of Religious Knowledge*. Grand Rapids: Baker Book House, 1949—53.

Jacobs, Henry E., and J. A. W. Haas, eds. *The Lutheran Cyclopedia*. New York: Charles Scribner's Sons, 1905.

James, Edwin Oliver. *Marriage and Society*. New York: Hutchinson's University Library, 1952.

James, William. *The Varieties of Religious Experience*. London: Longmans, Green and Co., 1902.

Juengst, Johannes. *Pietisten*. Tübingen: J. C. B. Mohr (P. Siebeck), 1906.

Kiefer, Otto. *Sexual Life in Ancient Rome*, 6th prtg. London: Routledge & Kegan Paul, 1953.

Kinsey, Alfred C., et al. *Sexual Behavior in the Human Female.* Philadelphia: W. B. Saunders Co., 1952.

———. *Sexual Behavior in the Human Male.* Philadelphia: W. B. Saunders Co., 1948.

Kirkpatrick, Clifford. *The Family as Process and Institution.* New York: Ronald Press, 1955.

Kittel, Gerhard, ed. *Theologisches Wörterbuch zum Neuen Testament.* Stuttgart: W. Kohlhammer, 1942.

Koch, Richard A. "Penicillin Is Not Enough," *Readings in Marriage and the Family,* eds. Judson T. and Mary G. Landis. New York: Prentice-Hall, 1952.

Koenig, John F. "De conjugio" in *Theologia positivo-acroamatica.* Vitembergae et Servestae: Sam. G. Zimmermann, 1755.

Köhler, Ludwig. *Hebrew Man.* New York: Abingdon, 1953.

Kramer, Frederick D. "Elementary Pupils and the Sixth Commandment," *Lutheran Education,* XCIV (June 1959), 495—502.

Kretzmann, Paul E. *The Problems of Adolescence and Youth.* St. Louis: Lutheran Literature Board, 1925.

Lähteenmäki, Olavi. *Sexus und Ehe bei Luther.* Turku, 1955.

Lambeth Conference, The, 1958: The Encyclical Letter from the Bishops Together with the Resolutions and Reports. Greenwich, Conn.: Seabury Press, 1958.

Landis, Judson T. and Mary G. *Building a Successful Marriage,* 3d ed. New York: Prentice-Hall, 1958.

Landis, Paul H. *Making the Most of Marriage.* New York: Appleton-Century-Crofts, 1955.

———. *Your Marriage and Family Living.* New York: McGraw-Hill, 1946.

Lawes, Frank. *The Sanctity of Sex.* Chicago: Good News Publishers, 1949.

Lea, Henry C. *History of Sacerdotal Celibacy in the Christian Church,* 4th rev. ed. London: Watts & Co., 1932.

Lehre und Wehre, XXIV (1878); XLVIII (1902); LII (1906).

Lenski, Gerhard E. *Marriage in the Lutheran Church.* Columbus, Ohio: Lutheran Book Concern, 1936.

Lenski, R. C. H. *The Interpretation of St. Matthew's Gospel.* Columbus, Ohio: Wartburg Press, 1943.

Letts, Harold C., ed. *The Lutheran Heritage* and *Life in Community,* Vols. II and III in *Christian Social Responsibility.* Philadelphia: Muhlenberg Press, 1957.

Lewin, Samuel A., and John Gilmore. *Sex Without Fear.* New York: Medical Research Press, 1950.

Lewis, Clive S. *Mere Christianity,* 5th ed. London and Glasgow: Collins Clear-Type Press, 1958.

———. *The Allegory of Love.* London: Oxford University Press, 1936 (1953 prtg.).

Licht, Hans. *Sexual Life in Ancient Greece,* 7th prtg. London: Routledge & Kegan Paul Ltd., 1953.

Ligon, Ernest M. *The Psychology of Christian Personality.* New York: Macmillan, 1953.

Lindesmith, Alfred R., and Anselm L. Strauss. *Social Psychology,* rev. ed. New York: Dryden Press, 1957.

Lövestam, Evald. *Äktenskapet i Nya Testamentet.* Lund: C. W. R. Gleerup, 1950.

Lueker, Erwin L., ed. *Lutheran Cyclopedia.* St. Louis: Concordia Publishing House, 1954.

Luther, Martin. *Dr. Martin Luthers Sämmtliche Schriften,* VIII, ed. Joh. Georg Walch. St. Louis: Concordia Publishing House, 1892.

Lutheran Scholar, XIV, No. 4 (October 1957), 577—584.

Lutheran Witness, V (Aug. 7, 1886); XLIV (June 16, 1925); LI (1932).

Lutheraner, Der, XVI (March 6, 1860); XIX (May 1, 1863); XLV (Sept. 24, 1889); XLVII (April 28, 1891); L (Dec. 18, 1894); LVII (Jan. 22, 1901); LX (Feb. 2, 1904).

Mace, David R. *Hebrew Marriage.* New York: Philosophical Library, 1953.

————. *Whom God Hath Joined.* Philadelphia: Westminster Press, 1953.

Mace, David and Vera. *Marriage: East and West.* Garden City, L. I., N. Y.: Doubleday, 1960.

McHugh, Gelolo. *Marriage Counselor's Manual.* Durham, N. C.: Family Life Publications, Inc., n. d.

McHugh, John A., and Charles J. Callan. *Moral Theology,* rev. and enl. by Edward P. Farrell. New York: Joseph F. Wagner, Inc., 1958.

McNeill, John T. *Modern Christian Movements.* Philadelphia: Westminster Press, 1954.

Magazin für ev.-lutherische Homiletik, I (1877); IV (1880); VI (1882); XI (1887); XII (1888); XIII (1889); XIV (1890); XVII (1893); XXIV (1900); XXV (1901); XXVII (1903); XXVIII (1904); XXIX (1905); XXXI (1907).

Magoun, F. Alexander. *Love and Marriage.* New York: Harper & Bros., 1948.

Maier, Walter A. *For Better, Not for Worse,* 3d ed. St. Louis: Concordia Publishing House, 1939.

Maleske, Harold J. "The Writings of the United Lutheran Church in America on Marriage and Family Life" (unpublished research summary, 1953).

Marquardt, Edward W. *Why Was I Not Told?* St. Louis: Concordia Publishing House, 1939.

Marriage, The Magazine of Catholic Family Living, XLI (Sept. 1959), 38—43; XLIII (Jan. 1961), 6—10.

Marriage and Family Living, XV (Aug. 1953), 234—249; 249—254; XXI (Feb. 1959), 1. Publ. by National Council of Family Relations, Minneapolis, Minn.

Marriage, Divorce, and Remarriage, American Lutheran Church Convention, Blue Island, Ill. (Oct. 4—11, 1956).

Mattson, Alvin D. *Christian Ethics.* Rock Island, Ill.: Augustana Book Concern, 1938.

————. *Polity of the Augustana Lutheran Church.* Rock Island, Ill.: Augustana Book Concern, 1952.

Mayer, Frederick E. *The Religious Bodies of America,* 3d ed. St. Louis: Concordia Publishing House, 1958.

Meily, Clarence. *Puritanism.* Chicago: Charles H. Kerr and Co., 1911.

Messenger, Ernest C. *Two in One Flesh,* 2d ed., in 3 vols.: *Introduction to Sex and Marriage; The Mystery of Sex and Marriage in Catholic Theology; The Practice of Sex and Marriage with Illustrations from the Catholic Liturgy.* Westminster, Md.: The Newman Press, 1950.

Michel, Ernest. *Ehe, Eine Anthropologie der Geschlechtsgemeinschaft.* Stuttgart: Ernst Klett, 1948.

Migne, J. P. *Patrologiae cursus completus.* Paris: D'Amboise, 1844, and Garnier Fratres, 1878 seq.

Minutes, Arkansas-Tennessee Pastoral Conference, April 3, 1888. File, Concordia Historical Institute, St. Louis, Mo.

Minutes, "Gesamtgemeinde," St. Louis, Nov. 5, 1860, to May 18, 1875. File, Concordia Historical Institute, St. Louis, Mo.

Minutes, Northern Illinois Pastoral Conference, Aug. 26—28, 1879. File, Concordia Historical Institute, St. Louis, Mo.

Minutes, Saginaw Special Conference, Aug. 6—7, 1879; Aug. 3—4, 1881; Aug. 5—6, 1884; April 17—18, 1885. File, Concordia Historical Institute, Saint Louis, Mo.

Minutes, Southern Indiana Pastoral Conference, April 19, 1858; May 2—4, 1862. File, Concordia Historical Institute, St. Louis, Mo.

Minutes, Trinity Lutheran Church, Eighth and Soulard, St. Louis, Dec. 9, 1850; Aug. 30, 1858. File, Concordia Historical Institute, St. Louis, Mo.

Minutes, Trinity Lutheran Church, Thiensville, Wis., June 8 to Oct. 5, 1879; Dec. 12, 1897, to June 9, 1907. File, Concordia Historical Institute, Saint Louis, Mo.

Minutes, Zion Lutheran Church, Cleveland, Ohio, March 2, 1858; Sept. 1858 to June 1869. File, Concordia Historical Institute, St. Louis, Mo.

Morgan, Edmund S. *The Puritan Family*. Boston: The Trustees of the Public Library, 1944.

Morley, John. *Oliver Cromwell*. London: Macmillan and Company Ltd., 1901.

Mueller, Karl. *Die Forderung der Ehelosigkeit aller Getauften in der Alten Kirche: Sammlung gemeinverständlicher Vorträge und Schriften aus dem Gebiet der Theologie und Religionsgeschichte*, No. 126. Tübingen: J. C. B. Mohr (Paul Siebeck), 1927.

Neill, Alexander S. *The Problem Family: An Investigation of Human Relations*. New York: Hermitage House, 1949.

Neve, Juergen L. *A Brief History of the Lutheran Church in America*, 2d rev. and enlarged ed. Burlington, Iowa: The German Literary Board, 1916.

Neve, Juergen L., and Otto W. Heick. *A History of Christian Thought*, Vol. II. Philadelphia: Muhlenberg Press, 1946.

Noesgen, Karl F. *Die Evangelien nach Matthaeus, Markus und Lukas*. München: C. H. Beck, 1897.

Nötscher, Friedrich. *Biblische Altertumskunde*. Bonn: Peter Hanstein, 1940.

Oberholzer, Emil, Jr. *Delinquent Saints: Disciplinary Action in the Early Congregational Churches of Massachusetts*. New York: Columbia University Press, 1956.

Oraison, Marc. *Union in Marital Love*. New York: Macmillan, 1958.

Oyen, Hendrik van. *Liebe und Ehe*. Basel: Friedrich Reinhardt, A. G., 1957.

Patai, Raphael. *Sex and Family in the Bible and the Middle East*. New York: Doubleday, 1959.

Peel, Albert, and Leland H. Carlson, eds. *Cartwrightiana*. London: George Allen and Unwin Ltd., 1951.

———. *The Writings of Robert Harrison and Robert Browne*. London: George Allen and Unwin Ltd., 1953.

Perkins, William. *The Whole Treatise of the Cases of Conscience*. London: T. Pickering, 1611.

Peterson, James A. *Education for Marriage*. New York: Chas. Scribner's Sons, 1956.

Pike, James A., and W. Norman Pittenger. *The Faith of the Church*. Greenwich, Conn.: Seabury Press, 1951.

Piper, Otto. *The Christian Interpretation of Sex.* New York: Charles Scribner's Sons, 1955.

Pittenger, W. Norman. *The Christian View of Sexual Behavior.* Greenwich, Conn.: Seabury Press, 1954.

Plummer, Alfred. *An Exegetical Commentary on the Gospel According to St. Matthew.* London: Elliott Stock, 1909.

Polatin, Phillip, and Ellen C. Philtine. *Marriage in the Modern World.* Philadelphia & New York: J. B. Lippincott Co., 1956.

Qualben, Lars P. *A History of the Christian Church.* New York: Thomas Nelson & Sons, 1933.

Quenstedt, Johann Andreas. *Theologia didactico-polemica.* Wittenberg: John Ludolph Quenstedt, 1701.

Reuss, Carl F. "Statement on the American Lutheran Church and Its Teachings on Marriage and Family Living" (unpublished research summary, 1953).

Rice, John R. *The Home — Courtship, Marriage, and Children.* Wheaton, Ill.: Sword of the Lord Publishers, 1946.

Richter, A. L. *Die evangelischen Kirchenordnungen des sechzehnten Jahrhunderts.* Weimar: Landes-Industrie Comptoirs, 1846.

Roberts, Alexander, and James Donaldson, eds. *Ante-Nicene Fathers.* American Reprint of the Edinburgh Edition, rev. and chronologically arr. by A. Cleveland Coxe (New York: Christian Literature Co., 1896), photolithoprinted, Grand Rapids, Mich.: Wm. B. Eerdmans Publ. Co., 1953.

Rowley, Harold H. *The Faith of Israel.* London: SCM Press, 1956.

Russell, George Lawrence (Gilbert). *Men and Women.* Greenwich, Conn.: Seabury Press, 1954.

St. Louis Lutheran, Sept. 20, 1958.

Schaff, Philip, ed. *Nicene and Post-Nicene Fathers of the Christian Church,* First Series. New York: Chas. Scribner's Sons, 1886. Photolithoprinted, Grand Rapids, Mich.: Wm. B. Eerdmans Publ. Co., 1956.

Scharlemann, Martin H. "The Biblical View of Sex," *The Lutheran Scholar,* XIV, No. 4 (Oct. 1957), 577—584.

Schmauk, Theodore E. *A History of the Lutheran Church in Pennsylvania (1638—1820).* Philadelphia: General Council Publication House, 1903.

Schmiedeler, Edgar. *Marriage and the Family.* New York: McGraw-Hill, 1946.

Schmieding, Alfred. *Sex in Childhood and Youth.* St. Louis: Concordia Publishing House, 1953.

——. *Understanding the Child.* St. Louis: Concordia Publishing House, 1945.

Schneider, Carl E. *The German Church on the American Frontier.* St. Louis: Eden Publishing House, 1939.

Schreiner, Helmuth. *Ethos und Daemonie der Liebe.* Gütersloh: C. Bertelsmann, 1950.

Schroeder, H. J. *Canons and Decrees of the Council of Trent.* St. Louis: B. Herder, 1941; 3d prtg., 1955.

Schwarz, Oswald. *Women: The Variety and Meaning of Their Sexual Experience,* ed. A. M. Krich. New York: Dell Publishing Co., Inc., 1954.

Seiler, Karl. "Ich bin ja so in dich verliebt," of the series, *Unser Weg in die Ehe.* München: Claudius Verlag, 1955.

Seligman, Edwin R. A., ed. *Encyclopedia of the Social Sciences,* III, VI, XIV. New York: The Macmillan Co., 1937.

Sheen, Fulton J. *Peace of Soul.* London: Blandford Press, 1950.

Small, Dwight Hervey. *Design for Christian Marriage.* New York and West-wood, N. J.: Fleming H. Revell Co., 1959.

Smith, Chard Powers. *Yankees and God.* New York: Hermitage House, 1954.

Social Hygiene Papers, A Symposium on Sex Education. New York: American Social Hygiene Association (now the American Social Health Association), 1957.

Social Pronouncements of the Augustana Lutheran Church and Its Conferences. Rock Island, Ill.: Augustana Book Concern, 1956.

Soe, N. H. *Christliche Ethik.* München: Chr. Kaiser Verlag, 1949.

Sorokin, Pitirim A. *The American Sex Revolution.* Boston: Porter Sargent, 1956.

——. *The Crisis of Our Age: The Social and Cultural Outlook.* New York: E. P. Dutton, 1942.

——. "The Depth of the Crisis: American Sex Morality Today," *Christianity Today,* IV (July 4, 1960), 3—5.

Spaude, Paul W. *The Lutheran Church Under American Influence.* Burlington, Iowa: Lutheran Literary Board, 1943.

Summerfield, Arthur E. "The Challenge of Obscenity — A Major Threat to Our Children," *American Lutheran,* XLIII (May 1960), 6—8, 30.

Synodal-Berichte (Synodical Proceedings)
 Canada Distrikt, 1906.
 Freikirche in Sachsen, 1894.
 Illinois Distrikt, 1906.
 Michigan Distrikt, 1907.
 Minnesota- und Dakota-Distrikt, 1892; 1894.
 Nebraska-Distrikt, 1900.

Terman, Lewis M., et al. *Psychological Factors in Marital Happiness.* New York: McGraw-Hill, 1938.

Thayer, Joseph H. *A Greek-English Lexicon of the New Testament.* New York: American Book Co., Copyright by Harper & Bros., 1889.

Theological Quarterly, III (1899); VII (1903).

Thomas, George F. *Christian Ethics and Moral Philosophy.* New York: Charles Scribner's Sons, 1955.

Thompson, W. Taliaferro. *An Adventure in Love.* Richmond, Va.: John Knox Press, 1956.

Triglot Concordia: The Symbolical Books of the Ev. Lutheran Church. St. Louis: Concordia Publishing House, 1921.

Trillhaas, Wolfgang. *Der Dienst der Kirche am Menschen.* München: Chr. Kaiser, 1950.

Troeltsch, Ernst. *The Social Teaching of the Christian Churches.* London: Allen and Unwin, 1949.

Truxal, Andrew G., and Francis E. Merrill. *Marriage and the Family in American Culture.* New York: Prentice-Hall, Inc., 1953.

Van de Velde, Theodoor H. *Ideal Marriage: The Physiology and Technique of Marriage,* trans. F. W. Stella Browne. New York: Friede Covici, Inc., 1930.

Veenstra, Rolf L. *Christian Marriage.* Hamilton, Ont., Canada: Guardian Publishing Co. Ltd., 1957.

Vollmer, Philip. *New Testament Sociology.* New York: Fleming H. Revell Co., 1923.

Walker, Mary Alice, and Harold Blake Walker. *Venture of Faith: A Guide to Marriage and the Home.* New York: Harper & Bros., 1959.

Wallis, Reginald. *New Man.* New York: Loizeaux Bros., Inc., 1931.

Walther, C. F. W. *Lutherische Brosamen.* St. Louis: Concordia Publishing House, 1897.

———. *Tanz und Theaterbesuch.* St. Louis: Concordia Publishing House, 1885.

Walther, Wilhelm. *Für Luther wider Rom.* Halle: Niemayer, 1906.

Wayne, T. G. (pseudonym of Thomas Gilbey). *Morals and Marriage: The Catholic Background to Sex.* London: Longmans, Green & Co., 1952 ed., 1958 impression.

Weatherhead, Leslie D. *The Mastery of Sex Through Psychology and Religion,* 17th ed. London: SCM Press, Ltd., 1954.

Weber, Hans Emil. *Reformation, Orthodoxie und Rationalismus.* Gütersloh: C. Bertelsmann Verlag, 1951.

Weber, Marianne. *Ehefrau und Mutter in der Rechtsentwicklung.* . . . Tübingen: J. C. B. Mohr, 1907.

Webster's New International Dictionary of the English Language, 2d ed. Springfield, Mass.: G. and C. Merriam Co., 1949.

Weinhold, Karl. *Die Deutschen Frauen in dem Mittelalter,* I, 2d ed. Wien: Druck und Verlag von Carl Gerolds Sohn, 1897.

Whitman, Howard. "Science Takes a New Look at Sex in America," *This Week Magazine* (Oct. 25, 1959). United Newspaper Magazine Corp., 485 Lexington Ave., New York 17, N. Y.

Winch, Robert F. *The Modern Family.* New York: Henry Holt & Co., 1952.

Workers Quarterly. Chicago: The Walther League, July 1958, 8, 9, 20.

Wylie, William P. *Human Nature and Christian Marriage.* London: SCM Press, 1958; New York: Association Press, 1959.

Wyrtzen, Jack. *Sex and the Bible.* Grand Rapids, Mich.: Zondervan Publishing House, 1958.

Young, Kimball. *Sociology.* New York: American Book Co., 1942.

Zorn, Carl M. *Die heimliche Selbstbefleckung.* Tract 64 (English No. 27). St. Louis: Concordia Publishing House, undated.

———. *Questions on Christian Topics.* Milwaukee: Northwestern Publishing House, 1918.

Indexes

INDEX OF TOPICS

INDEX OF SCRIPTURE PASSAGES